Colin –

    Just to remind you a little of us now you are at La Ressonie –

    With love from all the family

      John – Go

Christmas 1987.

Timpson's England

a look beyond
the obvious

at the unusual,
the eccentric, and
the definitely odd

JOHN TIMPSON

JARROLD

TIMPSON'S ENGLAND

Designed and produced by Parke Sutton Limited, 8 Thorpe Road, Norwich NR1 1RY
for Jarrold Colour Publications, Barrack Street, Norwich NR3 1TR

First Edition Copyright © 1987
Jarrold Colour Publications

ISBN 0-7117-0307-8 cased edition   ISBN 0-7117-0324-8 paperback edition

Printed in Great Britain
Text typeface 10pt Berkeley Old Style Medium

PICTURES *left to right*
- Anti-undergraduate post box? Cambridge, Cambridgeshire.
- Unusual chimneys at the vicarage, Morwenstow, Cornwall.
- Bowerman's Nose, near Moretonhampstead, Devon.
- Carved elephant, St John the Baptist Church, Danbury, Essex.

Timpson's England

a look beyond
the obvious

at the unusual,
the eccentric, and
the definitely odd

JOHN TIMPSON

JARROLD

PICTURES *left to right*
- The birthplace of William Wordsworth, Cockermouth, Cumbria.
- The 15 arch bridge, Berwick-upon-Tweed, Northumberland.
- 'The Sugar Loaf', Brightling Park, East Sussex.
- Monument to Thomas Gray, Stoke Poges, Buckinghamshire.
- Italian style lychgate, St. Endellion Church, Cornwall.
- Samurai in the Green Room, Snowshill Manor, Gloucestershire.

Contents

Contributors

AUTHOR
John Timpson O.B.E.

RESEARCHER
Jan Tavinor

DESIGNER
Geoff Staff

PHOTOGRAPHERS
John Brooks, Lynda Freebrey, Alan Gutteridge, Neil Jinkerson

ILLUSTRATOR
Libby Turner

A

DESCRIPTION

OF THE

SCENERY OF THE LAKES

IN

THE NORTH OF ENGLAND.

———————

THIRD EDITION,

(NOW FIRST PUBLISHED SEPARATELY)

WITH ADDITIONS,

AND ILLUSTRATIVE REMARKS UPON THE

𝔖𝔠𝔢𝔫𝔢𝔯𝔶 𝔬𝔣 𝔱𝔥𝔢 𝔄𝔩𝔭𝔰.

———————

By WILLIAM WORDSWORTH.

———————

LONDON:

PRINTED FOR

LONGMAN, HURST, REES, ORME, AND BROWN,

PATERNOSTER-ROW.

1822.

● Shortened title for the third edition of William Wordsworth's guide to the Lakes.

Introduction

I suppose it all started with my introductions to Radio 4's 'Any Questions?' It is usual on this programme to say a few words not only about the panellists but about the places we visited. It seemed a little predictable just to say: "This week we are in Wolverhampton in the West Midlands. The oldest parts of the church date back to the 15th century and it has a fine municipal art gallery . . ." So I recalled that Wolverhampton produced the first traffic lights in England and the first car to travel at 200 mph, which perhaps was why they needed the traffic lights. It was also celebrating the thousandth anniversary of its charter and the 25th anniversary of the last time Wolves won the Cup . . .

If we went to Stratford-upon-Avon I would avoid the obvious reference to the Immortal Bard and mention instead another local resident, John Harvard, who emigrated to America and left £779 17s 2d (in very old money) to found Harvard University. In Cambridge I would skip the university and recall Thomas Hobson, who hired out horses but would not let his customers select which they wanted, they had to take what he gave them. It was the original Hobson's Choice.

Cockermouth, famous for being Wordsworth's birthplace, was also the home of Fletcher Christian, Captain Bligh's mutinous mate. If I mentioned Wordsworth at all it would be to commend his lesser-known work with the longest title:

● The gazebo in Fletcher Christian's garden, Cockermouth, Cumbria.

"A Guide Through the District of the Lakes in the North of England with a Description of the Scenery etc, for the Use of Tourists and Residents".

Just about everywhere we went had something a little different about it, which the average tourist guide or even the average resident would probably not think of mentioning. So I started to accumulate little-known facts about well-known places. I covered thousands of miles each year – which went up to tens of thousands after I moved to Norfolk, that most inconvenient of starting points for going almost anywhere. As I travelled I kept an eye open for odd buildings and the odd stories that went with them; for parish churches with eccentric effigies, stately homes with quirky corners, village pubs with unlikely spirits, communities devoted to curious crafts.

On the roadside there were odd obelisks and mysterious milestones, strange signs and trees with a tale to tell. Even a mundane object like a water tower can be worth a second glance if it is disguised as a house; and what of a house made out of a helter-skelter, or in the shape of a coffin, or adapted from a public lavatory?

I mention in this book some famous railway bridges, but only to lead you to the 'Virgin Viaduct', the bridge which the railway never reached. I refer to Chesterfield's famous crooked spire, but only to point out another one, just as crooked, but given much less publicity. And I have noted the location of an AA box for you, not in case you break down but because it is a listed building under the official protection of the Department of the Environment.

I might have included stately homes like Althorp, not because it is the family home of the Princess of Wales but because one of her ancestors, the second Earl Spencer, invented a waistcoat which inspired his friend Lord Sandwich to write:

> *Two noble earls who, if I quote,*
> *Some folks might call me sinner,*
> *The one invented half a coat,*
> *The other half a dinner . . .*

But I have tried only to mention places where there is something still to be seen of the story that is told, and the Spencer family may not want to show you one of the Earl's original waistcoats, still less one of Lord Sandwich's sandwiches. I commend to you instead the secret room at Markyate where the original Wicked Lady changed into her highwayman's clothes, the five marks at the entrance to Benthall Hall which may have been the original "five-for-the-symbols-at-your-door" – and the obelisk at Mount Edgcumbe in memory of the Countess's pig . . .

This then is a look beyond the obvious at the unusual, the unlikely and the undeniably odd. It is far from comprehensive, just a very personal choice, but I hope it will give you a view of England you have not had before, and tempt you to take a closer look. If it amuses you also, so much the better.

● The Earl of Spencer's 'half a coat'.

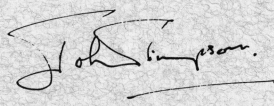

JOHN TIMPSON O.B.E.

Finding that oddity

Should the more intrigued reader wish to find a particular item referred to, a map section is included at the back of this book.

Below is a section from one of those maps showing how to locate that particular place of interest.

Also included at the back of the book is a comprehensive subject index.

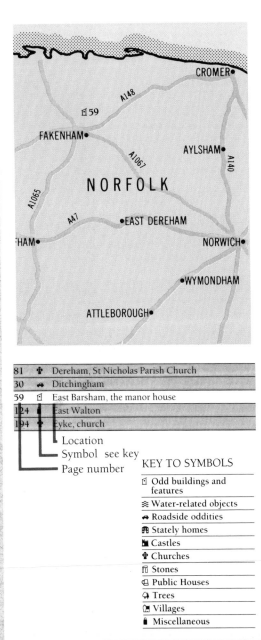

The information appearing on the maps is believed to be correct at the time of printing. Nevertheless, the publishers cannot accept any responsibility for errors or omissions, or for subsequent changes in the details shown.

● 🏠 59 East Barsham Manor, Norfolk

● Detail of its chimneys

81	♁	Dereham, St Nicholas Parish Church
30	⚓	Ditchingham
59	🏠	East Barsham, the manor house
124		East Walton
194		Eyke, church

Location
Symbol see key
Page number

KEY TO SYMBOLS

🏠 Odd buildings and features

≋ Water-related objects

⚓ Roadside oddities

🏛 Stately homes

🏰 Castles

♁ Churches

🗿 Stones

🍺 Public Houses

🌳 Trees

🏘 Villages

🕯 Miscellaneous

On the verge of the unexpected

Some of the strangest features of the English countryside can be seen without leaving the road. There they are, on the verge. It may be a massive monument to some great benefactor, or a tiny tombstone for a marmoset monkey. It may be a ten-foot-high milestone erected by an ostentatious landowner, or a two-foot-high castle built by American Army engineers. It may be a signpost still pointing to Londinium, or the arm of a gibbet pointing to Kingdom Come . . .

You may find that some of them take a little spotting, like the small decorated milestones on the road from Cambridge to Royston. Others, like the memorial at Norman Cross to French prisoners-of-war, you can hardly miss. All of them are worth a glance. Just keep right on to the side of the road.

Nowt so odd as folk – and their memorials

Of all the assorted obelisks that decorate our roadsides, perhaps the most appropriate stands not by a road but by a causeway. It is in memory of a traveller's benefactor, a minor patron saint of pedestrians. She was Maud Heath, a 15th century farmer's wife who lived near Chippenham in Wiltshire and took her farm produce to market across the wide and shallow valley of the Avon, which was often flooded during the winter and spring. After years of trudging through the wet she resolved to build a causeway, so that those who followed her could cross dry-shod.

Some say it was built in her lifetime, others that she left all her money for that purpose in her will. Either way, the causeway still stands, over four miles long, on nearly 70 small arches, and the locals still use it to pass between **Wick Hill** and **Langley Burrell**, where she died.

At the eastern end of the causeway there is a stone obelisk erected to her memory two hundred years after her death, by the trustees of the fund which she left for the maintenance of the causeway – presumably they had had a repair-free year. They did not merely record her public spirited generos-

Maud Heath's Causeway, near Chippenham in Wiltshire, built with her money across the water meadows so that other travellers could walk to market dry-shod. The obelisk recalls her story.

The causeway is four miles long, incorporating nearly seventy arches. Maud Heath' left enough money in her will to ensure it survived to the present day.

ity, they graced the obelisk with four sun-dials, one on each side, regardless of the fact that only one of them could actually function.

They also conjured up some rather turgid verse, directed at the unsuspecting passer-by. To justify all those sundials, for instance, there is this gloomy reminder:

Oh early Passenger, look up, be Wise,
And think how, night and day, Time
onward flies!

And in case the passenger was still insufficiently depressed, they followed up with this little thought:

Haste, Traveller! The sun is sinking now;
He shall return again – but never
thou!

I am not sure if the good-hearted Mrs Heath would have approved. It is difficult to tell what she would have thought from the rather primitive statue which was erected on top of Wick Hill much later, in 1838, by the Marquess of Lansdowne who lived at nearby Bowood House. It certainly depicts a lady in a bonnet sitting beside her shopping basket, but the details of the features are sketchy – probably because nobody had any idea what she looked like and it was 350 years too late to find out. But here again they could not resist the chance to offer us an uplifting thought. This time it was the Vicar of Bremhill who took to verse. He had some difficulty fitting 'Maud Heath's pathway' into the metre, but he very nearly made it:

Thou who dost pause on this aerial
height,
Where Maud-Heath's-pathway winds in
shade or light,
Christian wayfarer, in this world of
strife,
Be still and ponder on the Path of Life.

Another public benefactor is remembered at **Barwick Park**, a mile south of Yeovil, by four of the weirdest memorials in the country. If you ask the way to Barwick, incidentally, remember to call it 'Barrick'. The memorials, or obelisks, or whatever, are on a stretch of parkland just off the A37 road from Yeovil to Dorchester. They were built in the early years of the last century by a local philanthropist called George Messiter, giving employment to a number of men whose work in the glovemaking trade in Yeovil had ended.

Apart from that motive they are remarkable for their complete pointlessness. One of them does actually look like an obelisk, but it is so thin and crooked it has been described as a neurotic stiletto. Another is a cone with holes in it, standing on top of Gothic-type arches, like an enormous dove-less dovecote. A third is called the Fish Tower, a thin tower with a carved drum top about 50 feet high, which used to have a large weathervane in the shape of a fish.

The monument to Maud Heath, farmer's wife and travellers' friend

Giving the wind direction would have been the only useful feature of the entire collection, but it has long since disappeared.

Oddest of all is the fourth in the group, Jack the Treacle Eater. Like the others it is made of rough rubble, and it takes the shape of a shouldered arch, with a little tower with a conical roof perched on top. On top of that is Jack himself, said to be a youthful employee of Messiter who lived in the tower and trained on treacle to run messages to London. Less romantic folk say it is just another statuette of Mercury or Hermes, but there are still some locals who will tell you – probably with some difficulty, since it is not easy to speak with your tongue in your cheek – that if a basin of treacle is left by the arch overnight, Jack will have licked the basin clean by morning. Or perhaps a sweet-toothed rabbit?

At **Lindale**, two miles from Grange-over-Sands in Cumbria, there is an obelisk commemorating a man with much more practical achievements. John Wilkinson was one of the great ironmasters of the 18th century. He launched the first iron ship, on the River Winster, in spite of considerable scepticism from those who said iron could not float. He became known as 'Iron Mad' Wilkinson, a nickname he justified by asking to be buried in an iron coffin.

The obelisk, therefore, is also made of iron, an early example of box casting. For some years it lay neglected in a shrubbery after being struck by lightning (iron does have its hazards), but it has been restored and replaced in the village, freshly painted and bearing the tribute that

his different works in various parts of the United Kingdom are lasting testimonies of his unceasing labours.

Not every roadside memorial has such a happy history. On **Holcombe Moor** in Lancashire, just off the Rossendale Way, there

Two of Messiter's monuments – his doveless dovecote, and Jack the Treacle Eater's Tower, with Jack himself on the pinnacle.

Scene of a murder. A cairn of stones marks the spot where a young woman was murdered by her lover (though 'lover' seems hardly the word) after a day out at the local fair. It is beside the road on Holcombe Moor in Lancashire, just off the Rossendale Way.

Two very contrasting roadside memorials. 'The Boy's Grave', a young suicide, at Kentford in Suffolk, and the iron obelisk in Cumbria to the builder of the first iron ship, 'Iron Mad' Wilkinson.

is a cairn to the memory of Ellen Strange. It marks the spot where she was murdered by her lover Billy the Pedlar while on their way home from Haslingden Fair. Billy pleaded guilty at his trial in Lancaster and his body was hung on a gibbet at Bull Hill, not far from the scene of the murder. Local people built the cairn of stones in memory of Ellen.

Suicides were often buried on the roadside at crossroads – the latest recorded instance was at St John's Wood in London in 1823. The idea was to prevent the unhappy spirit from wandering. Needless to say, few of these graves can still be seen, but there is one at a crossroad on the main Bury St Edmunds road near **Kentford** in Suffolk which is still tended and provided with flowers. It is known simply as 'The Boy's Grave'. The boy was a young shepherd who hanged himself after being accused of sheep stealing, either from guilt or more likely from fear of transportation. He has not been forgotten.

The memorial in
Botusfleming to William
Martyn, who preferred a
pyramid across the road
to a tombstone in the
churchyard.

Not every roadside grave has such a sad history; although some people preferred it that way. In the village of **Botusfleming** in Cornwall, across the road from the church, is a pyramid marking the grave of William Martyn who died in 1762. The inscription explains why he crossed over. He was "a Catholic Christian, in the true, not depraved Popish sense of the word", and he had "no superstitious veneration for church or churchyard".

Formal memorials, not graves, are found on roadsides all over the country. There are grand ones like the 1939–45 Polish War Memorial at **Ruislip** in Middlesex on the A40 Oxford road, next to Northolt RAF Station from which so many Polish airmen flew, and the Cyclists Memorial at **Meriden** in Warwickshire, off the A45 Coventry-Birmingham road, dedicated to cyclists in the Services who died in the first World War; and there are humbler but no less respected memorials to local casualties which stand on so many village greens. But there is an unusual memorial beside the Great North Road to the dead of an earlier war.

As the A1 trunk road heads northward through Cambridgeshire it curves gently to bypass the village of Stilton, associated

The memorial at Meriden
to cyclists who died on
active service in the First
World War.

throughout the world with fine English cheese. Do not go in search of the factory. Stilton cheese was never actually made in Stilton, it came from Leicestershire and was merely brought to the village to connect with the London coach.

Press on instead to **Norman Cross**, a mile or two further north, where there is a concrete reminder of what else the English did when they were not making cheese – in this case, making war with the French. Just outside the village is a bronze eagle on a column, erected in memory of 1800 French prisoners-of-war who died there, for reasons their captors could hardly be proud of, during the Napoleonic Wars. The prison itself has gone, but the Commandant's house is still standing on the road to Yaxley, a three-storey building with parapet walls and bays.

Much more unusual, and rather less depressing, is another column which stands a few miles away at **Holme Fen**, Whittlesey Mere, the last great area of water to be drained in the Cambridge Fens. Land which had been six feet under water became available for ploughing, and the farmers moved in.

Unfortunately as the peat below the mere was exposed, it dried out and shrank – and kept on shrinking. The ground level started dropping at the rate of an inch a month. This was bad news for the farmers, but fascinating for the ecologists. To measure the shrinkage they sank into the peat, so that only its top showed, a cast-iron column, the sort that was used that year to build the Crystal Palace for the Great Exhibition.

That year was 1851. By the 1860s the column was sticking well out of the ground, the farmers had given up ploughing and planted coverts instead – and the peat was still shrinking.

By the beginning of this century the farmers had abandoned the land altogether. The area was taken over by birch trees, the column was now halfway uncovered – and the peat was still shrinking.

By 1957 so much of the column was exposed that they had to keep it up with guyropes. A second column was erected beside it, marked with the dates and the measurements of the shrinkage. They stand there still, but be warned: the peat is still shrinking . . .

A war memorial at Norman Cross in Cambridgeshire – not to the British, but to their old foes the French. It commemorates French prisoners-of-war who died in captivity during the Napoleonic Wars.

A monument to an ecological experiment which went wrong. When the Cambridge Fens drained there was more land for the farmers – but the peat kept shrinking and the land kept sinking. This cast iron column was nearly buried in 1851 . . .

They went that-a-way – milestones and signposts

A 'lady-size' milestone – the White Lady of Esher (now not so white and not much like a lady) at Esher in Surrey.

A Trinity milestone erected by the Master of Trinity College between Cambridge and Royston, thanks to a royal bequest in the 18th century.

Milestones came to England with the Romans, and they have been lining our road sides ever since, but they now measure a different mile. The Romans based theirs on one thousand military paces, milia passuum, and the average Roman squarebasher must have had either very long legs or quite a spring in his step, because in one thousand paces he covered 1620 yards. The average Anglo-Saxon would probably have been hard pressed to cover more than one yard per pace.

The mile has extended a bit further since then, somehow adding on another 140 yards to bring it up to the familiar 1760. But already on the athletics field the mile has become obsolete, and if the EEC continues to increase its influence, so will the milestone. We shall have kilometre-stones instead.

A rebus milestone on the London to Eastbourne road – note the bow and bells for Bow Bells – ho-ho . . .

MILE TO GREAT SAINT MARIES CHURCH CAMBRIDGE

So let us cherish those that we have got, particularly the more historic ones. Most milestones are fairly humble affairs, lumps of stone sunk in the grass verge, or in the years after the Industrial Revolution, made of cast iron, sometimes triangular, sometimes cylindrical. But some of them are quite fancy affairs, and others tower above the roadside, with a wealth of information about distances and places.

For a fancy milestone take the A10 road south from **Cambridge**. Between there and **Royston** you should spot a number of 'Trinity milestones', which were put there by the Master of Trinity College in 1728. They bear a crescent and rings within an ornamental shield, denoting their association with the college. They were put there as a result of a royal bequest of one thousand pounds, which in those days should have bought enough milestones to last all the way to London.

There are a number of other decorated milestones on the main **London** to **Eastbourne** road – the easiest to spot is probably the one near **Horsebridge**, twelve miles north of Eastbourne, which is particularly well preserved. There are more between **East Grinstead** and **Forest Row**. They are cast-iron plates attached to stones or wooden blocks, and display the mileage and a little bow and pendant of three or more bells. These are the 'rebus' or puzzle milestones, a rebus being a picture representing syllables or words, often using a pun. In this case the bow and the bells are a pictograph of Bow Bells; most southbound roads from London were officially measured from Bow Church in the City.

By contrast, **Esher** in the neighbouring county of Surrey has one of the biggest milestones in the country. It stands outside the Orleans Arms just north of the town, and it is known as the White Lady of Esher, though its whiteness has faded over the years into a dreary grey. It stands nearly ten feet high and is three feet thick, the result of the private enterprise of a Duke of Newcastle in the 18th century who owned an estate near Esher. To ensure that visitors from London did not miss the turning to his estate, in what was then open and empty country, he erected this obelisk of a milestone, giving the mileages to a score of different places, including his own house a mile away. The longest distance it records is to Portsmouth, 57 miles away, down what is now the A3.

But even the Duke of Newcastle's ostentation is outdone by the 18-foot milestone at **Craven Arms** in Shropshire, marking the junction of the A49 to Shrewsbury with the B4368 to Clun. On its sides it has the mileages to 36 different places, some of which seem somewhat superfluous. While it is useful to learn that London is 150 miles away, and Ludlow is 7½, would those early travellers really want to know that it is 223 miles to Newcastle or 295 miles to Edinburgh? No matter; it is one of our more attractive milestones, with its tall tapering sides, and not to be mocked.

We are more fortunate in our old milestones than in our old signposts. In these days of fast travel we want clear information rather than elegance, and our signs are designed accordingly. But there are still signposts about from a more leisurely age, and I particularly like the old one that stands on the A44 between Oxford and Evesham, at **Chipping**

The milestone at Craven Arms in Shropshire, 18 feet high and packed with (pointless?) statistics.

Campden. You may not recognise it straight away because it stands ten feet high, so the writing is just the right height for a stage-coach driver. And you may not benefit immediately when you do see it, because the distances are shown in Roman figures, and by the time you have worked out all the 'V's and 'X's you will probably have passed wherever it was you were going. Again, no matter; we are lucky it is still about.

Incidentally there is another signpost with a Roman flavour on Stane Street, **Bignor Hill**, where it crosses the South Downs Way in West Sussex. It points to Londinium in the north-east, which is reasonably clear, and Regnum in the south-west, which is not. Who would connect Regnum with Chichester – except a Roman?

The Chipping Campden signpost – designed for stagecoach drivers – and the Bignor Hill signpost – designed for Romans.

Thereby hangs more than a tale

The Steng Cross Gibbet –
with demonstration head.

Our forefathers were particularly adept at devising unpleasant ways of killing each other – not in the heat of battle or with murderous intent, but in the alleged cause of justice. Crucifixion, burning at the stake, hanging-drawing-and-quartering, were some of the more lingering methods. But death was not the final act. They dreamed up macabre epilogues, demonstrations of what they had done and what they would do again if the mood took them.

Impaling the head of the deceased on a spike was one way of impressing the populace. Dangling the dead body in chains was another. And for the latter purpose they invented the gibbet.

A gibbet is not necessarily the same as a gallows. In general the gallows was where they hanged people, the gibbet was where the bodies were hung. Not many of the former survive, but on lonely roadsides in many parts of the country you may find a sinister one-armed signpost, pointing – as it were – to the Hereafter.

Northumberland and the Border Country was particularly rich in these roadside ornaments, thanks to the frequency with which Border raiders had to be despatched. There still remains the Steng Cross Gibbet, also called Winter's Gibbet, which stands high on a mound beside the B6342 road, eight miles east of **Otterburn**, in desolate country which has been only partially tamed by the Forestry Commission. The arm of the gibbet is 18 feet above the ground, high enough to ensure plenty of clearance for the bodies, and well out of reach of any grieving relatives.

The present gibbet replaced the original on which the body of William Winter was hung in chains after he had been hanged at the West Gate in Newcastle in 1791 for murdering an old woman in a lonely cottage near Whiskershield Common. It was not a first offence by Winter; he had only just returned from transportation. Urged on, it is said, by two travelling tinker-women, who had experienced an old woman's hospitality, they broke into her cottage, killed her, and loaded her goods on their donkey. But this bizarre little group had been spotted in the vicinity the previous day by a shepherd boy, and Winter was tracked down and brought to justice, though there is no mention of what happened to his accomplices.

A curious tradition is attached to Winter's Gibbet, which seems to have no connection with Winter's crime. It is said that toothache can be cured by cutting a splinter of wood from the gibbet and rubbing it on the offending tooth – an uncomfortable form of treatment which has yet to receive the blessing of the British Dental Association.

Gibbets were not always placed in lonely spots. **Bilstone** in Leicestershire, about 15 miles west of Leicester, has a gibbet post standing on the outskirts of the village. The last person to be suspended from it was John Massey, who murdered his second wife in 1801, then tried to drown his ten-year-old daughter. The judge ordered the body to be sent for dissection, but Massey must still have had friends in the village; they cut him down and buried him between his two wives.

The gibbet at **Caxton**, a village on the main road from Royston to Huntingdon, west of Cambridge, was last used for the son of a former landlord of the local inn. He murdered three of the guests and hid the bodies in a well under the stairs. The name of the pub – the Caxton Gibbet.

The gibbet which stands three miles east of **Brigg** on the A18 in Humberside may not have been used at all. It was erected in the reign of James I, early in the 17th century, as a warning rather than a punishment. There was bitter rivalry at the time between two local families, the Rosses of Melton Ross and the Tyrwhitts of Kettleby. After a savage fight in which many members of both families died, the king ordered the gibbet to be erected as a warning that any further killings would be treated as murder. Whereupon the Rosses cut their losses and the Tyrwhitts stopped acting like Twhitts . . .

At **Millom** in Cumbria only a memorial stone remains to mark the socket in which a gallows post once stood. The Huddleston family, as lords of the manor, had the right to execute felons without bothering with the courts, and the gallows was the handiest method. There is a reminder of those days on **Inkpen Downs**, where Wiltshire, Hampshire and Berkshire meet. A tall post stands there, formerly a gallows post and, although it is no longer in use, it is a condition in the lease of a nearby farm that it has to be properly maintained. Presumably the lord of the manor never knows when it may come in handy . . .

Assorted gibbets – the warning gibbet at Brigg (above, left), the Caxton Gibbet, which had a pub named after it, (above, right), and the Bilstone Gibbet, which speaks for itself.

Historic holes and stately boxes

Think of the historic attractions of **Grasmere** in the Lake District and, if you are energetic, you will think of lakeside walks to Rydal Water and hill-climbs over Helm Crag and Alcock Tarn and Swinescar Hause. If you are literary, you will think of Wordsworth and Dove Cottage, where he lived and worked and entertained Coleridge and De Quincey and Southey. What you will not think of, I suspect, is an AA Box.

Drive a few miles out of the village on the A591 and there it is, a little black and yellow sentry box beside the road, which is officially designated as a Grade II listed building of architectural and historic interest.

These days the motoring organisations put their emergency telephones under modest little canopies which protect your head from the elements, and very little else. Bleakest of all are the motorway telephones, generally located on the most windswept, unwelcoming sections of the hard shoulder, where you can be deafened by the engines and submerged by the spray. That AA box outside Grasmere, now under government protection, is a reminder of a more gracious age, when we did not drive, we motored, and when the motor failed, an AA box would offer us sanctuary as well as succour. Our much-prized AA key would unlock this tiny cabin, and we could make our phone call in comfort.

Reprehensibly, I kept my key long after my AA membership expired, and such is the perverseness of human nature, I rather hoped I would have a breakdown so I could use the facilities of an AA box for nothing. Happily from all points of view, the breakdown never occurred, so my conscience was never put to the test. I can contemplate that Cumbrian callbox without a qualm.

The Department of the Environment has not always displayed such serendipity in its choice of listed buildings. While you are motoring around Cumbria – and assuming you have not had need of that AA box – head north beyond it, with Helvellyn soaring up on your right and Lake Thirlmere flanking the road on your left. Take a minor road off the A66 and you may eventually find yourself in the village of **Welton**, which achieved a fleeting moment of glory over its maypole.

The Department's experts were captivated by this maypole. Manifestly, they said, it dates

back to the 19th century, an historic relic of the days when young folk danced around it on May Day, intertwining their ribbons and tangling themselves up as well, and having no end of a time.

So the maypole went down on the list of 'buildings of historic interest', a bizarre concept in itself, since one does not normally think of a pole as a building, historic or not. Just how bizarre it was became apparent when the older inhabitants of the village pointed out that the 'maypole' was not actually a maypole at all, nor was it a century old. It

A Grade II listed building of architectural and historic interest – the AA Box near Grasmere in the Lake District.

was in fact a metal flagpole, erected for some local celebration not too many years before, and nobody had bothered to take it down. The experts made an excuse, and left. Some time later Her Majesty's Secretary of State for the Environment found himself signing an order de-listing a pole. The pole did not long survive this ignominy and rusted away, but its remains still lie there, so far as I know, a reminder of how conservationists can sometimes go a little over the top. Incidentally it was only in 1986 that the Secretary of State at that time, Nicholas Ridley, was advised by his office that his own front gate posts were being listed as historically valuable. This somewhat surprised him as he had actually erected one of them himself. So he wrote a letter to himself, pointing this out, and the Secretary of State acceded to his request and de-listed them.

If a pole or a gate post is an odd listed building, how about a hole? There are two that I know of. One is hardly worth visiting – it is an eight-foot deep, water-filled hole on a farm in **St Audries**, Somerset which the Department claims is all that remains of an unusual private gasworks built in the 1850s to provide lighting for the local Hall. It is a rather boring hole, and nobody is more bored with it than the farmer who owns it. He wanted to built on it and found it was illegal

to build on a 'listed building'. As he observed rather sourly, "I didn't realise I owned a stately hole".

But another water-filled hole on the Department's list is well worth a visit. It is actually the village duckpond at **Otford** in Kent. Nearly all the houses in Otford are listed, and presumably the Department decided to make a clean sweep and listed the duckpond as well. It sits on a roundabout in the centre of the village, and the ducks provide a regular hazard to motorists by trying to walk under their wheels. One can understand the ducks feeling suicidal at times; as residents of a 'listed building' I assume they can hardly pull up a weed without getting planning permission . . .

There are some five hundred thousand entries in the Department's list, and they range from St Pancras Station to an 18th century milestone. But my favourite is to be found at **Bishop's Tawton** in North Devon. Bishop's Tawton lies alongside a main road on the outskirts of Barnstaple, and attracted little aesthetic admiration until the Department's inspectors hove by and spotted Mr Ernie Smith's three-seater outside lavatory. Mr Smith pointed out to them that this ageing convenience had not been put to practical use for 30 years, and indeed the brambles which had encroached inside it would have made its use singularly uncomfortable.

No matter, said the inspectors. Here was an outstanding example of toilet togetherness which must be preserved for future generations. Mr Smith's three-seater is now a Grade II listed building, and well worth a pilgrimage – though if you are really in need of such a facility, I suggest you bear in mind the brambles and head for Barnstaple . . .

Why did the ducks cross the road? To take a break from their 'listed building', the village duck pond at Otford in Kent.

Most of the residences in Otford are listed buildings, so why not the ducks' residence too?

The historic 'three-holer' at Bishop's Tawton in Devon.

More roadside rarities – unlisted (so far)

Where will you find a green telephone box, a bus shelter with a horse on the roof, an obelisk made out of horseshoes, a two-foot-high castle built by American Army engineers, a memorial to a marmoset? These are some of the roadside rarities which can be enjoyed without even getting out of your car.

The green telephone box must have been a victory for the local burgher of **Okeford Fitzpaine**, a picturesque village in Dorset some seven miles north-west of Blandford Forum. It was felt that a red telephone box would be a jarring note among the pleasant huddle of cottages, some thatched, some with

One that slipped through the red-and-white net – the green phone box at Okeford Fitzpaine.

attractive alternate bands of flintwork and brickwork in their walls. So it was painted a more discreet green, and green it remains.

The bus shelter topped by the model horse must have started life as something much grander, but it is certainly a bus shelter now, complete with standard issue wooden seat. It is in the form of a most imposing stone arch, in the village of **Londonthorpe**, near Grantham in Lincolnshire. Why the horse is perched on it is a mystery; perhaps it started as a horse-bus shelter.

Much more recent is the obelisk of horseshoes at **Scarrington** in Nottinghamshire, some eight miles east of Nottingham on the A52. It consists of about 35,000 old horseshoes, each one carefully laid with its 'toes' pointing outwards and the nails left in. The village blacksmith started to construct it in 1946 and built it to a height of over fourteen feet, on a base five feet across. It neatly tapers to a width of about three feet at the top, and it is rounded off to a cone. It is tempting to think that if one horseshoe was removed from the bottom the whole lot would come down, but they are so firmly interlocked it would probably take a bulldozer to shift them.

Londonthorpe's equestrian-flavoured bus shelter – a throwback to the horse-bus, or just a Victorian planning department gone mad?

The Americans were here – but why? An unlikely wartime memento in Oxfordshire.

The miniature castle stands by the B481 road from **Stoke Row** to **Nettlebed** in Oxfordshire. It has two towers with simple windows and a central doorway over which is inscribed "343 Engrs US Army 1942". The engineers have long since departed, leaving no obvious explanation of their creation. Was it their billet, somewhere they blew up, a child's plaything? One thing I can say – it is singularly ugly.

Not far from this miniature folly, beside the main **Henley** to **Oxford** road, is a sad little reminder of a pet monkey. It is a memorial to a marmoset, buried there in 1937 by its grieving owner, a lady who used to wrap him round her neck like a fur. The inscription is more moving than one might expect.

"Jimmy," it says, "a tiny marmoset . . . There isn't enough darkness in the world to quench the light of one small candle".

This is not the only roadside reminder of a deceased pet. There is another, more practical one in the main public car park at **Bodmin** in Cornwall – a dog's drinking trough presented to the town by Prince Chula of Siam "in memory of his friend Joan, a wirehaired terrier who died in 1948 in her 17th year".

If you are visiting Blickling Hall, the splendid Jacobean mansion which is one of Norfolk's finest architectural treasures outside its churches, spare a moment to drive to nearby Cawston to find on the side of the B1149 a memorial to one of the lesser known activities of the Hall's founder. Sir Henry Hobart was Chief Justice of Common Pleas in the reign of

PRESENTED BY
HIS ROYAL HIGHNESS
PRINCE CHULA. OF SIAM,
IN MEMORY OF HIS FRIEND.
JOAN,
A WIRE HAIRED TERRIER
WHO DIED IN 1948
IN HER 17TH YEAR.

A princely tribute to his pet, a memorial dog-trough at Bodmin.

James I, but he sometimes took the law into his own hands. At **Cawston** is the Duel Stone, a stone ball on a plinth erected to commemorate a duel he fought with one of his neighbours, Oliver La Neve of Great Witchingham Hall. It was brought about by an election quarrel. The details are sketchy, but since there are a great many Hobarts in Norfolk today, and according to the telephone directory not a single La Neve, one can perhaps guess at the outcome. Certainly Witchingham Hall has not maintained its dignity in quite the same way as Blickling; it has achieved fame in more recent years as the original headquarters of those Boo'iful Norfolk turkeys.

A rather smaller stone ball on a considerably larger plinth – it is shaped like a cone and stands ten or twelve feet high – is in the market square at **Hallaton**, midway between Uppingham and Market Harborough in Leicestershire. Its shape is misleading, it is actually the market cross. On 364 days of the year it can be observed and examined in comfort, but on Easter Monday it is the focal point for the ancient bottle kicking and hare pie scrambling competition between Hallaton and the neighbouring village of Medbourne.

The Duelling Stone at Cawston in Norfolk – the National Trust tells it all.

Hallaton's 'cross' in the market square.

Casting the sack containing the hare pie for the crowd to dive in.

Diving for the hare pie.

Goal! Someone scores with the bottle (small barrel) reaching the stream.

The procession moves off, with the teams holding the 'bottles' aloft.

Finally, a mad scramble in the stream, with no obvious reason.

The Greatstone-on-Sea Listening Device, the radar that never was.

This involves a free-for-all in which any passerby can take part. Pieces of hare pie are scrambled for and three 'bottles', which in fact are small barrels of ale, are kicked around for a considerable period. Whichever side is judged to have won gathers beside the conical 'cross' and drinks the ale out of the barrels, which by this time must be in just the right condition to mix with the hare pie.

Finally let me commend to you a wall. We are not without walls on our roadsides, but this one is weirder than most. It stands all alone on the sands near the road to **Greatstone-on-Sea** in Kent. It is made of concrete and shaped like a bow, 25 feet high and 200 feet long. Nothing is on top of it, nothing is joined on to it. It just stands there.

This was the Greatstone-on-Sea Listening Device, the unsuccessful fore-runner to radar. It was built in 1928 to reflect the sound of enemy aircraft and pinpoint their where-abouts. They found they could spot them much quicker with the naked eye and ear, and since we were not due for another war anyway for another decade, the Device was left to its own devices.

"Give us a sign, Harry!"

A village sign, the sort you pass on the roadside just before reaching the 30-mile limit, is generally an unromantic affair. It tells you where you are, and perhaps how far you still have to go to find somewhere really

St Felix and the Beaver Bishop of Babingley.

BABINGLEY

interesting. It may reveal the name of a village in the depths of the Dordogne or the back end of Bavaria with which it is twinned, for reasons known only to those local burghers who enjoy the exchange visiting, but can hardly interest the passing motorist. Villages with a greater sense of civility and an eye to the tourist trade may also bid you welcome. But I confess the only one I ever stopped at to get a closer look was in North Yorkshire, at a time when my younger son was devoted to those engaging rodents, the Wombles. It was a long way from Wimbledon Common, but my son was in no doubt that we had tracked them down. I photographed him with his toy Uncle Bulgaria, standing by the sign at Wombleton.

There is however another sort of village sign, generally found in a prominent central position instead of on the outskirts, which has quite a different purpose and deserves a more detailed inspection. It depicts not just the name but the history of the place, its famous sons, the local legends. They are to be found in great profusion in East Anglia, probably greater than anywhere else in the country, thanks to the talents of one man.

Harry Carter was a schoolmaster who could not only carve wood with great skill, but enjoyed interpreting local history in pictures. He came into prominence in the 1950s, a time when villages wanted to mark the Queen's Coronation in some permanent form, particularly on the Royal Estate at Sandringham. As the idea caught on, other villages remembered anniversaries they should commemorate, or local dignitaries they should honour. Or they just wanted to keep up with the village next door. The cry went up, "Give us a sign, Harry!" And Harry gave them a sign.

It reached the stage where the only noteworthy thing about a village was its sign. Take for instance the tiny community of **Babingley**, on the edge of the Sandringham estate. There was nothing much at Babingley except a farmhouse, a few cottages, a corrugated-iron church – and a legend. This was the site of the first Christian church in East Anglia, founded by St Felix in AD 600. The legend went that after he had sailed safely all the way from Burgundy he was shipwrecked in Babingley River.

Since the river is now little more than a rivulet a little scepticism may be forgiven. But there is more to come. The saint was saved, so it is said, by a colony of beavers, and out of gratitude he made the head beaver a bishop.

This could perhaps have been the earliest equivalent to the Wombles or the inspiration for 'Wind in the Willows'. But Babingley takes it seriously – if it loses the legend it loses everything – and Harry Carter took it seriously too. A village sign now stands beside the main coast road from King's Lynn to Hunstanton, more striking than the village itself, which is easy to miss. It shows St Felix, and above him sits the beaver bishop, mitre on head and crook in hand, history's episcopal answer to Roland Rat.

Not far from Babingley, also on the Royal Estate, is the immaculate village of **Anmer**, with another striking sign. It was a gift to the Queen from the Norfolk Boy Scouts Association, for the help she has given to the movement, and it shows, predictably, a life-size Boy Scout. But Harry remembered Anmer's earlier history too, when it was more involved with Romans than Royalty, and back-to-back with the Scout is a Roman centurion, with the Latin version of the motto Julius Caesar could have done with: "Be Prepared".

But Harry was at his best with legends. In his home town of **Swaffham** he depicted the story of the Pedlar of Swaffham, who went to London with his dog in search of a fortune, and met a man on London Bridge who told

What do a Roman Centurion and a Boy Scout have in common? Yes, they are both 'prepared' – and they both stand guard at Anmer.

him he would find a crock of gold in his own back garden. He came home and found not one but two; he became a great benefactor of the town.

In **Dereham**, twelve miles away, is perhaps his most ambitious sign, spanning the High Street and illustrating the story of St Withburga and the deer which gave the town its legend and its name. But his work is equally worth seeing in little villages such as **Griston**, said to be the home of the babes in the wood. His sign shows them hiding from their wicked uncle Robert de Grey.

At **Ditchingham** he made a pyramid-shaped sign in honour of Rider Haggard and his book on Cleopatra; at **Taverham** he com-

memorated another saint, St Walstan, one of the earliest English mystics who nevertheless worked in the fields as a labourer all his life. And to demonstrate that there is more to village signs than saints and sinners, at **Trowse** on the outskirts of Norwich he tried his hand at a gentle pun. Trowse comes from the Old English Tre-hus, and he duly made a sign showing a man in the branches of a tree, peering down from a 'tre-hus'.

For me, incidentally, the name has always conjured up a different image. Ever since I worked on the nearby 'Dereham & Fakenham Times' in Norfolk I have wanted to launch a companion paper and call it the Trowse Press.

Signs with a story – St Walstan smiles in Taverham, the 'Tre-hus' man lurks in Trowse. Two of Norfolk's distinctive village signs.

Wondrous ways with water

Show an engineer a stretch of water and if it is narrow enough he will build a bridge over it, if it is rough enough he will build a lighthouse on it, and if it is drinkable he will build a water tower to store it.

Most of these structures are quite straightforward. A bridge is basically a road on legs, a water tower is a tank on very long legs, and a lighthouse is a lamp on a very long leg indeed.

But some engineers have not been satisfied to leave it at that. They have built bridges with chapels, water towers with windows and chimneys, lighthouses with no lights. They have all served their purpose (except perhaps the Virgin Viaduct at Tadcaster, built for the railway that never arrived) but they have that extra unexpected ingredient which makes them worth a second glance – and a place in this chapter.

One more river to cross – and another, and another . . .

Ever since the first Ancient Briton found a treetrunk lying across a stream and realised he could reach the other side without getting his feet wet, the English have had a lot of fun building bridges and others have had a lot of fun admiring them.

We were well behind the Egyptians, of course, as in so many other things. They built one across the Nile in about 2650 BC, and there was a very fancy affair across the Euphrates four thousand years ago with stone piers and a timber roadway which could be pulled up like a drawbridge. Many modern bridges use much the same idea.

But we were still traipsing over treetrunks and slithering over stepping-stones by the time the Romans turned up to show us a thing or two about bridge building, using timber and stone. They were good at roads and walls too, which lasted rather longer than their bridges. When the Roman Empire collapsed and the legions pulled out, it was not long before we were back to treetrunks again.

We had to wait for the monks of the 11th and 12th centuries to get the bridge building industry back to work. One of them in particular, Peter of Colechurch, had the bright idea of providing London with a bridge across

The Pulteney Bridge at Bath – better viewed from the river than to view the river from . . . But a reminder of what London Bridge looked like in the 1800s.

the Thames. It took him 30 years, but the bridge itself lasted for 650.

It was built, as so many early bridges were, to be lived on as well as to be crossed. It was lined with shops and houses and booths. The nearest we have to it today is Pulteney Bridge in **Bath**, built by Robert Adam under the patronage of Sir William Pulteney in 1769, with two-storey houses on each side of the 30-foot wide roadway. There are many other sights to be seen in this most celebrated of English spas, from the Roman baths to the Royal Crescent, but the Pulteney Bridge is not to be missed. On the other hand, if you want to see the river, the bridge is not much use to you – the buildings are in the way.

The same applied to Peter of Colechurch's bridge in London, and although it was much repaired and altered and generally messed about with over the centuries, its original framework remained unchanged until 1831, when it was replaced by a new London Bridge.

Alas, you won't see that one either. A passing American rather fancied it and bought the whole thing. The existing Thames bridges are too well-known to need further mention here. Much more interesting are some of the old bridges which do still survive elsewhere.

Take, for instance, Tarr Steps on **Exmoor** (if you are an American, please *don't* take it!). It requires quite an effort to get there, in one of the wildest areas of the moor, surrounded by bogs and unwelcoming hills. The Steps bridge the river Barle below Winsford Hill, and you have to walk a mile or so along a

footpath from the Challacombe-Simonsbath road, the B3358.

You can spot the footpath because it starts opposite the Caratacus Stone. Who Caratacus was and why he planted a stone there is not too clear, but the experts say it is 5th century Celtic and pretty important. To most of us, I suspect, it is pretty boring. Off you go down that footpath for the Tarr Steps.

Tarr Steps on Exmoor (above) and the builder? (below).

The Caratacus Stone – a Celtic memorial, and latterday pointer to the Tarr Steps.

Like the Caratacus Stone, not much is known about who put the bridge there. I have seen it described as prehistoric, dating from a thousand BC. Certainly it was used as a packhorse bridge in early times, and if indeed it goes back that far then its builders put the average early Brit to shame, because while he was toying with treetrunks they were humping chunks of stone weighing five tons or more, to build the 17 spans of the bridge.

There is another theory which is much more dramatic. The story goes that the stones were placed there by the Devil, in the space of a single night, after he had been challenged to a contest of strength by a local giant.

Some early bridges have lasted longer than the streams they were built to span. One of the most remarkable, at **Crowland** in Lincolnshire, was built by the monks of Crowland Abbey some seven hundred years ago. Its official name is Trinity Bridge, but it is locally known as the Three-Ways-to-Nowhere Bridge, and it is easy to see why. The monks doubtless wanted to symbolise the Trinity with its three intersecting arches, but its practical purpose was to span the three streams that ran through the village, the Catwater, the Welland and the Nene.

Now it stands high and dry while the streams have taken themselves off elsewhere.

The Three-Ways-to-Nowhere Bridge at Crowland in Lincolnshire (right) with its lonely traveller (above) probably originating from Crowland Abbey (below).

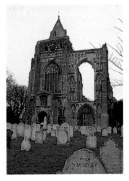

Yet those streams were so substantial that Edward the Fourth was able to reach the bridge by boat, on his way to Fotheringay Castle. Legend has it the waters disappeared into a raging whirlpool that lies somewhere below the bridge.

Apart from being unable to hold its water, the bridge has fared rather better than the abbey, which went through a very trying time in its early days. It was begun by King Ethelbald in 716 and was burnt down in 930. The monks rebuilt it and it was burnt down again in 1091. Again the monks rebuilt it, determined to be more careful with their matches in future – whereupon an earthquake gave it an extremely nasty turn in 1117. There was yet another fire in 1146, but by this time the monks must have had their wheelbarrows of cement on permanent stand-by, and up it went again in 1190.

Since then it has crumbled fairly steadily, and much of it is in ruins, but the north aisle is still used as the parish church. From those ruins a couple of hundred years ago someone removed a figure which now stands on the bridge. Some say it represents Christ carrying the world in his hands, but at a casual glance it looks like a forlorn traveller, waiting on the bridge for the boat that will never come, along a river that no longer exists.

Some old bridges emphasise their religious connections by having a built-in chapel as an integral part of their design. Let me commend two of them, one in Cambridgeshire, the other in Wiltshire.

I first saw **St Ives** bridge from the water, by far the best position from which to view it because the bridge itself is only wide enough for one line of traffic, and pedestrians have to thrust themselves against the parapets to avoid being mown down, first from one direction then the other as the lights change. You can also get a much better view of the 15th century bridge chapel which perches above the central point of its six arches like a little watchtower guarding the approaches to the fens.

We used to see it from our battered little cabin cruiser 'Mañana'. It was battered because it kept running into the bank when the engine broke down, and even when it worked I had great difficulty controlling the steering. It was called 'Mañana' because it came after 'Today' – when the programme ended we would head for the marina at St Neot's and take it down the Ouse to St Ives. We seldom ventured further than that terrifying lock beyond the bridge, where the river drops almost out of sight into the mysterious flat Fenland that stretches to Ely and the Wash. St Ives bridge, we felt, was the final frontier of civilised commuter life.

The town itself, incidentally, is a pleasant little place where you will find a statue of Oliver Cromwell because he once owned a farm there (he had farms like Queen Elizabeth had beds). You will not however find a statue of St Ives, because the name of this very English town comes from a Persian bishop, St Ivo, to whom the local priory was

The bridge chapel at St Ives in Cambridgeshire, a welcome sight for river travellers as they emerged from the featureless Fens five hundred years ago – and still a boundary marker between the sophisticated and the simple.

The old bridge between Huntingdon and Godmanchester – a fine example of 'by guess and by God'. They started building it from each side of the river, and hoped for the best . . .

dedicated. It would have saved confusion (and prevented the wrong mail going to that other St Ives in Cornwall) if they had kept to the name of the original village. It was called Slepe, not because it was dozy but because it was a slippery landing place. Even so, it would have been nice to set off in 'Mañana' with the farewell cry, "We're going to Slepe!"

Before you leave that stretch of the Ouse, there is another bridge up-river linking **Huntingdon** and **Godmanchester** which is worth a second glance. You will see there is an awkward curve in it which might make a modern civil engineer become rather uncivil to his builder. But back in the 14th century, when it was built, it was quite lucky if the two ends met at all – and in this case it was very lucky indeed. The story goes that they started work on opposite sides of the river without any common plan to work from. It is nice to think that if they had missed each other in the middle, as they very nearly did, they would have just kept going and finished up with two bridges instead of one.

My other notable chapel bridge is at **Bradford-on-Avon**, which also qualifies for a mention under notable churches and notable buildings. It has one of the few almost complete Anglo-Saxon churches in the country

and one of the biggest tithe barns, 168 feet long, a reflection of the medieval prosperity of this cloth town, and of how well the church did out of it.

To get to the barn from the church one must cross the Oratory Bridge. Two of the original 14th century arches remain, the other nine are 17th century. The little domed oratory, or chapel, is built on to a pier, not in the centre as at St Ives, but at one end of the bridge.

It was built as a shrine to St Nicholas, who was very fond of the humble gudgeon. Normally this little fish only serves as bait for anglers, but the good saint took it as his emblem, and it has been hoisted aloft on the copper weather vane of the chapel, a saintly symbol to the knowledgeable traveller, a source of some confusion to seekers after fish and chips.

It has also in its time been an emblem of incarceration. For many years the chapel was used as a lock-up and, instead of referring to people going 'inside', the locals talked of being "under the fish and over the water". John Wesley spent an uncomfortable night there in 1757, having antagonised the local hierarchy with his preaching. St Nicholas would not have been too happy about that, and nor I suspect was Dr Wesley. He was probably in high dudgeon under the high gudgeon . . .

It is unusual however for a bridge chapel to be put to such an unattractive use. Their original purpose was to collect offerings from passing travellers, a sort of voluntary toll, and the Church encouraged the better-off to endow bridges on the principle that this was a pious work, like building churches.

The bridge over the River Tweed at **Coldstream** in Northumberland actually went one better than just having a chapel. It had the Marriage House, where runaway couples were able to get married without going through the usual preliminaries. The House is still there but it has not seen a marriage since 1856, when the practice was stopped and elopers had to keep going until they reached Gretna Green.

In places such as **Ely**, where bridges and causeways were the only way of entering or leaving the city, an official road hermit was appointed to maintain and care for them. His duties have now devolved upon Cambridgeshire County Council.

Bradford-on-Avon bridge

The bridge over the River Tweed at Coldstream (above) and the Marriage House at one end of it, where runaway couples could 'do a Gretna' until 1856.

In Dorset bridges were so highly valued that in many places, such as **Sturminster Newton**, there is still a plaque which says sternly,

> *Any person wilfully injuring any part of this county bridge will be guilty of felony and upon conviction liable to be transported for life by the court. P. Fooks.*

It is admittedly a very handsome bridge, one of the most handsome in Dorset, but Mr Fooks does seem to have gone a bit over the top in protecting it . . .

Most bridges are symmetrical affairs – they have to be, generally, to stand up. But there are a couple at opposite corners of England where each arch is of a different size. One is in the far South-West in Bideford, the other in the far North-East at Berwick-on-Tweed.

Bideford bridge is nearly seven hundred feet long and has 24 arches, each one of a different width – and five hundred years after it was built it did start to fall down and had to be closed for three months for repairs. That was in 1968, a period of great frustration for drivers and considerable prosperity for the local boatmen, who provided the only link between the two sides of the river.

The bridge at Berwick (top), 'a herd of elephants crossing the Tweed' and Sturminster Newton bridge (above), so highly valued that anyone damaging it could be deported (left).

The bridge is wider and stronger now, but some of the original stonework still remains, dating back to the days when sturdy Bideford men tramped across it to the quayside, to man some of the ships which sailed against the Armada. The cannons which protect the bandstand in the nearby park are said to have come from captured Spanish galleons.

The war with the Spaniards is just history now in Bideford, but in **Berwick**, home of that other bridge with the variable arches, the Crimean War against the Russians is still technically in progress. Berwick had a special status as a free borough and merited a separate mention in certain Acts of Parliament. The town was specifically named in the declaration of hostilities, along with the rest of Britain – but when the rest of Britain signed a peace treaty two years later, Berwick was not mentioned. It has been officially in a state of war with Russia ever since.

The bridge itself connects Berwick, the northernmost town in England, with Tweed-mouth on the south side of the estuary. It was built in 1634. Its 15 arches all vary in height and width, and give it the appearance, as someone unkinder than me once put it, of a herd of elephants crossing the Tweed.

Nevertheless it is a lot more interesting than the concrete creation beside it, the Royal Tweed Bridge, which now carries the heavier traffic. And there is a third bridge, built in 1850 with 28 soaring arches, which is the product of a different era in bridge construction, the era of Telford and Stephenson and Isambard Kingdom Brunel. It is the bridge which carries the railway across the border into Scotland.

Bridgebuilders had already moved on from stone to iron when the railways came. No need to remind you of the world's first iron bridge, built in the 1770s across the Severn at Coalbrookdale in Shropshire, and such a significant historical landmark that the area is simply known as **Ironbridge**. It is nearly two hundred feet long, it has one major span of

It is called Ironbridge and that is what it is, the first iron bridge in the world, built across the Severn in Shropshire in the 1770s – the start of a new era in bridge building.

The Royal Albert Bridge across the Tamar – but never mind the quality, look at the height. Brunel had to allow a hundred feet clearance between the bridge platform and the water. Only the Admiralty knows why.

one hundred feet with two smaller ones, and it weighs 380 tons, a figure difficult to dispute, since how can you weigh a bridge?

It is restricted to foot traffic now, because the river banks are moving gradually closer together, squeezing the centre of the bridge upwards. It is a process well worth watching, if you have a year or two to spare. But iron had proved its worth to the bridge builders, and with the coming of the railways they went berserk. More than 25000 railway bridges were built in Britain in 70 years. They still used stone and brick for long viaducts across low or marshy ground, but mostly they used iron – first cast-iron, then when it was found to be too brittle, wrought-iron.

The first famous British bridges were built outside England. Glasgow had the first wrought-iron girder bridge, the Menai Strait in Wales was spanned not only by Robert Stephenson's famous tubular railway bridge but also Telford's first great suspension bridge. And the Forth Bridge, built in 1889, is still the second longest cantilever bridge in the world.

It was left to Brunel to provide England with its most well-known Victorian railway bridge, the Royal Albert across the River Tamar at **Saltash**. It is a familiar sight to travellers by rail between Devon and Cornwall, but they may not be so familiar with the main problem faced by Brunel in building it. The Admiralty, for reasons best known to itself, insisted there should be a clearance of one hundred feet between the bridge platform and the water at high tide. It was presumably expecting some very tall ships or some very low-flying aircraft.

Brunel found that as well as allowing for this height he also had to sink the central pier to a depth of 80 feet below high water level before he could strike solid rock. He met the challenge and the bridge was built, but he became too ill to supervise the final stages and he died the same year – though not before he had added his 'signature' to his final creation. The name 'I K Brunel' is emblazoned in massive letters on the arched entrance to the bridge.

If that is a sad tale of a bridge builder, at

least it ended in a successful and much-used bridge. Spare a tear for the 'Virgin Viaduct' at **Tadcaster** in North Yorkshire, a town famous for its breweries and its removable church – it was taken to bits in the 1870s and moved five feet higher to avoid the risk of being flooded by the River Wharfe. The 'Virgin Viaduct' was built alongside an earlier road bridge across the Wharfe in preparation for the coming of the railway. But the railway never quite made it to Tadcaster, and the viaduct remained unsullied and unwanted.

Finally three bridges which are unremarkable in themselves but have strange tales to tell. At **Cromford** in Derbyshire, where Richard Arkwright built his first mechanised textile factory, there is a stone on the bridge which recalls the daredevil feat of a man on horseback who jumped over the side and into the river 30 feet below. He did it in 1697, 80-odd years before Arkwright's mill helped to start the Industrial Revolution, and gave

The Tadcaster bridges (above and left). The road bridge, which has a road, and the rail bridge, which has no rails. 'The Virgin Viaduct' still waits for the railway that never came. (Below) Cromford bridge in Derbyshire, scene of a daredevil leap which is still commemorated (below left).

Wansford Bridge –
another odd feat
remembered.

Cromford a different claim to fame. **Wansford** in Cambridgeshire, just off the A1 trunk road between Peterborough and Stamford, has a bridge across the River Nene, which was liable to sudden flooding. Passers-by on the bridge were surprised one morning to find a local rustic floating underneath it on a hayrick. He had fallen asleep and the rick had been swept up in the floodwater.

"Where am I?" cried the poor fellow, not knowing how long he had slept or how far he had swept. "You're at Wansford," they shouted. "What, Wansford in England?" he asked. And the village has been labelled 'Wansford in England' ever since. The sign on the Haycock Inn portrays the story.

Then there is the happy story of Lovers' Bridge in **Glaisdale**, a village which stands on

the North Yorkshire Moors Railway, one of the prettiest lines in the country. But long before the railway was built, there was no bridge over the River Esk at Glaisdale, and a local lad called Thomas Ferris used to wade or swim across it to meet his sweetheart. According to legend he went to America to make his fortune and vowed that when he did he would return and not only marry his sweetheart but build a bridge to mark his old crossing point. He made a fortune, he married his sweetheart, and there stands the bridge, with the initials 'T F' and the date 1619.

Glaisdale Bridge, a
romance remembered.

Lights fantastic

The English word for the science of lighthouse construction is almost as odd as some of the lighthouses it has produced. 'Pharology' originates, as it sounds, from Egypt, but the word is derived not from the Pharaohs, who were more interested in pyramids than lighthouses, but from the Pharos of Alexandria, the first lighthouse in the world (apart from Vesuvius, Etna and the like, which may have acted as a night guide to mariners but were not exactly custom-built).

For once it was not the Egyptians themselves who introduced the idea. Alexander the Great, conqueror of Egypt, not only created the port named after him, but built the lighthouse too, on the island of Pharos at the port entrance.

Its precise date and specifications are matters for debate. Even a single work of reference contains two versions. On one page it is dated 280 BC and six hundred feet high, on another the date is 285 BC and the height is only three hundred feet. We shall never know which is right, because it fell down in an earthquake six hundred years ago (or was it seven?). But it was impressive enough to be rated one of the seven wonders of the world. The wooden fire on its summit was said to be visible for 30 miles.

England's first lighthouse was probably built by the Romans at Dover, and since then the more treacherous corners of our coastline have become a pharologist's paradise. They had a field day, for example, at **St Catherine's**

The present lighthouse at St Catherine's Point (below left) and a couple of its unlikely predecessors – the Mustard Pot and the Pepper Pot on St Catherine's Down.

Point, on the Isle of Wight, where two examples of their earlier and odder efforts still remain, as well as the modern lighthouse which stands 136 feet above the sea, with a light that can be seen for 18 miles. (Can you hear Alexander on top of his Pharos saying "18 miles? Peanuts!")

On the summit of St Catherine's Down, above the point, are two derelict buildings, one of which was definitely a lighthouse, the other carries some doubts. Let's take the doubtful one first. It is an octagonal affair with splayed foot buttresses and a pyramid-shaped roof, known locally as the Pepper Pot. The popular story is that it was built as a penance by a local worthy a couple of hundred years ago after it was discovered that a consignment of wine, looted from one of the many wrecks in Chale Bay, had ended up in his cellar. Then opinion divides. Some say the building was intended to be a lighthouse, to save other ships being wrecked on that coast, others say it was an oratory, because the wine

he acquired was the property of the church, and he had thus offended against the laws of God as well as man. Either way, it was the home of a holy man for some years – whether he acted as lighthouse keeper also is a moot point.

As it turned out, there was not much point in putting a lighthouse there anyway, as was soon discovered when the second building, known as the Mustard Pot, started to be put up in 1785. They never bothered to complete it, because St Catherine's Down is subject to frequent fogs at that height, and the light would not have been visible anyway.

To complete the cruet there ought to be a Salt Pot too, and indeed there is a third tall structure on St Catherine's Down which is also associated with an emperor called Alexander. But this is not another successor to Alexander the Great's Pharos, it is a pillar erected to mark the visit to Britain by the Emperor of All the Russias in 1814.

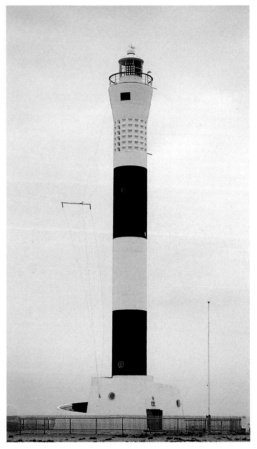

The Dungeness lighthouses, past and present, in pursuit of the sea.

Forty years later we were at war with Russia and, ironically, the pillar was used as a war memorial. A tablet was placed on it, commemorating the British soldiers who died in the Crimea.

Spurn Head on Humberside has been another happy hunting ground for pharologists over the centuries. This thin finger of land, three-and-a-half miles long, is so exposed to storms and tides that the sea is constantly encroaching on the land – and on the lighthouses. Quite a number have had to be built there, each one a little further west than the last, to keep ahead of advancing waves.

Quite the opposite problem affects **Dungeness** in Kent, where the shingle promontory is constantly extending out to sea because of the debris from the eroding cliffs. So successive lighthouses have had to chase after the sea instead of backing away from it. The latest bears a plaque taken from an earlier one which explains:

> *This (stands) instead of the old lighthouse which originally stood 540 yards to the northward, and which by means of the land increasing from the violence of the Sea became useless to navigation.*

Pharologists must have found it very frustrating . . .

The **North Foreland** lighthouse in Kent, between Margate and Ramsgate, has experienced changes not in position but in power supplies, from solid fuel to oil to electricity. Some of the earliest experiments with electric lighting took place there, but when it was first built they used to light a coal fire on top of the tower. Progress was not without its problems. In the 18th century someone had the bright idea of enclosing the coal fire in glass. This did not do much good to the glass, or the fire.

The North Foreland lighthouse, fighting the gloom since it relied on a coal fire for light.

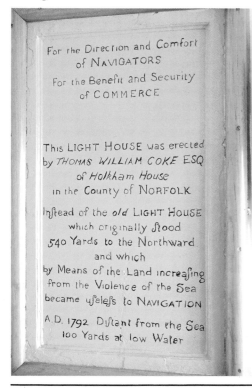

For the Direction and Comfort of NAVIGATORS
For the Benefit and Security of COMMERCE

This LIGHT HOUSE was erected by THOMAS WILLIAM COKE ESQ of Holkham House in the County of NORFOLK Instead of the old LIGHT HOUSE which originally stood 540 Yards to the Northward and which by Means of the Land increasing from the Violence of the Sea became useless to NAVIGATION

A.D. 1792 Distant from the Sea 100 Yards at low Water

Thanks to Trinity House the services of modern lighthouses are provided free, but it was not always so. **Burnham-on-Sea** in Somerset still has a 19th century lighthouse, standing on wooden legs, which was built by an enterprising curate as a profit-making concern. His idea was to take tolls from passing ships to pay for two wells which he hoped would establish the town as a spa.

He did manage to collect enough money from those ships which were civil enough to stop and pay up, to sink two wells. The water turned out to taste singularly unpleasant, but Burnham became a popular holiday resort without needing to be a spa. As for the curate's modest attempt to capitalise on the forces of nature, a much more successful effort has been achieved just along the coast – Hinkley Point nuclear power station.

Another seaside resort with an unlikely lighthouse is **Teignmouth** in Devon. At the south end of the promenade there is a little 25-foot affair, built in 1845 for reasons which no one has precisely discovered.

Private enterprise in
Burnham-on-Sea . . .

. . . miniature mystery in
Teignmouth.

Devon can also offer a lightless lighthouse at **Froward Point** near Kingswear, which serves the same purpose as the more conventional sort, but only in daylight hours. It is a hollow octagonal tower, standing on eight pointed arches, the whole affair about 80 feet high. There is no way of climbing it, but it was not intended to be climbed. It is a Daymark, erected by the Dart Harbour Commissioners in 1864 as a landmark for seafarers.

There is another Daymark in the Scillies, an even larger structure with red and white stripes, and I wish I could say I had seen it, but there was a thick fog when I visited the islands, and I must have wandered within one hundred yards of it without spotting it. If I had been a seafarer it would not have been a great help. Daymarks are of use on fogless days only.

The principle of erecting a lofty light to guide night-time travellers is not confined to the sea. There is a lighthouse in Northamptonshire, and you cannot get much further from the sea than that. It is in the village of **Weldon**, where the local quarry provided the stone for Old St Paul's Cathedral and King's College, Cambridge.

Many years ago the village was surrounded by dense woodland and was known as Weldon-in-the-Woods. It is said that a traveller became hopelessly lost in the forest, then spotted the tower of the village church above the trees. In gratitude he paid for a lantern to be placed at the top of the tower, to create an inland lighthouse for other tree-farers.

A lightless lighthouse – the Kingswear Daymark

A land locked lighthouse – the Weldon Lantern.

Two symbolic lighthouses – not guides to travellers but monuments to local heroes. Sir John Barrow's memorial outside Ulverston (left) (he was founder of the Royal Geographical Society) and the Ammersdown column in memory of Thomas Samuel Jolliffe (right) (Thomas Samuel who?)

For a real inland lighthouse – at least it looks real – you can go either to Cumbria in the north or Somerset in the south. Neither of them is there to guide travellers, but to commemorate earlier ones.

On the summit of Hoad Hill, behind the Cumbrian town of **Ulverston**, stands a splendid traditional lighthouse, one hundred feet high and dominating the whole area. But it is a lighthouse without a light. It was built as a monument to Sir John Barrow, founder of the Royal Geographical Society, Secretary to the Admiralty for 40 years, and notable globetrotter. It provides a rather more imposing reminder of this local hero than the cottage where he was born, which now serves as a sweetshop.

Down in Somerset, near the stone built village of **Kilmersdon**, and 27 miles from the nearest coast, stands a replica of the Eddystone lighthouse, complete with stone spiral staircase lit by ten tiny portholes leading up to the glass lantern at the top. But instead of waves dashing against its base, it has stone animals guarding the four points of the compass.

It is half as high again as the Barrow memorial, and in case you are not familiar with the feats of the man it honours, Thomas Samuel Jolliffe, there is a lengthy eulogy to his "genius, energy and brilliant talents" inscribed on it in English, Latin and French.

It is known as the Ammerdown Column and has stood in Ammerdown Park since 1853, an object of wonder to many and of envy to one – a Mr Turner, who lived next door to the Park. He decided to go one better, and hastened to build an Italianate tower on his own land, some 30 feet taller than the lighthouse. More haste, less speed – the tower was almost immediately declared unsafe and most of it had to come down, leaving the imitation Eddystone a clear field.

Towers of strength – or high water larks?

I hesitate to be unkind about water towers. In my early days in the Norfolk countryside we relied for our water supply on a rotary pump in the wash-house – 150 pumps to fill the tank, and the penalty for taking a bath was an extra hundred pumps. There was also an old-fashioned pump outside the back door, which produced some rather brackish water from the well below. It was exactly the same water we got from the rotary pump, but somehow the fact that that came out of a tap instead of an old pump made it more respectable. As for sanitation, we relied on a bucket at the bottom of the garden and the weekly visit of the 'night-soil' men – generally in the middle of breakfast.

So it was a great satisfaction, not to say relief, when a massive concrete mushroom was constructed on the top of a nearby hill, the pipelayers moved in and we were put on the mains. The mushroom stands there still, serving the water needs of several villages, but I confess that its usefulness is not matched by its beauty. Your average modern water tower is a great concrete lump, either standing on legs like an invader from Mars or poised on a central stem like a giant golf tee. Either way, it does nothing to improve the scenery.

The Victorians did this sort of thing rather better. Faced with the challenge of designing, say, a pumping station, they would produce a turreted, buttressed castle such as the one at **Stoke Newington** in North London with a different shaped tower at each corner, which seems to have a closer affinity with werewolves than water supplies.

They built their water towers square and sturdy, generally in red brick. There is a fine example in **Epping** High Street, with a thin stair turret and whitestone castellations, mellowed now with a covering of ivy. **Chelmsford** has another, built in 1888. But the daddy of them all is the 105-foot tower at **Colchester**, made of one-and-a-quarter million bricks, 369 tons of stone and 142 tons of iron, with a capacity of 230,000 gallons of water, and known universally as 'Jumbo' – not just because of its size, but in honour of a real Jumbo, a six and one-half ton African elephant which at the time of the tower's erection was in every sense the biggest attraction at London Zoo.

Jumbo, pride of the London Zoo in Victoria's day (above) and the water tower at Colchester named after him (left). The Zoo's Jumbo was taken away to join Barnum & Bailey's Circus – the Colchester Jumbo lives on.

"The fairies really own this house . . ." The House in the Clouds at Thorpeness, actually a water tower with all mod cons.

There was an outcry when Phineas Taylor Barnum bought him from the Zoo for his circus in America. Queen Victoria was among those who appealed to him unsuccessfully to let Jumbo stay in London with his mate Alice. When Jumbo sailed away, the people of Colchester still had his namesake to cherish. That was not much help to Alice . . .

A water tower is not an easy object to disguise, short of encasing it in a sham castle like the Stoke Newington pumping station. But it has been achieved most effectively – if somewhat eccentrically – at **Thorpeness** in Suffolk, home of the 'House-in-the-Clouds'.

The entire village of Thorpeness, some three miles north of Aldeburgh, was built as a speculative holiday development by the playwright and barrister G Stuart Ogilvie. In 1923, when it came to providing mains water, Mr Ogilvie installed a postmill to pump the water, which was attractive enough, and a water tower, which wasn't. However, he had already disguised his own domestic water tower as a dovecote, and he set about converting the Thorpeness tower into a five-storey house. The tank on top was made to look like a clapboard house with imitation windows and a pitched roof perched 60 feet up in the air.

With an eye to the family holiday trade Mr Ogilvie first named it 'The Home of Peter Pan', thus giving a new meaning to the pipes of Pan. He found tenants who were undisturbed by their gurgling, or by the thought of living under thirty thousand gallons of water, and one of these, a Mrs Malcom Mason, gave him a better idea for a name. She wrote a children's poem dedicated to her curious home, which began:

> *The fairies really own this house – or so the children say – In fact they all of them moved in upon the self same day . . .*

She called the poem 'The House in the Clouds'; Mr Ogilvie adopted it for his water tower forthwith.

The tower itself no longer functions. Thorpeness proved such a draw that a bigger tank was needed in 1929. It was camouflaged this time as a sort of Norman tower, standing in a parade of mock Tudor houses – not an inspired combination. Then came mains water, and both tanks became redundant. But The House in the Clouds still stands rising from a little copse of silver-birch and shrub, not the most elegant of structures but rather more interesting than a concrete mushroom.

There's no place like **my** home

"The ornament of a house," wrote Emerson, "is the friends who frequent it". Which was all very well for Emerson, who probably had a lot of friends, and ornamental ones at that. But not all of us are satisfied with this philosophical approach to decorating our homes. We like to display something a little more tangible, something that makes our home a little different from the rest.

It may just be a fancy knocker or a brass coachlamp in the porch. On the other hand if we have enough spare cash we may start from scratch and build a special sort of house. These days the planning laws discourage any major eccentricities, but in days of old when builders were bold, and sometimes a little barmy, they produced some very strange buildings indeed.

So here is a selection of these buildings, some of them oddly embellished, others odd in their own right, like Church Farm at Bidston in the Wirral, which has every one of its 13 windows at a different level. I have not included Follies, those 18th century equivalents of the garden gnome, serving no useful purpose except to amuse the guests and impress the neighbours – though I was tempted by the Folly at Newton Linford in Leicestershire, built by Lord Stamford in the shape of a drinking mug, complete with handle, in memory of a well-known local drinker (not Lord Stamford). There are however follies with a small 'f' which do have a practical purpose, like the Egyptian pyramids planted as memorials in the heart of the English countryside, examples of eccentric decorative buildings brought on by pyramania . . .

Be it ever so peculiar . . .

Most popular tourist resorts these days lay claim to having 'The Smallest House in Britain', even if they have had to build one specially for the tourists. So let us look at some of the lesser-known and perhaps more genuine claimants.

The most dramatic, perhaps, is the 'House-in-the-Cliff' at **Porthcurno** in Cornwall, three miles south-east of Land's End. It was built into a cleft in the cliffs which overlook the white sands of Porthcurno Bay. It has a 'basement' and stone steps leading to the

A house-in-a-cliff at Porthcurno (above and on previous page) and a house-on-a-bridge at Ambleside (right), two contenders for the title of smallest house in England.

narrow door of the only other room. Conditions are cramped but the view is tremendous. It is also very handy for the Minack Theatre, carved out of the face of the cliff two hundred feet above the sea.

In much less exposed surroundings, but with almost as good a view, is Bridge House at **Ambleside**, up in the Lake District. It is not so much a house as a tiny cottage, built on a bridge across a little beck. There is a delightful story that it was built by a Scottish family to avoid paying ground rent. Actually it was a summerhouse to Ambleside Hall, but it qualifies as a lived-in home because in Victorian times a family was squashed into it. It does claim to be the smallest in England.

At the other end of the scale is **Knole House**, more of a village than a house, and claimed to be the largest private house in England. It has a room for every day of the year, a stairway for every week and a courtyard for every day of the week. With judicious numbering the whole place could be used as a residential calendar. As it is, the Sackville family looked after it for four hundred years then handed it over to the National Trust, so you can make the standard stately home tour and count them all up for yourself.

Not everything about Knole is on such a massive scale. Keep an eye open for a little octagonal building in the park, now a gamekeeper's cottage, which is known as The Birdhouse. Before the gamekeeper it was occupied by pheasants brought back from China by Lord Amherst. They were so grateful they took his name.

From sizes to shapes. Cornishmen used to like their houses round. The village of **Veryan** has two round houses at each end and one in the middle. The inconvenience of trying to fit straight furniture against round walls, so familiar to the occupants of converted windmills, was more than offset by the protection against the Devil. A cross on the roof warned him not to carry them away. The round walls presumably made it difficult for him to get a grip.

The Veryan round houses (above and below left) – a devil of a job to take away. (Below) One of the seven stairways at Knole House.

For any Cornishman who still hankers after a round house, may I suggest a visit to **Potter Heigham** on the Norfolk Broads. A few hundred yards downstream from the bridge, among the more mundane bungalows that line the bank, there is a circular building which looks as if it has been sliced off the top of a windmill. It is actually the top of a helter-skelter which used to provide entertainment on the Britannia Pier at Yarmouth before the first world war. As holidaymakers became more sophisticated the helter-skelter trade declined, and it is said that a local bookmaker bought it and converted the top storey into a

The Helter-Skelter House at Potter Heigham.

holiday chalet. For a Cornishman it would be home from home.

There is another circular house at **Gayhurst** in Buckinghamshire they might not fancy so much if they knew its history. It is an elaborate affair with mullioned windows in the pointed roof and two stone dogs standing on the summit. Indeed it is called 'The Dog House'. It was actually built by a Victorian architect as an outdoor lavatory for the men-servants of Lord Carrington. If it ever comes on the market, instead of a 'Sold' sign I assume it will just say 'Engaged'.

Rather more macabre in appearance is the Old Coffin House at **Brixham** in Devon, but it actually has a story with a happy ending. The father of a local girl is said to have told her suitor – as many a father has done before and since – that he would sooner see her in her coffin than married to him. The suitor, being sharper than most, duly constructed a house in the rough shape of a coffin. The father was so impressed by his ingenuity that he re-lented, and the couple lived happily in their coffin ever after.

The Dog House at Gayhurst (left) and the Coffin House at Brixham (right). One developed from a loo, the other from a bill and coo . . .

Let's decorate the house . . .

Even the most modest of dwellings can be given a distinctive touch to make it stand out from its neighbours, if it is nothing more than a colourful windowbox. In centuries gone by it was more often some sort of carving. There is a good example on the Whitchurch road outside **Bunbury** in Cheshire – so good in fact that it is known as the Image House. The walls of the cottage are decorated with a host of carved stone figures, and there are more in the garden.

The story goes they represent the sheriff and his men, and were put there by a poacher who returned to the cottage after serving a term of transportation. It is not clear why he immortalised his old enemies in this way.

Spot some of the figures lurking on the walls of this Image House, near Bunbury. Which one is the sheriff?

One theory is that he spent many a happy afternoon sitting in his garden loudly cursing these minions of the law, without fear of reprisal. The good folk of Bunbury would not have approved of such goings-on – there is a strong methodist tradition in the village, in which John Wesley himself had a hand.

A less lurid history is attached to some carvings on the gable end of The Old Lime House at **Goudhurst** in Kent. It stands next to a row of medieval weavers' cottages, but its occupant in later years followed quite a different trade. William Apps was the village stonemason and he wanted to leave behind a reminder of his work. Again it is not certain what the carvings represent but they are known locally as 'Adam and Eve and the Soup Tureen', an unlikely but ingenious guess.

An artist at **Yoxford** in Suffolk had much the same idea, though I suspect his cottage was decorated more with an eye to advertisement than immortality. He painted one blank brick wall of his cottage with a most convincing portico-ed door, complete with a letter protruding from the letter box. There are realistic 'windows' and even a painted peacock to provide the authentic stately home flavour. The painting has his 'signature' in the form of a circular plaque painted on the wall, bearing his name.

A different form of decoration was adopted by Frederick Attrill, who worked at Osborne House on the Isle of Wight but lived more modestly in a semi-detached villa in **East Cowes**. In 1916, at the age of 78, Mr Attrill took it into his head to cover the walls of his semi with seashells. When he ran out of shells he used plates, bits of porcelain, mosaics –

'Adam & Eve and the Soup Tureen' – or whatever! The village stonemason leaves a conundrum at Goudhurst.

What you can do with a plain brick wall! An elegant bit of paintwork at Yoxford in Suffolk.

The high point in the life – and death – of Henry Trigg. A ploy to avoid the body-snatchers, now a deposit with the NatWest Bank.

almost anything small, shiny and available. This hobby kept him alive for another ten years, long enough to cover the front, side and back of his house. What his neighbour in the other semi thought of all this is not recorded, but it has provided Cowes with one of its stranger tourist attractions for the past 60 years.

On the other hand the decorations on a cottage near **Henfield** Church in Sussex have been an attraction – and in their early days, a distraction – since the 16th century. In those days the church had a cat and the owner of the cottage had a canary. The two met, with fatal results for the canary. Its owner, enraged at such unecclesiastical behaviour, made some iron effigies of the cat eating the canary, tied them on a wire, and rattled them at the vicar each time he went to church. Fortunately for the present vicar the iron cats are now firmly cemented into the cottage wall.

For the most macabre decoration I commend the barn of Henry Trigg, one-time grocer at **Stevenage** in Hertfordshire. Mr Trigg had a dread of body-snatchers – it is said he saw some at work in the churchyard on his way home from the local pub, and decided to ensure that his own remains should not suffer the same fate. In his will of 1724 he instructed his brother, his executor, to lay his coffin on a roof beam in his barn – otherwise he would not inherit his estate. His brother happened to be a parson and could hardly have approved, but the call of duty to the deceased – not to mention the estate – overcame any scruples, and the coffin was duly installed in the rafters.

A century later the coffin was observed to be falling into disrepair, and rather than allow Mr Trigg's remains to be precipitated to the floor they were installed in a new coffin which was again placed in the roof. At some stage after that his bones were finally removed – one hopes to a more appropriate resting place – but the coffin is still there. Along with the barn it became the property of the National Westminster Bank – one of their odder long-term deposits.

Cat-a-walling? No, they have been silent for centuries, but they used to rattle the Vicar. A reminder of a village feud at Henfield.

But the smoke goes up them just the same

To most of us a chimney is just a flue that smoke escapes through, preferably without leaving too much soot behind. It is the most ordinary of appurtenances, superfluous in smokeless zones, and with central heating installed in most new properties it is something of an endangered species.

But there was a time when architects, and builders, and the people who employed them lavished much care and money on their chimneys. The Tudors in particular liked them tall, and ornate, and imposing. Sometimes they liked them to be assorted as well.

Sir Henry Fermor was a 16th century chimney buff. He built the manor house at **East Barsham** in Norfolk, a splendid sight as you come down into the village on the road from Fakenham. It is worth seeing just for the bands of ornament in moulded brick, the patterning of the windows, the vertical buttresses and the battlemented top. But the highspot – literally – is the chimneys.

East Barsham Manor and its crowning glory – the astonishing assortment of chimneys.

There is a group of ten, each one carved differently from its neighbours and together making a most dramatic picture. Whether they are actually used I cannot tell – the hall is in private hands and not open to the public – but they earn their keep just as decorations.

While you are in East Anglia there is another pair of chimneys worth a visit, attached to the old Moot Hall at **Aldeburgh** in Suffolk. It was built about the same time as Barsham Manor but in a very different style, timber framed with brick walls at each end. Much of it was restored by the Victorians, but the lofty twin chimneys, tall and round with wider bases and tops, like a couple of up-ended sewer pipes, have remained unchanged for 450 years.

Whether they will last for another 450 is not so certain. The sea is gradually encroaching on Aldeburgh sea front – if it comes much closer the Moot Hall may be left on a Moot point. But when I was there the locals were busily raising money to preserve it; I am sure they will not let those marvellous chimneys go to pot.

Certainly an early Earl of Northampton went to some lengths to preserve his. **Compton Wynyates** in Warwickshire is considered to be one of the finest Tudor houses in England. It has a splendid porch bearing the arms of Henry VIII and Catherine of Aragon above the original door with its strangely contrived locks, and Henry slept in one of its one hundred rooms, behind some of its three hundred windows. But not least among its remarkable features are its twisted chimneys, standing high above the battlemented roof.

All this could well have come to grief during the Civil War, when the Roundheads besieged the house. They had already completely destroyed the church. Rather than see his home destroyed too the earl and his family agreed to go into exile. Four hundred Parliamentary troops were billeted there, but the building – and the chimneys – were unscathed.

Two years later, having paid a fine of £20,000 and filled in the moat, the family got it back, intact up to the last chimney.

The lofty 'drainpipe' chimneys on Aldeburgh's Moot Hall.

After the Tudors had gone, builders began to lose interest in chimneys. Indeed in the early 18th century a builder called Colin Campbell managed to eliminate them altogether. He built **Mereworth Castle** in Kent, one of the best examples of the Palladian style still standing in England. It was modelled in fact on Palladio's Villa Capra at Vicenza in Italy, and it looks like a temple with its circular, domed, chimneyless hall. Yet inside there are normal looking fireplaces with normal looking fires. In this case you will have to take my word for it – I gather visitors are not welcome.

Campbell's trick was to build the chimneys into the ribs of the dome, all leading up to a single outlet at the apex. This provided not only a warm fireplace but a warm ceiling, and left the roof free of any non-Palladian protuberances.

It took a man like the Reverend Robert Stephen Hawker to bring chimneys back into the public eye. He was Vicar of **Morwenstow** in Cornwall in the last century, and in the year of Victoria's ascension to the throne he built Morwenstow Vicarage, a perfectly normal home for a Victorian parson except for

Rare choice chimneys, at Compton Wynyates, built by a Tudor mason with an eye to a left-hand screw.

the chimneys. Each one was a model of a church tower which had taken his fancy, some turreted, some with battlements, some with fake windows set in the sides.

There was one exception, the kitchen chimney. It is a copy of his mother's tomb. Presumably in spite of all these external embellishments, the smoke went up the chimney just the same.

Factory chimneys are often imposing enough in their own right, but let me commend one which is rather different from the norm. The Marshall Mill at **Holbeck**, near Leeds, was built by one Ignatius Bonomi, who spent eight years in Egypt studying the Pyramids and came back with a slight touch of Egyptomania. You will find his pyramids mentioned elsewhere, particularly the 45-footer he planted in the back garden at Blickling Hall in Norfolk. But for the Marshall Mill he not only created a building on the lines of an Egyptian temple but stuck on top of it a chimney shaped like Cleopatra's Needle.

To add to the mill's bizarre appearance the flat roof was covered with earth and grass to keep the workroom warm below – and to keep down the grass a flock of sheep grazed on the roof. Perhaps to the relief of passing travellers, who may have feared for their sanity at such a sight, the practice was discontinued when one of the sheep fell through the roof and into the machinery. Repairs were

Morwenstow Vicarage (right) adorned by chimneys in the shape of church towers, except for the kitchen chimney (above), which the vicar shaped like his mother's tomb.

carried out and the mill is still in commercial use. Not much could be done for the sheep. The chimney has now been demolished, but the rest of the building remains, well worth seeing in its own right.

Not every chimney is attached to a building. There is a freestanding chimney alongside the Customs Quay at **Falmouth**, on the south coast of Cornwall. It stands 30 feet high, built of brick on a stone plinth in four tiers – an unlovely object, and certainly unloved by smugglers. It was known as 'The King's Pipe', and the Customs men used it to 'smoke' contraband tobacco. It was burned in the chimney, providing a most unsoothing aroma for its erstwhile owners.

Finally there is a chimney on the Black Downs near **Portesham** in Dorset which is actually not a chimney at all. Indeed opinion varies on whether it even looks like one.

Theories range from a peppermill to a candlestick telephone. The most popular description, though, is a factory chimney wearing a crinoline.

It is in fact Hardy's Monument, erected not in memory of Thomas Hardy in spite of his famous connection with the area, but Admiral Sir Thomas Masterman Hardy, he of the well-known deathbed scene on board HMS Victory at the Battle of Trafalgar.

Did Nelson say "Kiss me" or "Kismet"? We shall never know for certain, any more than we shall know whether the designer of this monument, a Mr Troyte, meant it to be a chimney or a chesspiece. I did consult the National Trust, who have owned the thing since 1900, but all the Handbook says is: "This viewpoint is suitable for visitors in wheelchairs".

'The King's Pipe' at Falmouth, where the customs men 'smoked' contraband tobacco.

Bonomi's Egyptian mill at Holbeck. Its chimney was shaped like Cleopatra's Needle.

Hardy's Monument in Dorset – no, not Thomas Hardy, and no, not exactly a chimney!

Never mind a garden gnome – let's have a pyramid

A very odd appurtenance to a stately home – the Bonomi pyramid at Blickling Hall

The ancient Egyptians, you will recall, were terribly keen on pyramids. The ones they went in for were not so much king-size as Pharaoh-size. The Great Pyramid of Gizeh was big enough to take the Houses of Parliament and St Paul's Cathedral with room to spare, if indeed there had been any room at all. Actually the centre was of solid rock; the whole thing took over two-and-a-quarter million pieces of stone, each weighing up to fifteen tons.

This sort of vast bulk greatly impressed visiting Egyptologists, almost as much as the treasures they found underneath. Pyramid mausoleums started springing up in English churchyards, on a rather smaller scale but with much the same object – to protect the dead and impress the natives.

One of the most enthusiastic pyramid-builders was Ignatius Bonomi, whose Egyptian-style mill in Yorkshire is mentioned elsewhere. While he was fascinated by all things Egyptian, he specialised in putting up four-sided buildings which came to a point at the top.

If you visit **Blickling Hall** in Norfolk, having marvelled at the splendid Jacobean building with its very English gardens, you may be startled to find a large pyramid in the grounds, a most un-English edifice which would have given quite a shock to Anne Boleyn's family, who used to live there. This is a Bonomi special, considered to be the finest pyramid in England, 45 feet high and housing the remains of the second Earl of Buckingham and his two wives. It has a massive portico with the earl's arms over the top, more suited perhaps to a town hall than a pyramid, but the experts are very pleased with it, and so I am sure was the earl.

Where the Earl of Buckinghamshire led, Mad Jack Fuller was not far behind. Mad Jack was a famous English eccentric who was in his forties when the earl's pyramid was built. There is no evidence he ever saw it (Norfolk was even more inaccessible in those days than it is now), but a few years later he decided that he too should be entombed in this way. Well, not quite in this way. It is reported that he asked to be seated fully dressed in an iron chair in the centre of the pyramid, with a bottle of port and a roast chicken in front of him, waiting in comfort for the Resurrection. The floor of the pyramid was sprinkled with broken glass, it is said, not to deter any mortal invaders but to cut the hooves of the Devil if he attempted to snatch him away.

Mr Fuller had the pyramid built in the churchyard at **Brightling**, his home in Sussex. It has been suggested that he got the vicar's consent by moving his pub, the Green Man,

'Mad Jack's' pyramid at Brightling, where he sits with a bottle of port and a roast chicken, awaiting the Day of Judgment.

from opposite the church to a converted barn elsewhere in the village, which is now called the Fuller's Arms. The real explanation is rather more mundane. According to the parish register he erected a new stone wall for the churchyard, with a couple of pillars and an iron gate, a sufficient inducement for the parson to stretch a point.

The idea caught on. A 15-foot pyramid is to be found at the west end of **Nether Wallop** church in Hampshire. Dr Francis Douce endowed a school in the village on condition that the pyramid be properly maintained.

A Norfolk solicitor, who died in 1929, had much the same idea, except that he endowed a library instead of a school, and his memorial pyramid in **Attleborough** churchyard is rather more modest. Melancthon William Henry Brooke, or Lawyer Brooke as he was better known, gave detailed instructions in his will for the pyramid's precise measurements (it stands about six feet high) and for the stone that should be used (white limestone). His will also revealed a minor domestic disagreement in his household. To his housekeeper Florence Curtis he bequeathed "the sum of £20 free of legacy duty. This legacy would have been £100 if she had complied with my wishes and continued to wear for service the whitecap and apron

Lawyer Brooke's pyramid at Attleborough.

Dr Douce's pyramid at Nether Wallop.

A mount's memorial on Farley Mount. The pyramid in memory of 'Beware Chalk Pit'

For criminals with pointed heads – the village lock-up at Wheatley.

which became her so well". Happily he had second thoughts and added a codicil increasing the amount to £50.

Pyramids have sprouted in churchyards elsewhere, but one of the finest is not by a church but on a hilltop, and it commemorates not a human but a horse.

It is in Hampshire on **Farley Mount**, between Winchester and King's Somborne. Unusually, one can go inside it – three of its porches are blank, but the fourth is open, and there a tablet tells the story of this equestrian mausoleum.

> *Underneath lies buried a horse, the property of Paulet St John Esq, that in the month of September 1733 leaped into a chalk pit twenty-five feet deep a-foxhunting with his master on his back, and in October 1734 he won the Hunters' Plate on Worthy Downs and was rode by his owner and entered in the name of 'Beware Chalk Pit'.*

One regrets the horse is not running still, if only to hear a racing commentator baffling his listeners with cries of "Beware Chalk Pit!"

You may also be baffled by the pyramid which stands in the village of **Wheatley** in Oxfordshire. It would seem to be an incongruous setting for a mausoleum, and indeed it is. In the 19th century this pyramid was the village lock-up, especially designed no doubt for criminals with pointed heads.

Nature's jokes – with a little help from her friends

Whatever strange and wondrous objects may be produced by the hand of man, none can match the strange and wondrous works of Nature. But man can always embellish them with tales of the unnatural or the unlikely, so that an odd-shaped stone, or an unusual stretch of water, or a curiously-flowering tree is given a much greater fascination.

Loch Ness for instance would be just another loch without its monster. The Glastonbury Thorn would be just another thorn without the story that it grew from the staff of Joseph of Aramathea. The apricot trees which climb many of the cottages at Aynho in Northamptonshire would be just some more apricot trees if the Lord of the Manor had not demanded the apricots as rent. And the wishing well at Berwick St John in Wiltshire would be just another hole with water in it without the legend that the Devil would grant your wish if you walked seven times at midnight round the Iron Age fort outside the village, swearing as you went.

I have chosen some of these natural phenomena which have a history, or just a story, like the wild Scotch thistles which grow on the remaining earthworks of Fotheringhay Castle in Northamptonshire, and which are said to have been planted by Mary, Queen of Scots, while she was awaiting execution. And I have chosen some of Nature's tricks with trees and rocks and water – Nature's jokes, I am tempted to think – to which man has added the punchline.

Tree tales – turning over an old leaf

"No town can fail of beauty, though its walks were gutters and its houses hovels, if venerable trees make magnificent colonnades along its street," wrote Henry Ward Beecher. For those who had to live in the hovels or wallow in the gutters, that may have been too rosy a view, but there is nothing like a tree to improve a view and happily, in spite of the depredations of Tudor shipbuilders, Victorian property developers and present-day papermakers – not forgetting Dutch elm disease – we still have a fair number of venerable trees left in England, and some are very venerable indeed.

It ought to be possible to decide which is the oldest tree in England, just by counting its rings. But since in some very old trees the rings have merged, and to do a thorough job one would have to cut down the tree to count them, it is difficult to declare any out-and-out winner. The Americans did cut down a sequoia in California and count 1,335 rings, and that was only 276 feet high, whereas some of Australia's eucalyptus trees are over 300 feet high and so probably a lot older.

Here in England we are a little less ambitious. Our longest-living tree, judging by the claims of various villages, is not the romantic English oak but the undramatic yew, much favoured by bowmen, cabinet makers, topiarists and country churchyards. A yew rarely grows higher than 30 feet, it becomes unattractively obese, and it never sheltered any royal fugitives, so in fact anything a yew can do, oak can do better – except outlive it.

One thousand years seems to be a popular round figure for aged yews, but **Darley Dale** in Derbyshire claims to have one twice that age in its churchyard. It is 32 feet in girth, and was certainly well established long before the 13th century church was built beside it. But if it is the oldest it is not the fattest; at **Ulcombe** in Kent there is a yew measuring 34 feet seven inches round, at a height of five feet.

The girth of these old yews is so substantial that over the years enterprising burghers have built seats inside them to provide a sort of living bus shelter.

Much Marcle in Herefordshire has an eight-seater yew in its churchyard. This old tree survived the mysterious move of Marcle Hill in 1575, when for three days the hillside moved a distance of some four hundred yards, killing unsuspecting cattle and sheep,

Much Marcle's eight-seater yew tree – a lot bigger, but is it a lot older than . . .

. . . the Aldworth yew, which lost most of its branches in a gale in 1976 but still survives. They could both be a thousand years old.

flattening trees and hedges, and even destroying a small chapel – the chapel bell was unearthed by a plough some 250 years later. But the 13th century church and the yew survived. So did an effigy of a man lying cross-legged with hands clasped in prayer, carved out of a solid block of oak – one of the things oak can do better . . .

The thousand-year-old yew at **Aldworth** in Berkshire, a few miles from Goring, is in a rather poorly state. Most of it was blown down in a gale in January 1976, and all that remains is an unimpressive stump which has been likened to a giant fossilised sponge. But there is a single green branch growing from it, so it still qualifies. In this same churchyard is the grave of Laurence Binyon, the poet whose words are heard at every Remembrance Day service: "They shall not grow old as we who are left grow old . . ."

Stoke Gabriel on the Dart estuary in Devon has another ailing yew in its churchyard, incapable of standing by itself and having to rely ignominiously on props. It does however claim to be up to 1500 years old, so its seniority may justify the crutches.

Painswick's yews in Gloucestershire make up in profusion what they may lack in age.

The Stoke Gabriel yew, perhaps the daddy of them all – said to be 1500 years old. Like many of us it is very gnarled at close quarters (above) but looks quite handsome at a distance (left).

The churchyard is full of them, in all shapes and sizes, but always, it is said, totalling the same number – ninety-nine. The Devil apparently took exception to a round one hundred. The villagers make a great fuss of their ninety-nine and have a 'clipping ceremony' each year, in which the yews are tidied up and there is much holding of hands and dancing round the church. The more fanciful say that some of the yews lining each side of the church path, their branches meeting overhead, look like couples on their wedding day, en route from the church to the reception – but that thought generally occurs quite late in the proceedings.

The Marton Oak, now split into four with a wendy house tucked into its trunk. Could this have been the biggest oak in England?

Painswick's 99 yews – an excuse for puppy-dog pie.

The ceremony also used to involve the eating of puppy-dog pie. In more recent years the puppy-dogs have been china replicas, but tradition has it that a local landlord ran out of meat to supply the crowds at the clipping ceremony and filled his pies with some of the Painswick strays. Alas, that is probably as inventive a tale as the history of the clipping ceremony itself. A spoilsport has pointed out that the ceremony dates back to the early 14th century, whereas the yews were only planted in 1792. He maintains that the word 'clipping' has no connection with the yews, it comes from an early English word meaning 'to enclose', and the celebrations were probably something to do with the freeing of enclosed land. He will be telling us next that the Devil would be quite happy to allow that hundredth tree . . .

I know of only one cedar that has been entered in the league table of aged trees. It stands in the village of **Cropthorne**, off the Evesham-Pershore road in Worcestershire, and the locals claim it was planted before the Norman Conquest, which would put it close to the magic one thousand. But I suppose the title must go to **Stanhope** in County Durham, which boasts a fossilised tree stump removed from a local quarry and now to be seen through a gap in the churchyard wall. It is estimated to be over two hundred and fifty million years old . . .

The oak does not claim the longevity of the yew, but it can certainly challenge it in size. The biggest in England is said to be the one at **Marton** in Cheshire – or rather the four, because the trunk has now split into quarters. It had a girth of 58 feet at its base, and its biggest branch was eleven and one-half feet

The fossilised tree stump at Stanhope – said to be 250 million years old, so don't start counting the rings.

Elizabeth's oak at Hatfield House, where she heard she had ascended to the throne.

The Dunsdons' oak at Shipton-under-Wychwood, where they were hung in chains as convicted highwaymen.

The Northiam Oak, where Elizabeth changed her shoes and left the old ones behind (queens can afford to do that sort of thing). The shoes are still preserved.

round. When it split and became a mini-stockade, a local farmer used it as a pound for his bull.

The Boscobel Oak in which Charles II hid from the Parliamentary troops in the grounds of **Boscobel House** in Shropshire has long since gone, though you can always see the oak which now stands in its place – not quite the same thing. But the oak tree under which the young Elizabeth sat with her maid when news was brought that Mary was dead and she was Queen of England, still stands in the grounds of **Hatfield House** in Hertfordshire, country seat of the Earls of Salisbury.

Elizabeth seemed to have a particular affinity with oaks. She chose one to rest under at **Northiam** in East Sussex on a journey to Rye in 1573. Her feet, it seems, were killing her, because she changed her shoes there and left behind the offending pair, made of green silk damask with two and one-half inch high heels and sharp pointed toes – not the ideal wear for a day in the country. The oak still

stands, and the shoes were preserved at the nearby mansion of Brickwall, an object lesson for future generations of ill-shod hikers.

Shipton-under-Wychwood in Oxfordshire claims an oak tree with a more sinister history. Carved on the trunk are the initials H D and T D, and the date 1784. But this was no romantic tryst. Harry and Tom Dunsdon were 18th century highwaymen who were captured near this spot, taken to Gloucester and hanged. Their bodies were brought back to Shipton and the oak was used as a gibbet. The experience is said to have stunted the oak; the Dunsdons did not appreciate it either.

A massive tree at **Lydiate** on Merseyside served a more useful purpose. It was incorporated in a public house which was built around it, and it still holds up part of the roof. The pub was originally named the Royal Oak in its honour, but its name was changed after one of Bonny Prince Charlie's wounded men was said to have hidden there and been nursed back to health. It is now the Scotch

Part of the ancient oak tree which still helps to hold up the Scotch Piper at Lydiate.

Piper. The Moorcroft family held the licence for five hundred years, until the only surviving daughter sold it to a brewery in 1945.

The oak has not merely given its name – and in that case, its support – to pubs, but also to places from Oakham to Acton ('ac' is the Old English word for oak), and to patriotic festivals like Royal Oak Day, May 29th. It is a great symbol of British sturdiness, even though it actually grows all over Europe and parts of America, Africa and Asia. Indeed, of the three hundred different kinds of oak only two are native to Britain. No matter; Royal Oak Day is celebrated with suitable patriotism at places such as **Aston-on-Clun** in Shropshire, where on May 29th the Arbor Tree is festooned with flags and bunting, some of which remain there for the rest of the year.

There are two stories behind Aston-on-Clun's tree dressing ceremony. Some say it started as a celebration of Charles II's restoration to the throne, after his successful concealment in that other Shropshire oak at Boscobel. More likely the flags were first hung there to mark the wedding day of a local landowner, John Marston on May 29th, 1786. What makes the whole affair more confusing is that the tree is not an oak at all, but an ancient black poplar!

The Arbor Tree at Aston-on-Clun, annually dressed overall.

Let me offer you one more unlikely tree tale, from **Berry Pomeroy** in Devon. The whole story of how Berry Pomeroy Castle became a ruin is a little weird. It was built by the Norman de la Pomerai family but sold to the Seymours, who built a fine mansion within its walls. William of Orange was received here on his way from Brixham to London to be crowned king. But only 13 years later the local vicar wrote of the castle, "All this glory lieth in the dust, buried in its own ruins". Even the Seymours, who still own it, do not know the details. But in the grounds is a wishing tree which it is said will grant the wish of anyone who walks round it three times, backwards. Could this be Devil's work, I hear you mutter – or like the Marton Oak once was, is it just full of bull?

To counter that, go to **Tewin** churchyard in Hertfordshire and see the tomb of Lady Anne Grimston. Before she died in 1713 Lady Anne said the truth of the Resurrection would be proved if trees grew from her grave. The ash and sycamore trees that have pushed their way through her tomb bear lasting witness.

A tree that grants wishes
– at Berry Pomeroy Castle

Trees that prove a point –
in Tewin churchyard.

Weird waters – still running deep

Dozmary Pool – Excalibur's last resting place?

High on the list of natural phenomena which stir the imagination and inspire the poetic muse is a nice deep lake. There is of course the beauty of it, which prompted Sir Walter Scott to write about the "burnished sheet of living gold" and the islands "empurpled bright, floating amid the livelier light" and another five thousand lines of similarly ecstatic adjectives in his "Lady of the Lake". John Greenleaf Whittier was another to eulogise on "Lake of the hills, where cool and sweet thy sunset waters lie ... Walled round with sombering pines".

But there is more to a lake than inspiring poets to invent words like 'empurpled' and 'sombering'. There is a mystery about deep still water which has stirred the imagination of writers since Sir Thomas Malory wrote down the legend of King Arthur and his sword Excalibur. Remember how it appeared from the waters of the lake, held by an unknown hand – how it shone like fire in battle and its scabbard protected Arthur from losing blood from his wounds? And remember how the treacherous Mordred fatally wounded him (yes, in spite of the scabbard – don't ask me, ask Malory) and in response to his dying wish the faithful Bedivere hurled Excalibur back into the lake, where it was neatly fielded by the same mysterious hand?

The snag is, Malory omitted to say which lake. Since the sword was studded with rich jewels there has been no lack of searchers – it would have been interesting to locate that hand as well. But so far Excalibur has escaped detection. If you fancy your chances you might try **Dozmary Pool**, in Cornwall – 'a drop of sea' which is high on the list of 'possibles'. It is also rumoured to be bottomless, which is not encouraging, but take heart from the local cattle, which seem to wade about in it quite safely.

If you fail to see anything odd at Dozmary, you stand a better chance at **Siddington** in Cheshire. There is a large lake called Redes Mere, in the Capesthorne Hall estate, which has an island formed of peat in the middle. Visit Redes Mere when the wind is blowing strongly and you will see the island move. When I first heard this I recalled the April Fool story we once broadcast on the 'Today' programme of an island bird sanctuary in the Medway which was to be towed out of the way of passing shipping. But the Redes Mere island really does move, just a little, and if legend is to be believed, for a very strange reason.

A medieval knight thought that his girl-friend was being unfaithful, and swore he would never see her again until the island moved – presumably a medieval equivalent of "until Hell freezes over". His suspicions, however, were unfounded, and when he fell ill the faithful girl nursed him back to health. As additional confirmation of her fidelity, the island was uprooted and has floated on the waters of Redes Mere ever since . . .

If you think you can do better than that, there's an opening for a good legend at **Halberton** in Devon, which boasts another odd piece of water – not the Grand Western Canal, which passes through the village in a very ordinary sort of way, but the pond which lies down Pond Lane. However cold the weather, this pond never freezes. Could there be some supernatural explanation, some strange tale of another ancient vow? All right, so it's probably a hot spring, but a little flight of fancy always cheers up the guide books.

Redes Mere, where an island is on the move.

Halberton Pond, where the water never freezes.

Earthy stories – leaving no stone unturned

When it comes to stories about stones there are two front-runners who seem to have been the inspiration behind most of them – the Druids, and the Devil. The Druids' penchant for stones is well-known, of course, through their annual visit to Stonehenge, the most spectacular stones of all. But many legends associate them with earlier ceremonies and give them credit for remarkable feats with stones which probably came about through natural causes.

There is a notable example at **Blidworth** in Nottinghamshire, said to be the home of Maid Marian. It is also said that Will Scarlet is buried in the churchyard, and that near the village is a cave in which Robin Hood and his outlaws stored their food. With this super-abundance of Robin Hood folklore (some of it dreamed up, perhaps, by the Merry Men of Blidworth in one of their merrier moments) it is surprising that a massive boulder at the foot of the hill on which the village stands

The Blidworth Boulder – a sacred relic of the Druids or just another stone with a hole in it?

Devil's work:
disappearing boys at
Marston Moretaine (the
stone marks the spot,
near the church tower) . . .

. . . and disappearing
bells at Newington (only
his footprint remains by
the church gate).

does not turn out to be the one which Little
John rolled down the hillside in an effort to
crush the Sheriff of Nottingham. But as it is
90 feet round and 15 feet high, perhaps that
would push credulity too far. Instead the
villagers will point out the hole through the
middle of the rock and speak knowingly of
Druids and their strange ways.

In the main however it is the Devil who
gets the credit for any stones of an untoward
shape or in untoward situations. Judging by
the legends lingering around many of our
villages, he spent much of his time toying
with stones – throwing them, dropping them,
stepping on them, cursing them. In his efforts
to capture the hearts and minds of the rural
population he left no stone, as it were, un-
turned.

He also leapt about a great deal, either
carrying stones or leaving stones in his wake.
At **Marston Moretaine** in Bedfordshire, for
instance, he started his leaping from the
tower of St Mary the Virgin – we are not told
what he was doing there, but one can assume
he was up to no good. He took three great
leaps, the third taking him across a road and
into a field where a group of young boys were
playing. The boys, singularly unalarmed by
his arrival, and doubtless impressed by the
quality of his leaping, agreed to let him join in
their game of leapfrog. When it came to their
turn to leap over his back they leapt straight
into a hole and disappeared forever. Only a
stone, the Devil's Stone, remained to mark
their departure, a grim warning not to play
leapfrog with strange men with forked tails.

While we are uncertain what the Devil was
doing on top of Marston Moretaine's church
tower, we have a much clearer account of his
visit to **Newington** Parish Church in Kent. He
was incensed, it seems, by the sound of the
church bells. It is a problem which has
affected others who live close to churches,
but understandably he felt more deeply about
them than most. He also took more drastic
action than most.

One night, feeling in particularly good
leaping form, he leapt into the belfry, gathered up all the bells and put them in a sack. As
he leapt down again he uncharacteristically
overbalanced (the weight of the bells must
have been quite considerable) and left evidence of his visit in a footprint on a stone
near the church gate. The footprint is still
around, but those bells are not. They fell out
of the sack as he made his awkward landing,

rolled into a nearby stream and disappeared for ever.

At this stage you may start arguing about the Devil having hooves, not feet. But the evidence is quite clear, a 15-inch footprint on the stone. Surely you would not suggest a human could have that size foot, so who else could it be?

The Devil, as you might expect, had quite a fixation about churches. When he was not leaping off them he was throwing stones at them. We have evidence of this in **Rudston** churchyard, near Bridlington in Yorkshire. Among the gravestones is a lofty stone, 25 feet high and six feet round. The mundane explanation is that it is a markstone, dating back to before 1000 BC, but others know

better. They say it was thrown at the church by the Devil, but he had had a bad night and his marksmanship was poor. The fact that the stone was there long before the church has as much impact on their story as the stone had on the church.

Another Devil's Stone landed in the village of **Shebbear** in Devon, but it is not allowed just to lie there. Every November the Fifth, when other villages are lighting bonfires and letting off fireworks, there is the ceremony of turning the stone. Since it is a half-ton boulder this is quite a feat, but it is cheerfully tackled by the local bellringers, perhaps on behalf of their erstwhile colleagues at Newington who lost their bells to the Devil. Curiously enough there is a ceremony

1968 'Turning'

Devil's Stones: the missile he is supposed to have thrown at Rudston Church (something of a long shot?) . . .

. . . and the one that landed in Shebbear village green, giving the locals quite a turn. Now the stone gets quite a turn every November.

attached to this custom in which the Vicar blesses the Devil's Stone in what is thought to be an 'overturning' of pagan rites and insurance against the Devil throwing anything else at the village.

The effort put in by the bellringers of Shebbear is quite unnecessary on the stone at **Colwall**, a village in the Malvern Hills some four miles from Ledbury in Herefordshire. The Colwall Stone, a large chunk of limestone in the centre of the village, was of course put there by the Devil, and every midnight, for reasons no one has dared question, he turns the stone round. No one has dared watch, either, but the story is just as plausible as the alternative the locals will offer you – that a giant who lived in a cave beneath the nearby Herefordshire Beacon suspected his wife of infidelity and hurled the stone at her, killing her forthwith.

It may be as an antidote to the Devil's Stone story that Colwall is one of several Herefordshire villages which are said to have a thornbush grown from a cutting from the Holy Thorn at Glastonbury. It blossoms, it is said, at midnight on Twelfth Night – just about the time the Devil is turning his stone down the road.

Perhaps the most impressive impact from a Devil's Stone occurred in Cornwall. On this occasion the Devil had got bored with leaping and was actually flying over Cornwall, carrying a stone to block the entrance to Hell. We are not told whether he planned to keep the baddies in, or the goodies out. As it turned out, he never made it. He was intercepted during the flight by no less than St Michael – one can imagine the Devil muttering, "Angel One-Five". In the ensuing devilfight he dropped the rock, and 'Hell's Stone'

How a cunning cobbler saved the Cotswolds.

Cam Long Down Hill.

'Hell's-stone', dropped by the Devil during a battle with St Michael, now safely preserved in the wall of the Angel Inn at Helston.

The Devil's Chimney on Leckhampton Hill.

fell on the spot where **Helston** stands now. The stone itself, so they say, is built into the wall of a local hostelry – the Angel, no less.

Incidentally the town must have sprung up around the stone very speedily, because the inhabitants were already on hand to dance around the streets in celebration of St Michael's victory. The Floral Dance takes place each year, presumably with St Michael still in mind, but Marks & Spencer have not yet cashed in on the publicity.

Perhaps if the Devil had completed his mission and blocked his front entrance we would have had no Devil's Chimney on **Leckhampton Hill**, near Cheltenham in Gloucestershire. It is a 50-foot high limestone pinnacle, which may be the residue from centuries of quarrying all around it, but the locals say it rises straight from Hell.

But them Gloucestershire folk are well versed in the Devil's funny ways. They preserve the tale of how he once decided to cart away the Cotswolds to dam the River Severn, for some devilish purpose of his own. As he was wheeling a barrow load of the Cotswolds across Cam Long Down he met a cobbler and asked how far it was to the river. The cobbler, shrewd fellow, pointed to all the shoes he was carrying and said he had worn them all out on the walk from the river. The Devil, appalled at the prospect of such a long hike (presumably he had not regained his flying powers after the encounter with St Michael), gave up the idea and left the Cotswolds where

they still are today. This could also be the origin of the phrase: "A load of old cobblers".

Not every strange stone has been touched by the Devil's hand. There is one, for instance, which is supposed to be quite good for you. The **Men-an-Tol** stone in Cornwall is reputed to have remarkable healing powers; you have to crawl into it via a 'porthole' in the stone to get the full effect. If that fails you can always take a dip in the nearby Madron Well, close to the burial place of St Madern. The waters are supposed to be particularly beneficial to children's complaints – "shingles, tetters and wildfires". Unfortunately the treatment involves not only plunging into the water, but following that up by walking around the well nine times, then sleeping on the marshy ground beside it. No doubt the shingles, tetters and wildfires were often re-placed by rheumatism, hypothermia and double pneumonia.

It does not do, however, to mock these sacred relics. Elsewhere in Cornwall, a county rich in stone-lore, there is a basin-shaped stone which formed St Nun's Well at **Pelynt**. A sacrilegious farmer fancied the stone for use as a pig trough, and chained his oxen to it to drag it up the hill to his farm. Halfway up the chains broke and the stone rolled back down the hill (making a skilful right-angle turn in the process) to land back in its original position. Moreover the farmer was immediately struck lame and the oxen dropped dead on the spot. No one has tried to steal it again.

Another farmer had a weird, though not lethal, encounter with a strange stone at **Anwick** in Lincolnshire. He was ploughing

Kill or cure? The prescribed treatment for "shingles, tetters and wildfires" at the Madron Well.

near the church when his horses disappeared into a bog, which is unusual enough in your average ploughed field, but as they went in a drake flew out. Next day a huge drake-shaped stone appeared on the spot. An attempt was made to move it but again the chains snapped. Again the drake was seen to fly from the spot. Many years later, in 1913, the stone was hauled to the churchyard, but it broke in two at the entrance, and the two pieces still stand there, one about six feet long, the other half that size. It is said that two drakes are often seen sheltering beneath them. It is also said – here we go again – the stone was a Druids' memorial.

The **Rollright Stones** in Oxfordshire, third in the Special Stones league table behind Stonehenge and Avebury, go back to before 1500 BC, and are also said to have been involved in ancient ceremonies, but legend has it differently. A local king was told by a witch that if he could see the neighbouring village of Long Compton from the top of that hill he would be king of all England. Being familiar with those parts he thought he was on to a good thing. He led his men to the top of the hill, looked towards Long Compton, and found the witch had stirred up a mist which completely obscured the view. Whereupon he and his men were turned to stone. You will find the King's Stone, and the King's Men, and there is a third group of stones called the Whispering Knights, who probably passed on the story in the first place.

The Anwick Stones, with strange drake connections.

The Rollright Stones – all the King's Men.

Once the size of a small loaf – and the Blaxhall Stone still grows?

The Whetstone at Kingstone walks into deep water.

If you are the slightest bit suspicious of these tales – and there are some sceptical folk about – here is one you can check for yourself. The Blaxhall Stone, at **Blaxhall** in Suffolk, is said to be steadily getting bigger. Local people say that when it was first noticed about one hundred years ago it was the size of a small loaf. Now it must weigh about five tons, and it is still growing. The stone is easy to find – just ask for Stone Farm. Do keep an eye on it, and if nothing has happened after a few years, let me know. Similarly, you may care to stand guard on the Cock-Crow Stone at **Looe** in Cornwall, which turns round thrice when a cock crows, or the Whetstone at **Kingstone**, near Hereford, which walks into the River Wye to whet its stone whistle.

It must be confessed that some stones are not entirely above suspicion. There is for instance a completely bogus Avebury near **Weston Rhyn**, in north-west Shropshire. The slabs of stone stand in the same sort of circle, but they were actually put there by a Major West in the 1830s to enliven the view from his house, and no doubt provide a talking point over dinner.

There is an imitation Stonehenge near **Ilton** on the Yorkshire Moors, but at least there was a philanthropic motive behind it. William Danby was an eccentric author with a snappy line in book titles. His first work, "Travelling Thoughts", was followed up by "Thoughts Chiefly on Serious Subjects", and the more broadly-based sequel "Thoughts on

The bogus Avebury in Shropshire, to provide a view for the guests . . .

The imitation Stonehenge in Yorkshire, to provide some work for the locals.

Various Subjects". But he also had the more practical thought of providing work for the unemployed by erecting a northern answer to the pride of Salisbury Plain. His workforce was paid a shilling a day to put up an amazing assortment of altars and standing stone, and the like, enough to keep the average Druid happy for a lifetime. They stand now on Forestry Commission land, looking rather embarrassed among all that Sitka spruce, a rather forlorn monument to a kindly man.

The Rev Edward Atkyns Bray of Tavistock devised another generous way of utilising stone for the common good and his own immortality. He decided to inscribe a selection of superior poetry on the rocks in Dartmoor's **Cowsic Valley**, for the enlightenment and education of passing hikers. Unfortunately Dartmoor granite does not yield easily to an amateur stonemason, and Mr Bray had to settle for merely carving the names of his favourite poets without giving actual examples of their work. A careful search of the

The Ten Commandments on Buckland Beacon – carved by 'Moses'.

boulders should lead to the names of Milton, Shakespeare, Homer and Spenser, but latest reports indicate that the elements are showing little respect for the great names of English literature, and they are gradually being obliterated.

The efforts of a Mr Whitley on the top of **Buckland Beacon** have fared rather better – or more accurately the efforts of Mr W A Clements, the stonemason he employed to carve the Ten Commandments on two tablets. He was a hard taskmaster; during the month or more Mr Clements was on the job he had to live on the tor in a cowshed, supplied with a loaf of bread by Mr Whitley once a week. This was not the Middle Ages, this was 1928. However it seems Mr Whitley had a sense of humour too; he nicknamed the carver of the tablets "Moses".

A much more elaborate example of education in stone is on a cliff outside **Swanage** in Dorset. The Great Globe on Tilly Whim, a round stone ten feet in diameter and weighing 40 tons, is surrounded by stone slabs bearing all manner of fascinating statistics to exercise the mind of the unsuspecting picnicker. He will learn, for instance, that if the globe represents the earth, the sun would be 1,090 feet across, the moon a mere 33 inches. There is material to uplift the mind as well as exercise it: quotations from the poets, with Shakespeare again well to the fore, and Old Testament Psalms. The anonymous compiler of this anthology on rock has tossed in a few of his own efforts as well. "Let justice be the guide to all your actions," he urges. "Let prudence direct you, temperance chasten you, fortitude support you." Great stuff to go

The cryptic carving at Nether Silton. The inscription is on the next page.

with the pork pie and the cheese and tomato sandwiches. Did some Great Purpose lie behind all this, or was Tilly Whim just a silly whim?

Happily for their creator, the inscriptions are well preserved, due in no small part to the shrewd thinking of the local authority which has provided spare stones on which graffiti-minded visitors can scratch away to their hearts' content. Not nearly so satisfying to the true vandal, but the stone scribbling pads have been much used, while the Great Globe is comparatively unscathed. The idea has been adopted in some of our inner cities, but without the same response. An aerosol-can knows no frontiers.

Once people had started carving messages on stones it was inevitable that some joker would come along and carve a mystery message that nobody else understood. An 18th century Yorkshireman called Squire Hickes has left behind a cryptic carving on a stone which sits in a field behind the church at **Nether Silton** in North Yorkshire. The first

The Great Globe near Swanage, centrepiece of several stony statistics.

line reads: "H T G O M H S", the second "T B B W O T G W W G" and so on – I will not irritate you with the entire inscription. Some crossword enthusiast has worked out that these are not a code or an anagram, but the initial letters of words which the squire put together to describe in verse the building that stood on this spot.

According to this cryptographer the first two lines read: "Here the grand old manor house stood, The black beams were oak, the great walls were good". Whatever the object of Squire Hickes in leaving such a puzzle, it hardly seemed worth the effort of transcribing it. How much more exciting if it had

started off "H B T", standing for "Here be treasure . . ." As it is, here be just a stone.

There are some stones which are memorable enough without being embellished either by the stonemason or the stray hooligan. Near **Grange-over-Sands** in Cumbria is the Bowder Stone, a two-thousand-ton boulder (how *do* they work out these weights?) measuring 50 feet square. It stands on one of its corners, apparently about to topple over at any time, but it has stood in that position ever since it fell from its original perch.

On the other hand there is the Logan Stone on a headland near **Porthcurno** in Cornwall which rocks when gently pushed. On one

The Bowder Stone near Grange-over-Sands – much safer than it looks.

occasion in 1824 it was pushed too far. A bold naval lieutenant took a lunge at it and shoved it over the headland on to the beach below. This caused considerable irritation among the locals, who no doubt feared they had lost their major tourist attraction, and they insisted on him replacing the rock at his own expense. This he did – and has the consolation of knowing, wherever he may be now, that his expensive shove is immortalised on the sign of the Logan Rock Inn at Treen. Oddly enough the lieutenant's name was not Logan but Goldsmith. Perhaps Logan was the man from the Tourist Board who put the stone there in the first place.

On the coast near **Lulworth Cove** is another natural marvel in stone, the Durdle Door. Two wide bays are divided by a chalk headland, in which the sea has carved out a great arch – the Durdle Door is in fact a doorway. Further along the coast, incidentally, to the east of Lulworth, is another curiosity in stone, a 'fossil forest' – treestumps which have become fossilised over the centuries.

The Logan Rock near Porthcurno – inn sign and in situ.

The Brimham Rocks near
Pateley Bridge – strange
shapes in stone.

Whenever we are stumped for a legend about an unusual stone we try to dream up an appropriate name instead. There is a granite stack on Dartmoor, a few miles south of **Moretonhampstead**, which is known as Bowerman's Nose, named after a local charac-ter who lived rough on the moor. Judging by the shape of his nose he must have lived very rough indeed. But there are some more inge-nious and accurate names to be found among the **Brimham Rocks** in Yorkshire, not far from Pateley Bridge.

They cover some 60 acres on a high plateau, a collection of gritstone outcrops which the wind and the rain have carved into strange and sometime familiar shapes. The favourite among younger visitors is the Dancing Bear, which looks exactly that. There are other animal shapes, perhaps not quite so easily identifiable – the Tortoise, the Rabbit, the Rhinoceros, and even the Yoke of Oxen. Then we are back to the two old favourites again – the Devil's Anvil and the Druids' Altar.

Finally, two stones with genuine tales attached to them, which even I believe. At **Wolverhampton** in the West Midlands, in a corner of St Peter's Collegiate Churchyard, is a stone about five feet high which has a hole near the top just big enough to shake hands in. This is the Bargain Stone, and in the days

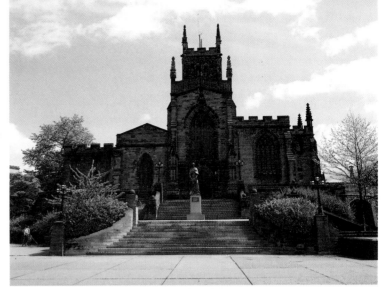

The Bargain Stone (left) in the churchyard of St Peter's Wolverhampton (above). A handshake through the hole meant the seal on a deal.

before contracts and computers, a buyer and a seller would clasp hands through the Bargain Stone, and the bargain would be sealed.

And at **Burrington Combe** in Somerset, in an area of dramatic rocks and exciting caves, there is one great stone in which the curate of nearby Blagdon sheltered during a thunderstorm and was inspired to write a hymn about it. The Rev Augustus Toplady died only three years later at the age of 38, but "Rock of ages, cleft for me" will be his lasting memorial, as well as the rock itself.

"Rock of Ages, cleft for me" – the stone in Burrington Combe which inspired the hymn.

The stately home circuit – by the back door

Yes, these are castles and stately homes, the sort you find in any self-respecting tourist guide, but while those guides concentrate on the architecture and the furniture and the family history I have tried to single out the stately oddity. I do not linger over Vanbrugh's Tuscan pillars at Seaton Delaval, I am more fascinated by that mystery sculpture of David and Goliath in the garden – and even more so by the tale of how one of the occupants of the family mausoleum, John Delaval, died in 1775 at the immature age of 20, "as a result of being kicked in a vital organ by a laundry-maid to whom he was paying his addresses"!

A mansion may have imposing halls and vast galleries but I always head for the secret room or the false chimney, or the vault where a fugitive was kept alive by a faithful servant, until the servant died and he starved to death too.

Sometimes it is the place itself which is odd – the 'medieval fortress' built in 1910, or the Oriental mansion with an onion dome on the roof and fake Brahmin cows in the garden, all deposited in the heart of the Gloucestershire countryside. Sometimes it is the occupants who are odd, filling a room with life-size Samurai warriors or erecting temples to their dead pets.

There is even one castle, St Briavels in the Forest of Dean, which our forefathers travelled to from all over the country just to pick a quarrel. Henry III alone ordered six thousand. They were the quarrels fired from crossbows, and though they have long since disappeared, the Tump on the village green is formed from the cinders of the fires in which they were forged.

Quirky castles and curious corners

The extinguished Sir Walter Raleigh.

The 'New Castle' at Sherborne where Sir Walter Raleigh experienced the hazards of smoking.

Where castles and stately homes are concerned, some people are never satisfied. Take Sir Walter Raleigh. In 1592, having made the odd penny on tobacco sales, he decided to rent the castle at **Sherborne** in Dorset. It had been built four hundred years earlier by Bishop Roger, who as Chancellor to Henry I was in a position not to stint himself. It was not good enough however for Sir Walter, who fancied a few modern conveniences. He built himself another one alongside it, and the two castles stood together for another 50 years until Cromwell's forces reduced the original one to ruins. They are still known as the Old and the New.

Sir Walter's sojourn in the New Castle was not without its eventful moments. It is said he was trying out some of the new tobacco he had brought back from Virginia, when his servant, unversed in such sophisticated habits and believing his master to be on fire, doused him with a mug of beer. Sir Walter's reaction is not on record.

Four centuries later another individualist appeared with strong views about castles and enough money to put them into practice. Julius Drew was one of the founders of the Home and Colonial Stores. He dreamed of building himself a castle on the site where he believed his ancestor, the Norman noble Dro-

go, once lived. It was nine hundred feet up, near the village of **Drewsteignton** in Devon and overlooking the wooded gorge of the River Teign, with splendid views over Dartmoor.

On a family picnic in 1910 he selected the spot where the driveway should start by pulling up a mangold. That was the cheapest part of the operation. He spent £50,000 on the castle and £10,000 on the grounds. He told Sir Edwin Lutyens he wanted "a medieval fortress to match the grandeur of the site". Sir Edwin got to work with the granite, and created what looks less like a medieval fortress than a modern prison. High square walls, small windows, all straight lines and sharp corners, and about as romantic as one of Julius's grocery stores. It is now preserved by the National Trust – more as a curiosity, surely, than as a place of beauty.

But at least Castle Drogo was completed. **Twizel** Castle, close to the Scottish border in Northumberland, never got that far. Sir Francis Blake had a similar idea to Julius Drew – he wanted to build a medieval fortress too. That was in 1770. Men worked on it for nearly 50 years, then they gave up. It reached five storeys, but it was never finished and never occupied. It stands in a majestic position overlooking the River Till just before it flows into the Tweed, backing on to a ploughed field.

Twizel Castle, a bogus medieval fortress, never completed.

Castle Drogo a bogus medieval fortress that was completed – for better or worse.

Oriental splendour in
Gloucestershire – Sir
Charles Cockerell's
domed house, Sezincote.

Sir Charles Cockerell had a rather better idea than Mr Drew's enormous granite biscuit-tin. He spent many years in India in the early 19th century, and decided to bring home a breath of the exotic Orient to the peaceful Gloucestershire countryside around Bourton-on-the-Hill and Moreton-in-Marsh. With the help of his brother Samuel Pepys Cockerell (a name that must have taken some living up to) he built a house at **Sezincote** which was English in plan but incorporated Oriental arches, an onion-shaped dome, and a pinnacled north wing with a greenhouse pavilion. Even the gardens were landscaped in Indian style by Humphry Repton, with shrines to Indian gods in the water garden and imitation Brahmin cows on the Oriental bridge.

Presumably the Prince Regent visited Sezincote because this was the inspiration for his Pavilion at Brighton. The Cockerells have a lot to answer for.

Another great house in Gloucestershire keeps its eccentricities to itself. From the outside **Snowshill Manor** looks like a typical Cotswold house, with not an onion dome to be seen. Inside, however, it is crammed with treasures and trinkets from all over the world. Charles Wade's coat of arms bears the motto "Nequid Pereat" – "Let Nothing Perish" – and he didn't.

It must be one of the country's largest collections of just about everything. Not just the rooms; the stairs and corridors and attics are all stuffed full. Mr Wade himself moved into a cottage in the courtyard to give the collection more space. Most spectacular items·

"Let Nothing Perish" –
and not much did.

are the 26 full-size Japanese Samurai dressed for battle with weapons poised, which greet you as you enter the Green Room. That's assuming you can get in.

The oddest thing about Hellen's, a fine Jacobean house at **Much Marcle** in Herefordshire, is its name, which makes it sound like a teashop. It actually derives from Walter Helyon, the steward who managed the estate for its owner, Yseult Mortimer Audley. But how much better to have preserved its original name – The Manor of Marcle Magna Purparty Audley. It might make an unwieldy letterhead, but it rolls off the tongue like the names of those firemen in Camberwick Green. One must not be too flippant about Hellen's, though. There is a sad episode in its history. At the turn of the 18th century Hetty Walwyn, the daughter of the house, ran away with a renowned scoundrel. Her father, it is said, died of a broken heart. When the inevitable happened and she returned, brokenhearted, her mother locked her in a barred room. All she had left was the diamond ring her lover had given her. With it she inscribed his name on a window. It is still there:

John Pearcel 170 2

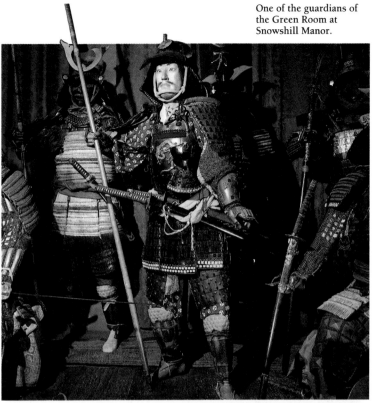

One of the guardians of the Green Room at Snowshill Manor.

Hetty Walwyn's room at Hellen's, and her farewell gesture to her lover – his name inscribed on the window.

Seaton Delaval Hall, the Palladian mansion which Sir John Vanbrugh built for Admiral George Delaval in Northumberland in the early 18th century, was burned twice, stood roofless for 50 years, and was occupied by the military in both world wars. It was nearly derelict when they started putting it together again in the 'Fifties, but some of its features survived unscathed, including one of the most intriguing pieces of sculpture in the country.

It stands in the gardens, an 18th century replica of an Italian work of art depicting David and Goliath which was completed two hundred years before. Nobody knows its history or the whereabouts of the original statue. Admiral Delaval may have known, but he did not live to see his mansion completed – he died from a fall from his horse – and the story probably died with him.

A rather more obvious decoration was left by the Countess of Shrewsbury – 'Bess of Hardwick' – when she had **Hardwick Hall** built in Derbyshire in 1591. Bess was extremely rich, having married four times, on each occasion to a richer husband. She must have many counterparts in modern times. Even though she left her fourth husband, the Earl of Shrewsbury, he bequeathed her all his money. But none of these gentlemen is featured at Hardwick Hall quite as dramatically as Bess herself. Her initials 'E S' are emblazoned along the roof tops.

Many stately homes have painted staircases, the status symbol of the 17th century, but few can equal the extravagance of Thomas Vernon, who built **Hanbury Hall** in Worcestershire. Sir James Thornhill, who later became famous for his work in St Paul's, had a fine time with his paintbrush, decorat-

David and Goliath at Seaton Delaval a replica of who knows what?

ing not just the staircase but the ceiling as well. The figure of Mercury links the two, his feet on the walls and his head on the ceiling. The feature to look for, however, is the object he has in his hand.

It is a portrait of Dr Sacheverell, a controversial character of the time who was found guilty of sedition. Mercury was apparently aware of this – he is about to plunge him into the flames lit by the Furies on the ceiling.

The painted staircase – and ceiling – at Hanbury Hall, where ancient Mercury has obviously had prior knowledge of Dr Sacheverell's misdeeds and is about to plunge him into the flames.

A feminist gesture of the 1500s. The Countess of Shrewsbury makes sure there is no confusion about who built Hardwick Hall.

"Five for the symbols at your door" – is this how it originated? Benthall Hall in Shropshire has the five marks in the porchway which are thought to have offered sanctuary to Catholic priests in the 16th century.

In the porchway to the main door of **Benthall Hall**, a few miles from Much Wenlock in Shropshire, you may spot five marks in the stone surround, arranged like a five in a pack of cards. This mark occurs in a number of 16th century houses; they are thought to indicate to strangers that the house was owned by catholic sympathisers and would offer sanctuary to priests. Could this be the original of that line in "Green Grow the Rushes O" – "Five for the symbols at your door"?

Dover Castle's odd feature is much more obvious. They called it Queen Elizabeth's 'pocket pistol', a cannon 24 feet long, elabo-

rately decorated with fruit and flowers. It is not so much the cannon which is odd as the ditty that went with it.

> *Use me well and keep me clean, I'll send a ball to Calais Green.*

It is a big cannon but not as big as that – its actual range was two thousand yards. But no doubt it kept the chaps cheerful.

While you are at the Castle, cast a wary eye at Peverell's Tower, which holds a guilty secret. Many years ago, when they were no better at building tower blocks than they are now, it was in the habit of falling down. The architects, surprisingly, blamed somebody else – in this case, the evil spirits. To placate them, an old woman and her dog were buried in the walls – alive. This unpleasant form of exorcism had its just revenge. The mason who carried it out fell to his death from the tower. I am sure it has nothing to do with this unfortunate lady or her dog, but I am bound to report that the tower has not fallen down since.

Queen Elizabeth's 'pocket pistol' at Dover Castle – "Use me well and keep me clean, I'll send a ball to Calais Green". Really?

Animal (ever so slightly) crackers

It may have led a dog's life, but in death, what glory! Lord Byron's memorial to his Newfoundland dog 'Boatswain' at Newstead Abbey.

Many a stately home was shared with a stately pet, and if it endeared itself sufficiently to its stately owners it finished up with a stately memorial. The gardens and grounds of some of our finest houses are bespattered with slightly bizarre tributes to four-legged friends of yesteryear.

Dogs, of course, are all over the place. They inspire some of the biggest memorials and some of the soppiest inscriptions. Even Lord Byron went a bit over the top with his monument to his Newfoundland dog 'Boatswain' at **Newstead Abbey**, his ancestral home near Nottingham:

Beauty without Vanity, Strength without Insolence, Courage without Ferocity, and all the Virtues of Man without his Vices.

Such paragons (of pets) were apparently commonplace among the aristocracy. At **Woburn** a former Duchess of Bedford erected a twelve-foot-high temple to her pekinese Che Foo. It has six Corinthian columns, a wrought-iron dome, and a bronze effigy of Che Foo on a stone plinth which bears another of Lord Byron's canine compliments:

In life the firmest friend, The first to welcome, foremost to defend.

One gets a splendid picture of the Duchess being defended against all comers by her daredevil Pekinese.

But never mind the dogs, whose devotion to their owners is only matched by their owners' posthumous devotion to them. Rather less likely are the memorials to horses, to a cow and a pig, and to a trout.

The memorial pyramid to a horse called 'Beware Chalk Pit' is mentioned elsewhere in this book, together with the explanation for that cautionary name. Another horse, the Earl of Yarborough's favourite hunter of the 1880s, called more explicably Dashaway, has an imposing urn in his honour at **Brocklesby** in Lincolnshire. Dogs, incidentally, have not been forgotten at Brocklesby – it has the oldest-established private pack of hounds in the country, in magnificent kennels which may also be the oldest, dating back to 1780. But horses have generally had pride of place. It is said that after dinner each evening the butler would announce "The horses are bedded, my Lord", and the guests would then troop off to the stables for an inspection.

CHE FOO (WUZZY)

BORN DECEMBER 1904-DIED JULY 28 1916·

WHEN THE BODY THAT LIVED AT YOUR SINGLE WILL,
WHEN THE WHIMPER OF WELCOME IS STILLED (HOW STILL!),
WHEN THE SPIRIT THAT ANSWERED YOUR EVERY MOOD
IS GONE – WHEREVER IT GOES – FOR GOOD,
YOU WILL DISCOVER HOW MUCH YOU CARE,
AND WILL GIVE YOUR HEART TO A DOG TO TEAR!

Temple to a pekinese (left) – the Duchess of Bedford's memorial to her pet, Che Foo (above). Che Foo himself (above, right) does not seem terribly pleased.

The memorial to Dashaway, the Earl of Yarborough's favourite hunter.

Memorial to an unknown horse (left), not in terribly good shape (right), and tombstone to a cow (below), not in a terribly good position.

Another horsey urn stands in the grounds of Longworth Hall Hotel at **Lugwardine** in Hereford. Its full story is not known; it was discovered in the cellar of the house in the 1880s (the urn, I hasten to say, not the horse), restored and re-erected. It stands beside a tree in a commanding position overlooking the River Frome.

The memorial to a cow is a much more modest affair, a simple tombstone which, when last seen, was propped rather forlornly against a wall in the grounds of **Rousham**, home of the Cottrell Dormer family. Faustina Gwynne was a shorthorn cow which died in 1882 at the age of 22, after a happy lifetime

terrorising the villagers, by chasing them down the street whenever she could get loose. Her much better behaved sister Goody Gwynne received no such commemoration – further proof that there is no justice in this world, even for cows.

However the Countess of Mount Edgcumbe made sure that justice was done in the case of Cupid, her devoted pig. Cupid was part of the social life of South Devon in the 18th century. He followed the Countess about wherever she went, even accompanying her on visits to London. Needless to say, this little piggy never went to market. He lived out his days in considerable comfort, and on his death the Countess erected a massive obelisk over his grave in the grounds of Mount Edgcumbe. It was later moved to a hill overlooking **Plymouth Sound**, where the River Tamar runs into the sea. I am not clear whether it was moved to give it greater prominence, or to get at the gold casket in which Cupid's remains were said to be buried.

Fish Cottage at **Blockley** in Gloucestershire is not perhaps the stateliest of homes, but it housed a family as devoted to a trout as the Countess was to her pig, and their sentiments were just as noble. The fish was the pet of a Mr William Keyte, who tamed it and trained it to rise to the surface, dolphin-like, whenever he approached. It may have done so from affection or just plain hunger, but there is no doubt about the Keytes' affection for the fish. When he died in 1855, aged 20, William's son Charles inscribed a memorial tablet "in memory of the Old Fish". The verse is admirably straightforward:

> *Under the soil the old fish do lie,*
> *Twenty years he lived, and then did die.*
> *He was so tame, you understand,*
> *He would come and eat out of our hand.*

At a stately home an obelisk to a pig (right), and at a modest cottage (below left) a memorial to a fish (below).

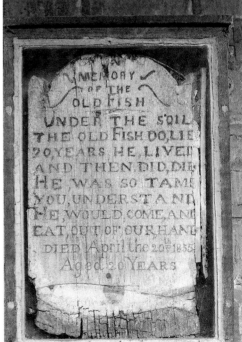

Hidden depths and familiar haunts

Our more illustrious forefathers had a great passion for secrecy. They loved hiding things – preferably people. And many of our very big stately homes have very small stately hiding places, custom-built for the errant earl or the fugitive friar.

Harvington Hall, a happy hiding ground with its false chimney (above), its false beam which swings forward to reveal a secret chamber (below) and its false stair (below, right).

They had good reason in those days, of course, to hide. There were several centuries when life seemed to consist of just one damn purge after another. If the Protestants were not purging the Catholics, the Roundheads were purging the Cavaliers. Considering the precarious condition of the monarchy a surprising number of people seemed anxious to acquire the throne. The number of beds that Queen Elizabeth slept in was only equalled by the number of secret rooms Prince Charlie hid in.

So part of the standard training for 16th and 17th century architects was a crash course in concealment, an S-level in secrecy. False ceilings, false walls, false chimneys, false floors – they offered their clients the slogan taken up by Star Wars, "The False be with you . . ."

As a result no self-respecting stately home was without its secret chamber. Some were so honeycombed that if anybody had given them a good shake, the whole place might have collapsed.

Harvington Hall in Worcestershire was probably built by the master of secret chamber designers, Nicholas Owen. It was the happy hiding ground for Jesuit priests in the reign of the first Elizabeth; false chimneys, a false step in a staircase, even a lavatory shaft were crammed with the chaps. There was also a hide over the bread ovens, but it was not too

popular when the fire was lit. Later the Franciscan St John Wall tucked himself into one of the hall's cunning corners, but to little avail. In 1679 he became the last Roman Catholic to die for his faith in England. Ironically, or perhaps fittingly, the house is now owned by the Roman Catholic Archdiocese of Birmingham.

Mr Owen created a spare supply of hiding places at nearby **Hindlip Hall**, and even made a ten-foot-deep hidey-hole at the Harvington gatehouse for the poorer class of fugitive. There are probably a few more yet to be discovered.

The Wicked Lady made famous on film by Margaret Lockwood was in reality Lady Katherine Ferrers of **Markyate Cell** in Hertfordshire. Just as in the film, Lady Ferrers donned men's clothing at nightfall and rode off to rob travellers on what is now the A5 trunk road. She used a secret room to hide, not herself, but her disguise. Her career ended when she was shot during the course of her work. She managed to get home, but died at the foot of the secret stairs leading up to the hidden room. Miss Lockwood herself could not have devised a more dramatic closing scene.

Between Fordham and Hilgay, two obscure little villages in the south-west corner of Norfolk, there is the 17th century **Snowre Hall**, sometimes spelt Snore Hall to reflect the general atmosphere. But Snowre Hall has seen some excitement in its time. Charles Stuart is said to have sheltered in one of its secret chambers before his surrender at

Markyate, home of the original Wicked Lady, who kept her highwayman's gear in a secret room and died in such dramatic circumstances that Margaret Lockwood could hardly have done better.

Newark. One hopes that for his comfort they did not put him in the smallest room in the house – not a loo but a hidden chamber just six feet long by three feet wide. You cannot see it these days because it has been boarded up, but if you visit Hilgay anyway don't miss its other claim to fame, the grave of George William Manby, school friend of Nelson and inventor of the rocket apparatus for saving life from shipwreck. You will spot his tombstone by the ship and anchor and mortar carved upon it. His is a name to be remembered as long as there can be a stranded ship, says the inscription, and it ends rather sourly:

The public should have paid this tribute

The saddest story of a secret hiding place must surely be the one linked with **Minster Lovell Hall** in Oxfordshire. It is said that Francis Lovell, a follower of Richard III, escaped to the Continent after the Battle of Bosworth, but was unwise enough to return a couple of years later to plot against Henry VII. Discovered and pursued by the authorities, he hid himself away in an underground room at the hall, blocked in by a faithful retainer

The ruins of Minster Lovell Hall (right), where a bride playing hide and seek hid all too successfully . . .

who brought him food. Alas, the retainer died without passing on his duties to a successor. Lovell's skeleton, and that of his dog, were discovered by workmen in 1718.

In another such tale, a bride of the Lovells hid in a chest during an innocent game of hide-and-seek. She was all too successful; nobody found her, and she could not open the chest herself. Another skeleton was added to the family history.

Only the ruins of the hall remain, but small wonder that there are stories of ghosts – of a suffocating girl, a starving man and no doubt an emaciated dog. Ghosts seem to follow naturally from secret chambers, and the 13th century **Chingle Hall** near Goosnargh in Lan-cashire, the first domestic building in England to be built of brick, has a profusion of them both. There are four priest holes, each with a full quota of restless spirits. It is said to be the most haunted house in Britain.

Certainly there have been strange goings-on there, even in recent times. One photo-grapher was taking a picture inside the Hall when the camera was snatched from him by an invisible hand and flung over a rafter in the ceiling. Another succeeded in taking the picture, but found that when he developed it strange images were visible on the print. Fortunately – or perhaps unfortunately – our own photographer was unmolested and her pictures were unaffected.

Chingle Hall (far left), said to be the most haunted house in Britain, where priests held illegal services. The candlesticks were kept hidden in the floor (below, far left) and the cross set into the wall (below, left) was hidden by a curtain. The priests themselves had various 'holes' in which to hide (below).

Assorted spirits at
Barnwell Abbey House.

For sheer variety in ghosts it would have been difficult to beat **Barnwell Abbey House** in Cambridge. There was a squire, and a White Lady, and a poltergeist, and a disembodied head. There was also the statutory clanking chain and, less likely, a ghostly squirrel and a hare.

It would have been interesting to hold a competition for combining all these elements into one comprehensive ghost story. The squire could have kept the White Lady chained up with only a hare and a squirrel for company until a poltergeist freed her by stunning the squire with a well-aimed head . . . But alas, it is too late. All that remains is a building called Cellarers Chequer and these restless spirits with their ghostly menagerie must have long since departed.

The Cellarers Chequer at
Barnwell Abbey House.

Not just a pretty facade

Villages, like people, can have a lot more to them than just a pretty face. They can develop peculiar talents, peculiar habits, peculiar reputations. They can even have their own peculiar secrets. For instance, Bisley in Gloucestershire may not be as famous as Bisley in Surrey, home of the National Rifle Association, but in Tudor times it is said to have nursed a secret that changed history. It would explain Elizabeth the First's reluctance to marry, and her receding hairline in later life. It is said she was staying as a child at Over Court, a private house in the village, when she suddenly died. Her hosts, understandably reluctant to break such devastating news to the volatile Henry VIII, found a replacement of similar age and build with the right crop of red hair. It just happened to be a boy. It is not explained how Henry failed to spot the substitution, let alone the Queen's several male admirers as the years went on, but the villagers of Bisley kept their secret well and as you can see from the history books, it was never discovered . . .

Not the greatest, just the mostest

It is always hazardous to claim that anything is the prettiest or the ugliest, the funniest or the dullest, the oddest or the quaintest. That is a matter of opinion rather than fact, and opinions can differ wildly. I have always tried to avoid judging competitions like best-kept villages; you make one set of friends and several sets of enemies. (In the case of baby competitions, incidentally, you can make enemies for life.) So I would hesitate to record, for instance, that **Castle Combe** in Wiltshire is England's most beautiful village, even though the residents of Castle Combe say it very firmly, and a great many guidebooks bear them out. The makers of the film 'Dr Doolittle' thought so too when they chose it for their location. But no doubt there are scores of other villages which would disagree. Through the eye of these beholders there would be less beauty in Castle Combe than in their own; whereas I am convinced there are half a dozen Norfolk villages which would knock spots off the lot.

So let us turn to more measurable qualities. **Flash** in Staffordshire claims to be the highest village in England, 1518 feet above sea level. There is not much to Flash and what there is can look pretty desolate, but it claims another distinction too. It has added its own meaning to the word 'flash' which, according to Collins Dictionary, has 33 meanings altogether, ranging from lights to news. Number 17 in the list is 'sham or counterfeit', and this is said to derive from the fact that Flash, being close to the point where three counties meet (Staffordshire, Cheshire and Derbyshire), was a popular haunt of thieves and forgers who could nip across a county boundary if the law appeared. They could be gone, as it were, in a flash – which is Meaning Number Three, 'a very brief space of time' . . .

Three miles from Zennor in Cornwall (which has good claim to the title of always being the last village to appear in a guide book index) is a village with a much more dramatic claim; it has the oldest village street

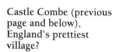

Castle Combe (previous page and below), England's prettiest village?

More 'mostest' villages – the oldest, Chysauster (left) and the highest, Flash (right).

in England. **Chysauster** was built somewhere
between the first century BC and the third
century AD, on the side of a hill rather than in
the fertile valley below, because in those days
the valley was so fertile it was probably
impenetrable. To cope with the Cornish
winds the walls of the houses were built
about 15 feet thick, which is why many of
them still remain, while the roofs have long
since disappeared. So have the inhabitants,
but they left evidence that they farmed and
smelted tin, and kept small gardens.

The area is full of relics of those early
Cornishmen. There is an artificial cave not far
away which was probably used as a cold-
store. There are old fortifications on Gur-
nard's Head, and an assortment of quoits,
which were not for playing games but for
burying people – they are tombs made by
putting two boulders on end with a flat one
across the top. Which gives the Chysauster
area another claim to fame; one of these flat
slabs is big enough to cover not one burial
chamber but two; it could be the biggest
burial-tomb boulder in the business.

Ashington in Northumberland used to be
given the not entirely enviable title of largest
mining village in the world, with 25,000

The largest mining village,
Ashington (above) and the
largest village square,
Bradworthy (left).

The longest names – but what about the hyphen?

people in the community who grew up around the pits. These days it is prouder of being the birthplace of Jack and Bobby Charlton. Another 'biggest' is claimed by **Bradworthy** in Devon, which is surrounded by several other 'worthy' villages – Dinworthy, Ashmansworthy, Chilsworthy, Pyeworthy. But they cannot equal Bradworthy's village square, which is recorded as the largest of its kind in Devon and probably in the country. It could thus also be the village with the smallest parking problem.

Blakehopeburnhaugh is another 'biggest' claimant, just because of its name. Although the village itself is tiny, it claims to have the biggest one-word name. Its 18 letters are outnumbered by nearby Cottonshopeburnfoot, with 19, but according to the Ordnance Survey there is a hyphen somewhere in the middle, and once the field is open to double-barrels the contestants are too numerous to classify.

Of all the 'biggest' claims, my favourite is the village of **Dymock** in Gloucestershire, which could well have the biggest variations in the way it is spelt. Maps and guidebooks offer two or three alternative spellings, but I

was presented with a mug which gives the complete range over the past nine hundred years: Denimock, Dimoc, Dimoch, Dymock, Dimmoc, Dymoke, Dimmukes, Dunmock and Dymmocke. On average they changed the spelling every century, a source of constant confusion to census takers and postmen. The village also caused some confusion when it decided to celebrate its nine hundredth anniversary in 1985, when it was actually built in 1088, but they found that a priest was first recorded in the area in 1085, which seemed a good enough reason for rejoicing. No doubt there will be more rejoicing in 1988.

There must be many contenders for the remotest village in England, particularly in the northern counties. I can only offer my own nomination. If you turn off the B5289 between Borrowdale and Derwentwater, up in the Lake District, and negotiate three miles of narrow twisting track, across a narrow packhorse bridge of deceptive width, you will find the hamlet of **Watendlath**, beside the tiny lake of the same name. It is a little hidden valley in the middle of nowhere, with the two thousand-foot High Seat peak towering above it. Hugh Walpole must have found his way

The remotest? Watendlath, in the Lakes.

A claimant for the biggest variety of spellings of a village's name – or is this just a mug's game?

there, because some of his novels are set in the area. So incidentally has the National Trust; they have installed a car park at Surprise View, on the way to Watendlath, and all but one of the stonewalled and stoneroofed buildings in the village are under their protection.

Finally the most off-putting title must go to **Pluckley**, a pleasant little hillside village in Kent between Charing and Biddenden, which is generally accepted to be the most haunted village in England. At the last count, some 20 years ago, there were a dozen spectral inhabitants, some of them belonging to the Dering family, who also left behind the 'lucky' Dering windows. During the Civil War a Dering Royalist escaped through one of these narrow round-arched windows framed by white bricks, and nearly every building in Pluckley now boasts them, largely due to the efforts of Sir Edward Cholmeley Dering, who added the brick facades with their Dering windows at the end of the last century.

The Dering manor house is now a burned-out ruin, said to be haunted by the White Lady Dering, while the Red Lady Dering is roaming the churchyard in search of her unbaptised child. There is also a Cavalier who presumably failed to avail himself of a Dering window and was caught and killed by the Roundheads. Much longer established is the ghost of a 'smiling monk' who had little reason for amusement, since he was executed at Tyburn in the time of Henry VIII.

The roads are patrolled by a highwayman who was pinned to a tree by the sword of a victim who declined to stand and deliver, and on the verge is a gypsy watercress woman who fell asleep while smoking her pipe and was burned to death. Meanwhile in the vicinity of the local brickworks is the 'screaming man', who came to an unpleasant end in the last century when he fell into a mixing trough filled with knives. A phantom coach and horses also rampage around the village, perhaps in search of more highwaymen to nail up.

I have to record however that in spite of this milling throng of lost souls in their midst, the present inhabitants of Pluckley seem singularly undisturbed. They mingle nonchalantly with their weeping, screaming, moaning neighbours, who have no doubt been joined by generations of giftshop and teashop owners, still crying all the way to the bank.

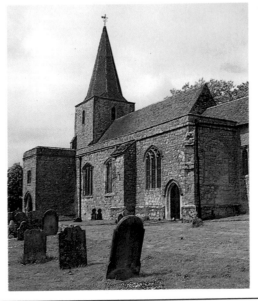

The most haunted village in England? Pluckley has a haunted churchyard, haunted houses, haunted streets – no doubt the pub has spirits too.

New villages for old – like it or not

New Houghton (below) an early example of compulsory town planning – Sir Robert Walpole knocked down the old village and built a new one outside his park.

The vast majority of English villages are a jumble of different styles from different centuries. New shops and cottages were tucked between and around the old ones, new streets were added to existing lanes and alleys, a wash-house was tacked on here, a chicken-house there. Many a village owes its charm to a total lack of any overall plan. They just grew.

But in the 18th century a new sort of village began to appear, the early rural equivalent of our present-day New Towns. Old villages were wiped out and the planners started from scratch. They were not acting for a planning authority or a development corporation; these were the lords of the manor, working not so much in the public interest as in their own. They put the villagers where it was most convenient for their own purposes – where they were handy enough to work on the estate, but far enough away not to spoil the view.

Probably the best known example is **Milton Abbas** in Dorset, because it is one of the most attractive. It has a single street of thatched semi-detached cottages, all identical and all sharing the same front lawn. A charming picture these days, but it must have been quite a jolt for the people who were moved into them in the 1770s by the Earl of Dorchester, who had wiped out their original little market town because it offended his eye. He did shift the original almshouses to the new village, and put up a church, but one marvels at the feudal powers which permitted a landlord to raze people's homes and plant them in new ones out of his way. One also wonders what happened to those who got left out of the allocation – the original town was much larger than the new village.

In Norfolk, where feudalism is still fairly well entrenched, they probably took it as a matter of course when Sir Robert Walpole, England's first Prime Minister, moved into his

newly built Houghton Hall, decided the village of Houghton looked untidy, scattered about on his parkland, and built **New Houghton** instead, outside the park gates. He could not do much about the church, which still stands deserted on its original site; indeed the family vault is there, and his ancestors might have objected to being shunted outside the gates with everyone else. In due course of time he joined them.

Elsewhere in East Anglia Lord Orford, First Lord of the Admiralty, did much the same thing at **Chippenham**, not far from Newmarket. When he set out his park he knocked down several cottages that happened to be in the way and built the village outside his lodge gates. In Derbyshire a century later on the Chatsworth estate the sixth Duke of Devonshire caught sight of the village of **Edensor**, decided it was an eyesore, and demolished it to create a new one with a castellated entrance lodge and villas rather than cottages.

In more recent times, of course, villages and towns have been transferred from area to area without disturbing a brick. The great local government re-organisation of 1974 changed county boundaries and invented new ones, while counties such as Rutland and Middlesex officially disappeared altogether.

Needless to say this proved singularly irksome to a great many people, not least those Yorkshire folk who suddenly found themselves living in the rival county of Lancashire, or even in Greater Manchester. There was much gnashing of teeth, for instance, in the area known as Saddleworth, actually a collection of seven villages scattered on the western slopes of the Pennines – Uppermill, Diggle, Dobcross, Delph, Greenfield, Denshaw and Springfield. What rankled most was the automatic disqualification of anyone born in **Saddleworth** to play cricket for Yorkshire – the club only accepts native-born Yorkshiremen, not nouveau-Mancunians.

Such was the outcry that Saddleworth achieved a special dispensation. Not only could it retain a white rose as its emblem, but Saddleworth children remained eligible to play for Yorkshire.

This is only one of Saddleworth's distinctions. It has the longest and highest canal tunnel in England, its band contests are nationally renowned, and its Saddleworth rushcart which is hauled through the streets on festival days, originated the expression, "on the wagon". Only someone quite sober could retain his balance on it.

Back now to that earlier form of village

Saddleworth was moved on the map from Yorkshire to Lancashire, but retained its rush cart (above) and its Yorkshire Cricketing status.

Edensor (below) was moved bodily by the sixth Duke of Devonshire.

transplant, which involved removing the buildings instead of just re-drawing the map. At least those 'ideal villages', as they have come to be known, were attractively built and fitted into their surroundings, even if in the early ones it was assumed that no family had more than two children and nobody ever had need of a lavatory. The industrial villages built by the tycoons of the Industrial Revolution were serviceable and practicable, but picturesque they were not.

The best attempt was made by Sir Titus Salt, who laid out the village around his massive Renaissance-style mill in streets which were designed to match the status of the occupiers – elaborate and substantial for the senior staff, more modest for the workmen, but all with plenty of open space and greenery. He demonstrated, as one expert put it, that industry and ugliness were not inseparable. He also demonstrated an admirable emphasis on cleanliness; **Saltaire** had its own public baths, its own Turkish bath, and its own steam laundry which could wash, iron, dry and fold clothes within the hour. That at least was the claim, though perhaps it should be taken with a pinch of Salt.

The last great tycoon to build his own English village must be William Whiteley, he of the stores, whose object was not to house his workpeople but to provide a haven for 'thrifty old people'. He was pretty thrifty himself. When he died he left one million pounds for the building of **Whiteley Village**, near Cobham in Surrey. It had chapels, shops, a licensed club, a village hall and a communal kitchen – but no garages. Mr Whiteley's architects presumably felt there was enough to occupy people in the village without having to drive elsewhere.

Incidentally the nearest thing to an idyllic 'ideal village' must be **Ardeley**, near Walkern in Hertfordshire, which has a ring of delightful thatched and whitewashed cottages, with village hall to match, and a village green with a well. What makes Ardeley surprising is that this quaint olde-worlde corner was actually created less than 70 years ago by the local Lord of the Manor; it thus has the benefits of 20th century plumbing built into apparently 16th century surroundings.

Many genuine old villages have fought successfully to fend off the developers who succeeded the unscrupulous landlords in the

Upper Slaughter – its most recent house was built in 1904.

business of wholesale demolition. They have been greatly helped of course by all the conservation bodies that have gathered so much support in recent years. So one can find places like **Upper Slaughter**, for instance, tucked away in a wooded valley in the Cotswolds, with its Elizabethan manor house and the parsonage where the Rev F E Witts wrote "The Diary of a Country Parson". True, the parsonage is now a hotel, but otherwise the village has hardly altered for a century; the last house to be built there was in 1904.

One can find other corners of England, which through force of circumstances rather than pressure from conservationists, the world has left behind. The little village of **Shotwick** in Cheshire, now without a shop or a pub, was once the port for Ireland and on a main route to Wales. It had a castle, an Elizabethan manor house, and a ford across the River Dee. Now the castle has disappeared, the manor house is a farm, and the River Dee has changed course and runs nearly two miles away. For the past two hundred years the village has remained virtually unchanged; even the arrival and departure of the nearby Shotton Ironworks, closed in 1980, has left it undisturbed.

Other villages have had difficulties in surviving at all. Some were wiped out by the Black Death, others like **Wycoller** in Lancashire were reduced to 'ghost villages' by the departure of workers in the Industrial Revolution, seeking jobs in the towns. Wycoller has achieved an element of immortality, however; its mansion appears in the pages of Charlotte Bronte's "Jane Eyre" as Ferndean Manor.

Wycoller, emptied by the Industrial Revolution.

Shotwick, once a port, now left high and dry.

In the case of **Cadgwith** in Cornwall it is just the elements that threaten its existence. This little fishing hamlet is only a couple of miles from Lizard Point, the most southerly tip of England, and greatly exposed to the gales that rage in from the Atlantic. Ill-advisedly, one might think, a number of the cottages have thatched roofs. To ensure they keep them, substantial chains have to be used to hold them down.

One village which did cease to exist was not hit by the Plague or the Industrial Revolution or an Atlantic gale, but by the War Office. **Tyneham** in Dorset was taken over during the Second World War, along with a

Cadgwith, a village in chains. It needs them to keep the thatch on the roofs during the Cornish gales.

Aisholt – a 'Thankful Village', with no casualties in the First World War.

vast surrounding area, and is still part of the Lulworth firing ranges, only open to the public on rare occasions so that former residents can return to tend their family graves.

While World War II gave Tyneham little to be thankful about, World War I produced 32 'Thankful Villages' in England. They were so called because all the menfolk who went to the war returned safely. Somerset has seven of them, including **Aisholt** where the poet Sir Henry Newbolt lived. It is a grim comparison between that total of 32 villages with reason to be thankful, and the thousands which have war memorials to their dead.

Sound guidance, stock punishments

Some villages are notable, not for their beauty of their location or their ruins that Cromwell knocked about a bit, but for a single item, an heirloom of history, a relic that revives the past. Sometimes it is still in use, sometimes it is preserved as a valued curiosity, sometimes it is left neglected in some corner of the village green. Almost always it is worth searching out.

You may have thought that the only place in Yorkshire to boast an official hornblower called the Wakeman, was **Ripon**, which in 1986 celebrated the 1100th anniversary of being granted its charter by King Alfred the Great, said to be in the form of a horn. That may be just another Ripon yarn, but a horn is still blown (though alas, not the same one), at nine o'clock every night by the market cross.

There is a period of the year however when the Wakeman's Horn finds an echo 30 miles away across the North Yorkshire Moors, be-cause at that precise moment, during the months between Hawes Back-End Fair on September 28th and Shrove Tuesday, there is an answering blast from the Wensleydale village of **Bainbridge**. Three blasts on the horn are blown nightly to each point of the compass, originally as a signal to bring in the sheep from the surrounding hillsides for safe-ty, and help the shepherd 'hear' his way in the dark. The traditional hornblowers are from the Metcalfe family of Nappa Hall, an old fortified farmhouse, but the horn is kept in the local Rose and Crown pub.

Bainbridge has two other distinctions. As it was originally a Quaker village it has no village church, just a Meeting House. It also has, so it claims, the shortest river in Eng-land, the River Bain. This will no doubt be strongly disputed, but they are understand-ably proud of their river – it is after all the Bain of their life – and anyway one does not argue readily with a Yorkshireman.

Historic horns – the Wakeman of Ripon (below, left) and the Bainbridge Horn (below), both sounding a nostalgic note over the centuries.

Malefactors' Corner at
Brent Pelham –
accommodation for six in
the stocks and the
whipping post.

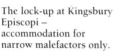

The lock-up at Kingsbury
Episcopi –
accommodation for
narrow malefactors only.

Early implements of punishment still abound on our village greens. Some have stocks, some have whipping posts – **Brent Pelham** in Hertfordshire has both. Brent means burnt, because a fire in the 1300s destroyed the original village. It was one of three villages owned by the Furneaux family; nearby are Furneaux Pelham and Stocking Pelham (stocking originally meant 'built of logs', not that the village was out on a limb). It is possible that all three villages sent their criminals to Brent Pelham for punishment because the stocks and the whipping post alongside them could accommodate six people at a time, which would amount to quite an alarming crime wave for such a small community.

While awaiting sentence to the stocks or the whipping post, malefactors were housed in the village lock-up, and a number of these still survive. **Kingsbury Episcopi** has one, with a narrow nailstudded doorway. And at **Hunmanby** in Yorkshire there is not only a lock-up with two cells and tiny barred windows, but beside it a circular stone pinfold, which was a lock-up for cattle. Until the late 19th century pinfolds were as common as lock-ups, but fewer of them remain. There is another example at **Raskelf**, dating from the 18th century and restored by the parish council in 1971. The little enclosure has battlemented brick walls with arched door and windows, all heavily barred. Stray cattle were kept there by the pinder or pinman until they were redeemed by their owners – presumably with a payment of pinmoney.

There are a few ducking stools still around, but they are rarer than stocks, and at **Fordwich** in Kent for example, while the stocks have been left outdoors to face the elements the ducking stool has been taken inside the Court Room in the Town Hall for protection. A town hall seems a bit of an extravagance for a place this size, let alone a courtroom, but Fordwich used to be the port for Canterbury on the River Stour, and the shipping no doubt brought miscreants as well as merchandise.

Village greens were not only equipped for punishment but also for entertainment. Maypoles still sprout throughout the country, but it is claimed there is only one genuine quintain left in England. The quintain was a horseman's equivalent of a boxer's punchbag; it was there primarily to provide a target but if you did not get out of the way in time, it

Wrestlers are held down by a pinhold – stray cattle at Raskelf were held in by a pinfold . .

Fordwich Court Room and Town Hall, where justice was meted out and punishment imposed.

Another ducking stool at the Weavers Arms, Canterbury. The sign reads "Unfaithful Wives beware . . . Butchers Bakers Brewers Apothecaries and all who give short measure . . .

could hit back. The target was on one end of a revolving arm, a sandbag was on the other. The quintain on the village green at **Offham**, near West Malling in Kent, has been provided with a helpful inscription which tells the whole story:

> *The pastime – originally a Roman exercise – was for the youth on horseback to run at it as fast as possible and hit the broad part in his career with much force. He that by chance hit it not at all was treated with loud peals of derision; he who hit it made the best use of his swiftness lest he should have a sound blow on the neck from the bag of sand which instantly swung round from the other end. The great design of this sport was to try the agility of both horse and man, and to break the board; which, whoever did, he was accounted the Chief of the Day's Sport.*

The quintain is still put to use every May day, but not quite so drastically. Girls take part instead of boys, and the penalty for slowness is not a sandbag in the back of the neck but a bucket of water over the head.

Medieval merrymaking also involved medieval meals, and another useful piece of village green equipment was the roasting spit. **Eyam** in Derbyshire may be best known as the Plague Village because of its unfortunate experience in the Great Plague, but it also has a mechanically operated roasting spit which is still put to use in the annual sheep-roasting ceremony in the late summer. For 'afters' they could have travelled north in the old days to **Askrigg** in Yorkshire, which for centuries has been the home of Wensleydale cheese. The wives of the dale farmers used a cheese press made of stone and wood before the factories took over, and one of these still exists in the garden of a farm cottage, though alas it is now in a sorry state, rusty and decaying.

The West Norfolk village of **East Walton** has an oven but it has nothing to do with food. It is a rare wheelwright's oven, used to heat the metal tyres which fitted on to the wooden wheels of farm waggons. The tyres were made from a flat iron strip which was run through a sort of mangle to bend it. The wheel itself was measured round its circumference, and a length of the strip was cut off, a

Early appliances for jousting and roasting – the quintain at Offham and the village spit at Eyam.

fraction shorter than the circumference to make sure it fitted tightly, and the ends welded together. The tyre was heated in the oven, a narrow brick affair with a rounded roof and a doorway in one end, looking like an outsize dog kennel. The red-hot tyre was put round the wheel while the metal was expanded by the heat, then doused with water to shrink before it burned the wood. It rarely needed a re-tread.

One can find quite ordinary-looking villages which have remarkable pasts. **Islip**, in the area of Oxfordshire which has been called "sleeping Otmoor, cast under a spell of ancient magic", was the birthplace of Edward the Confessor nearly one thousand years ago; his portrait is in the church with an excerpt from his will:

> *I have given to Christ and St Peter in Westminster ye little town of Islippe wherein I was born.*

For the most macabre village relic my nomination is **Plumpton Green** in East Sussex; where else would you find railway embankments which incorporated the bones of hundreds of men who died in the Battle of Lewes in 1264? The skeletons apparently became available to the contractors, who used them as ballast. Commuters may hear an extra rattle as they pass over these unfortunate 'sleepers'. . .

Edward the Confessor, who gave "ye little town of Islippe" to Christ and St Peter in Westminster. His likeness is preserved in the village church (left and below).

British Rail's 'skeleton service' at Plumpton Green.

Not a wartime shelter or an outsize kennel – the wheelwright's oven at East Walton.

Crafty communities, from crooks to cobbles

Thanks to the demand for agricultural diversification, backed up by exhortations from the local tourist boards, rural crafts are booming. Old mills which have not ground flour for 50 years have been repaired and restored and are grinding once again; old forges and smithies which have been defunct since the tractor took over from the horse have been refurbished to bash out wrought-iron gates and fancy doorlamps; garden seats and bird tables are lined up for inspection outside isolated cottages, barns are being turned into workshops, estates are being laid out as countryside parks where you can try your hand at identifying a tree or steering a Shire horse along a furrow. Sometimes it seems the entire countryside is being turned into an enormous open-air museum.

But there are some villages which have had no need of such a revival. They have been practising their crafts ever since the crafts were invented. Never mind those rather twee craft centres with the gentlemen in open-toed sandals and the ladies in shapeless woolly sweaters. These are the villages where for generations parents have passed on their skills to their children. "Learn a craft while you are young, that you may not have to live by craft when you are old," they probably never said, but that is what they had in mind.

One of the most widespread village crafts is basket-making, which has been going strong since the days when Moses was found in one among the bullrushes. The rushes are still used in villages along the Norfolk-Suffolk border, and you will find basket makers scattered throughout England's rural community, as far afield as **Totnes** in Devon, though the local craftsmen there are becoming outnumbered by the immigrant potters and silversmiths.

Another village craft which dates back to Biblical times and still exists today is the making of shepherds' crooks. The West Sussex village of **Pyecombe** was once a shepherds' village, and although the main London to Brighton road thunders through the parish these days, it still has the smithy opposite the church where Pyecombe crooks were made. Even the latch of the churchyard gate is in the shape of a crook, and it has been adopted for the village sign. The crooks them-

Pyecombe, a village hooked on crooks, even on the churchyard gate.

selves were said to be of a specially cunning design, just the right size to catch a ewe by the hind leg, and a lamb by the neck.

Calverton in Nottinghamshire still has a number of handknitters in the village in spite of the fact that this was the birthplace of the man who invented the stocking-frame, which could well have done them out of business. William Lee was an Elizabethan parson who was driven to inventing the machine when the lady to whom he was making amorous advances refused to desist from her knitting. He made the first device in the world to produce a knitted fabric, and he went on to invent a more refined version which made silk stockings. It did him little good financially; Queen Elizabeth refused to grant him a patent and the idea was eventually developed on a commercial basis in France. Whether it did him any good romantically is not recorded, but if he could not persuade the object of his affections to put down her needles, she probably found a stocking-frame even more engrossing.

Broseley in Shropshire became deeply involved in ironmaking in the days of the illustrious John Wilkinson, the ironmaster who built the first iron boat and the first machine which could bore a cylinder sufficiently accurately to work in a steam engine. His works, the New Willey Furnaces, were the major feature of Broseley's existence in the 1700s, but long before then it had been occupied with a very different form of manufacture, though it also involved smoke. It was a centre for making clay pipes ever since the smoking of medicinal herbs was introduced, along with Sir Walter Raleigh's tobacco, in the reign of Queen Elizabeth. Demand has somewhat slumped but if the odd churchwarden is in search of his traditional comforter, Broseley can still produce a pipe for him.

Not quite such a traditional product but a source of great enjoyment to many has been turned out by craftsmen at **Robertsbridge** in Sussex for over a century. In the early days of cricket a local enthusiast started making bats for his friends, and they became so popular the business developed into a major rural craft. One of the Robertsbridge bats was used to considerable effect by W G Grace; he scored two thousand runs off it, as a photograph and a letter in the workshops testify. For a period bats had to be a strict regulation size – not more than 38 inches long and 4½ inches wide, including the 14-inch handle. The Botham era seems to have allowed a certain variation in weight at least.

Coastal and riverside villages and towns have their own crafts connected with fishing, with netmaking well to the fore. But **Berkeley** in Gloucestershire, on the Severn Estuary, has its own speciality. The town is best known for the castle where Edward II was

The gentle art of putching, as practised in the Severn Estuary at Berkeley.

The putchers are set out on the wicker fencing to catch the salmon. Overleaf we putcher in the picture . . .

Contrasting styles of fishing: making putchers to catch salmon in the Severn (above and right), netting salmon from a cobble at Berwick (below). First they 'lay the net on', then they 'pick up the flue'.

murdered, Double Gloucester cheese and a nuclear power station, but it also has the putcher and the kipe. They are made from local willow by the fishermen, and an experienced putcher-maker can push a putcher into service at the rate of ten a day. It is in the shape of a giant ice-cream cone, used in the salmon season to trap the fish as the current takes them into the broad end of the cone and prevents them swimming out again. You have to remember, of course, to put your putcher facing the right way. A kipe is a sort of king-size putcher, a three-baskets-in-one version which traps other fish as well.

At **Berwick-upon-Tweed** in the far corner of England from Berkeley they cobble for their salmon. A cobble is quite a different craft, actually a flat-bottomed boat. Two men take one end of the net in the cobble, a third holds the other end on the shore. Once the net has been fully extended four more men join in to haul in the catch, which can often amount to 50 salmon at a time. The season lasts from mid-February to mid-September, a period when the fishermen must be tempted to cobble all night and cobble all day . . .

Other villages can offer other unusual crafts or memories of crafts – the little village of **Hartsop** in Westmorland still has at least three houses with spinning galleries under the overhanging eaves, and at **Castleton** in Derbyshire, in the mouth of the famous Peak Cavern, there used to live ropemakers who specialised in Hangmen's ropes. The Devil was said to approve of this craft – Devil's Cavern, where he sometimes stayed, is one of those which leads off from the Peak – and when heavy rains in the hills sent water pouring out of the cavern it was assumed that at times even the Devil had to relieve himself.

Beers, wines and all manner of spirits

There are nearly as many pub guides around these days as there are pubs to be guided to, but here I am not dealing with the way they keep their beer, how much they charge for their sandwiches or whether they allow children in the bar. I am only dealing with pubs which have something special about them – their name, their size or location, their history, or their ghost. Especially their ghost –there is nothing like a good shiver down the back to give a pub an extra piquancy.

Take for instance the Ostrich Inn at Colnbrook in Buckinghamshire, a traditional black-and-white timber-framed building which is something of a contrast to Heathrow's multi-bedroomed monsters down the road. I find it gives the beer an added bite to know that many of the pub's earlier customers finished up by being boiled in it. A landlord called Jarman and his wife used to put their overnight guests in a special bed fixed to a trapdoor. When it was opened the sleeper would be plunged into a cauldron of boiling ale in the kitchen beneath. They disposed of 60 customers in this way, and a great deal of ale, before they were found out and hanged. The brew is a little different now but one cannot help listening for the odd splash . . .

Ye oldest, ye highest, ye smallest . . .

The Ostrich Inn at Colnbrook scene of sinister splashing . . .

Nobody will ever agree on which is the oldest public house in England. If it was originally built for some other purpose and there are bits of the old building still in use, does that qualify? Or do you base it on the length of time a licence has been held there, regardless of whether the original structure still remains? I can only offer you some pubs which have laid claim to the title, and whether they hold it or not, they are jolly good pubs.

Take for instance Ye Olde Ferryboat Inn at **Holywell** in Cambridgeshire, a pub I called at many times during our boating days on the Ouse because it has free moorings and a direct route across the garden to the bar. Any pub called 'Ye Olde' something is a bit suspect, but there has been a building on that spot for over one thousand years, although originally it was a monastic ferry house. The monks no doubt took a discreet glass there to get strength for the row across the river, and the contents of the glass did not necessarily come from Holywell's Holy Well. The present bars do not exactly date back to that period, but there are plenty of old beams and timbers, and a couple of great open fires, one with a fish and an eel in a setting of rushes, moulded on to the chimney beam.

Ye Olde Ferryboat can also lay claim to another title – the pub with the oldest ghost. That story is told elsewhere.

Another frontrunner among the oldest pubs is another 'Ye Olde', the Fighting Cocks at **St Albans** in Hertfordshire. It was first opened as an alehouse less than four hundred years ago, but here again there are monastic connections going back nearly as far as the foundation of St Albans Abbey in 795. It had a succession of careers – the monks may have used it as a boathouse or fishing lodge, the Normans used it as a battlemented gatehouse, then it became a flour mill and possibly a silk mill. Even since it became a pub it has changed its identity. For three hundred years it was called the Round House, for a time it became the Fisherman (harking back to those monks again?) and now it is named after one

Front runners for the title of England's oldest pub – Ye Olde Ferry Boat Inn and Ye Olde Fighting Cocks (opposite page) formerly the Olde Round House. The 'Ye' is therefore no measure of antiquity . . .

Where you can get high on one drink – the Tan Hill Inn, highest pub in England.

of the corners in the building which in Stuart times was used as a cock-fighting pit. It is still there, down one of the assorted corridors and steps in and around the main bar.

Out of local loyalty I must mention the Adam and Eve, certainly the oldest pub in **Norwich** and with parts of the ground floor dating back seven hundred years. That cannot compete with the thousand years claimed by the other two, but at least it is not called 'Ye Olde . . .'

The highest pub is much easier to name. There is general agreement that the Tan Hill Inn up in the Yorkshire dales near **Arkengarthdale** holds the title at 1732 feet. It can also probably claim to be the most isolated, relying for its trade mostly on passing tourists and the annual hill sheep fair. It has the unlikely distinction of being owned at one stage by a former editor of the Good Beer Guide. He did not, alas, stay long.

The Nut Shell at Bury St Edmunds, which you may think is the smallest pub in the country – until you visit the Smith's Arms at Godmanstone, where they are in no doubt at all.

If we try to identify the smallest pub in England we are in trouble again. Should it be the smallest building, or the building with the smallest bar? And how do you define a bar anyway? The Nut Shell at **Bury St Edmunds** is one nomination, but I think I must plump for the Smith's Arms at **Godmanstone** in Dorset. Its front is just eleven feet wide and it has only one room – but not only that, it has a pleasant tale to tell.

This six hundred-year-old thatched building was originally a smithy, and it is said that Charles II was riding through the village (he covered a lot of ground in those days) and stopped there to have his horse re-shod. Feeling a thirst come upon him, he asked the blacksmith for a drink – and was so appalled when he learned that he had no licence that he granted him one forthwith. It has been licensed ever since.

Although the pub is inevitably cramped inside, it offers all the standard pub amenities – shove-ha'penny, darts, table skittles and the like, and serves a remarkable assortment of pub lunches. Fortunately there is a terrace outside to take the overflow of customers.

For the smallest bar in the world, let alone England, you must go to **Huddersfield** and look for the telephone kiosk at the Huddersfield Hotel, in the centre of the town. It was opened as a bar in May 1985, in spite of

opposition from the local fire officer who was concerned that it did not have an emergency exit!

As for the biggest pub, if it can be called that, the world title was claimed when it was built in 1819 by the Regent Hotel at **Leamington Spa** in Warwickshire. It had one hundred bedrooms – and one bathroom! The management would doubtless like me to emphasise that things have changed a bit since. The title has long since left this country and has now become the subject of a battle between the two super-powers. The United States claimed to have the largest in the world, the Las Vegas Hilton, which has 3174 rooms (complete with 3174 bathrooms) and a dozen international restaurants. But the Soviet Union claims the hotel with the most bedrooms – the Rossiya in Moscow, built in 1967, has 3200 rooms, putting them 26 ahead of Las Vegas, and can accommodate 6000 guests. All of which puts the Leamington Spa Regent into the small-country-pub class by comparison.

I think however that England still retains a claim to the oddest looking pub almost anywhere. **Combe Martin** is an otherwise unexceptional Devon village, straggling for over a mile down to the sea on the county's north coast. But in the midst of it is 'The Pack o' Cards', which experts have described as the most bizarre building in Devon. It has chimneys perched on a central turret with railings round the top, out of all proportion to the two-storey front of the building below. It was

The Regent Hotel at Leamington Spa. It was the biggest hotel in the world – one hundred bedrooms and one bathroom. Now the world has much bigger hotels, and the Regent has many more bathrooms.

"Hold the line please, I'm serving a customer . . ." A telephone kiosk has become England's smallest bar at the Huddersfield Hotel.

built, the story goes, by Squire George Ley in the early 18th century to celebrate a handsome win at the gaming tables. He gave it 52 windows (some of which were blocked up later to escape the window tax), four main floors including the turret, and 13 doors at ground level.

The story has been written on parchment and hung in the pub, but sceptics point out that the Venetian windows in the gable ends were not around in Squire Ley's time, and nor was the name of the pub. Old photographs show it to have been called the King's Arms Hotel. No matter; it is still a very startling vision.

One more modest contribution from Norfolk. In the spring of 1987 the landlord of the Boar Inn at **Great Ryburgh** converted a former outside gentleman's lavatory attached to his pub into a unisex hairdressing salon. He was proudly photographed at the opening ceremony having a haircut with a pint of bitter in his hand. Is this the only licensed barber's shop in England?

The Pack O' Cards at Combe Martin – 52 windows, 13 doors, 4 floors, and no doubt a square deal.

Have a ram jam dram – or a sortie to the rorty

For the connoisseur a pub by any other name would smell as sweet so long as the beer was good, but for the curious and the inquisitive there is a certain fascination about an unlikely or an incomprehensible pub name. Some mysteries are fairly easy to solve – all of those out-of-place Ostriches in West Norfolk have flown in via the coats of arms of the local aristocracy, for instance, and the combination of an elephant and castle, found on so many pub signs, probably originates from the Infanta of Castile. But what about the Ram Jam Inn at **Stretton**, the Rorty Crankle at Plaxtol, the Four Alls at **Welford-on-Avon**, the Wink at Lamorna . . .

I have driven past the Ram Jam Inn on the Great North Road in Leicestershire dozens of times, and stopped for a beer on occasions, but if I thought about its name at all I only assumed it had some Indian connotation. Not at all; it is a tale of 18th century guile involving a guest who lodged at the inn for a week and could not pay his bill. When the day of reckoning came he offered to show the landlady how to draw two different kinds of beer out of the same cask.

In the cellar he drilled a hole in the side of a beer barrel and asked her to ram her thumb in it to stop the beer coming out while he drilled another hole on the other side. She jammed her other thumb in that. While she was safely rammed and jammed in the barrel the guest departed, rejoicing.

The Ram Jam is not the only oddly-named pub in this small village. Just off the main road is the Jackson Stops, which took its name, not from any reluctant-to-leave customer called Jackson, but from the estate agent's sign which stood outside it for quite some time while it was up for sale. The inn sign itself still bears the original name, the White Horse, but everyone calls it the Jackson Stops, including the tourist books and the beer guides, and no doubt Messrs Jackson Stops are delighted with the publicity.

The Rorty Crankle at **Plaxtol** in Kent has been named thus, one suspects, very much with publicity in mind. It is claimed to be Anglo-Saxon for 'Happy Corner', and the message is emphasised in the bar, where the

The Ram Jam Inn, at Stretton – no Indian connotation, just a cunning guest.

The Rorty Crankle at Plaxtol – and a happy corner to you too. . .

The pub with the Four-All
bar at Welford-on-Avon –
a tribute to the tax-payer!

same phrase is repeated in more than 60 other languages. Perhaps it is to compete with the counter-attraction of Old Soar, the remains of a fortified home of a 13th century knight just up the road, which is the main local tourist attraction.

Welford-on-Avon in Warwickshire, some four miles from Stratford, is a picture-book village with timber-framed houses, a genuine maypole, and an ancient lychgate said to be the oldest in the county, but its oddest feature is the name of its pub, the Four Alls. Some say this is just a corruption of 'Four Ales', but there is a much more attractive explanation inside the bar. There are four portraits in stained glass of a soldier, a parson, a king and a countryman, with the legend: 'Fight All, Pray All, Rule All, Pay All', an early illustration of how the activities of royalty, the army and the church are paid for by the man-in-the-street.

And the **Lamorna** 'Wink'? One local belief is that it was the suggestive signal given by a customer in the days when it was only licensed as an alehouse and he wanted something a little stronger. But I am assured the wink comes from Kiddleywinks, the name given to alehouses in Cornwall. Incidentally, the games you can play at the Wink are listed as darts, pool, dominoes, cribbage and a fruit machine, but no tiddleywinks – so that theory is ruled out. But I can tip you the wink that in addition to some excellent beers it has one of the finest collections of warship mementoes, sea photographs and nautical brassware in the country.

A wink's as good as a nip – how they ordered something a little stronger at the alehouse in Lamorna.

A Trusty Servants portrait would you see
This Emblematic Figure well survey
The Porkers Snout not nice in diet shows
The Padlock shut no secrets he'll disclose
Patient the Ass his Masters wrath will bear
Swiftness in errand the Staggs feet declare
Loaded his Left hand apt to labour saith
The Vest his neatness Open hand his faith
Girt with his Sword his Shield upon his arm
himself and master he'll protect from harm

There are other apparently simple pub names with quite complicated explanations. The Trusty Servant in the New Forest village of **Minstead** in Hampshire is a fair example. The 'servant' on the inn sign has the head of a pig with a padlock round its snout, the feet of a stag, and various other peculiarities. Pupils of Winchester College will know what it is all about – the college has the original picture. The snout means the servant will eat any scraps, the padlock shows that he tells no tales (though it can hardly assist his eating), the stag's feet indicate a speedy messenger. The complexities of the sign would delight Sir Arthur Conan Doyle, who is buried in the nearby churchyard.

The Cuckoo Bush at **Gotham** in Nottinghamshire stands for much more than a cuckoo in a bush. It recalls the 16th century 'Merrie Tales of the Mad Men of Gotham', an enterprising band who put a cart on top of a barn to protect the roof from the sun, burned down a forge to get rid of a wasp's nest, tried to drown an eel, and, best of all, built a hedge round a cuckoo in a bush so that it might be Spring all the year round.

He eats any scraps, he tells no tales, he runs like a stag – the Trusty Servant at Minstead.

Were they really mad, or did they just lay it on a bit because they had heard King John wanted to build a hunting lodge in the middle of Gotham, and they thought he might be put off by an entire village of village idiots? Either way, the story and the pub give a little colour to a rather ordinary place devoted mainly these days to mining and plaster works.

Hawkshead in Cumbria is best known as the place where Wordsworth went to school before going on to Cambridge, and carved his name on one of the desks. He dreamed up some fine poetry while he was there – "And has the sun his flaming chariot driven", that sort of thing – but he could never have dreamed up the tale of the Drunken Duck, the pub just outside the village. It is said that beer seeped out of the cellar and into the ducks' feeding trough. The landlady found the birds lying about looking lifeless as well as legless. Making the best of it, she started plucking them for dinner, but as she did so, the ducks started sobering up. She could not do much for their hangovers, but she could make up for the lost feathers. The plucked ones were eventually returned to their quarters, wearing little knitted jumpers.

Legendary pub birds – the Cuckoo Bush at Gotham and the Drunken Duck at Hawkshead.

Pubs with gruesome connections – the Bucket of Blood at Phillack (above) . . .

The tale of the Drunken Duck could have had an unhappy ending. The Bucket of Blood at **Phillack** in Cornwall did. Two hundred years ago the landlord went to draw water from the pub's well and drew a bucket of blood instead. It turned out that a headless corpse had been thrown down it. Small wonder the pub is said to be haunted, though confusingly not by a headless corpse but by a headed monk.

The Last Drop Inn at **Bolton** in Lancashire was once reputed to be owned by Albert Pierrepoint, England's last hangman, which would give a gruesome flavour to the name. Actually it merely refers to an empty glass. But another of Pierrepoint's pubs can hardly have such a mundane explanation; it was called the Struggling Man.

Sherston in Wiltshire has its share of grue with its Rattlebone Inn, named after the hero Rattlebone who was wounded in a local battle before the days of the Norman Conquest. It is said that he held a tile to his ripped-open stomach to staunch the blood and preserve his innards. Certainly the story is commemorated on the church porch as well as at the pub.

. . . and the Last Drop Inn at Bolton.

Much more healthy is the sign of the Three Willows at **Birchanger** in Essex. There are many pubs connected with cricket, particularly around Hambledon where the game was born, but this is more imaginative than most. It shows three batsmen, one of 1780, one of 1900 (looking uncommonly like 'W G') and one of 1946.

Grantham has two of the best known coaching inns in England, the George Hotel which used to be the home of Sir Isaac Newton and the Angel and Royal founded by the Knights Templars. It has also produced a rather famous grocer's daughter and has been named – for no obvious reason – the most boring town in the country. More fascinating than any of this is the pub sign in **Castlegate**. The Beehive Inn has a real beehive, actually being used by bees and producing thirty

Bat and bee: cricketers producing runs through the ages at Birchanger, and the bees producing honey through the ages at Grantham.

Yes, there is still honey for tea at the Beehive, Grantham.

pounds of excellent honey a year. It is mounted in a lime tree outside the pub and has certainly functioned as its sign since 1830 and probably before that. It inspired the verse:

Grantham, now two rarities are thine, a lofty steeple (on St Wulfram's church, 272 feet high) and a living sign

Finally a sign which hangs, not outside a pub, but in the entrance hall. It was a source of some embarrassment to the Victorian landlord who had it painted. Originally the sign at the Swan Inn at **Fittleworth** in West Sussex portrayed a nude woman astride a swan – quite a traditional design. But there was consternation when someone noticed that the woman's face looked very like Queen Victoria's. The thought of displaying a naked picture of the monarch was too much for the landlord and his customers. The artist was recalled, and clothing was added forthwith.

The tale of the Swan at Fittleworth – how a skilful artist saved the blushes of the landlord.

Keeping their spirits up

If an attractive barmaid is hard to come by, then the next best attraction to draw in the punters is a ghost. If it makes interesting noises and moves things about, so much the better. If it actually appears, that really would be something, but somehow that rarely seems to happen except very late in the evening in front of unreliable witnesses. Most landlords are happy just to provide a good ghost story, summon up an occasional slamming door, and leave it at that.

One or two are a little inclined to overdo it. The 14th century White Hart Hotel at **Bailgate** in Lincolnshire has so many ghostly curiosities that it provides its guests with a list of likely sightings. There is the first-floor maid who roams the bedrooms regardless of doors and walls, the faceless highwayman, the young man who shot himself, the owner of a stolen vase who comes back to search for it – they are all there, queuing up for your attention. But like a restaurant that offers too long a menu, it is perhaps difficult to believe that all of it is top quality. I prefer the solitary roamer with a good tale to tell, and perhaps a fragment of evidence to support it.

A good example is Ye Olde Ferryboat Inn at **Holywell** in Cambridgeshire, already mentioned in these pages because of its claim to be the oldest pub in England. It could certainly have the oldest ghost, plus a sad, sad tale to go with it, and a tombstone close to one of the bars for authenticity. It marks the grave of

Juliet Tewsley, who committed suicide because of her unrequited love for the local woodcutter, Tom Zoul (whose family, with a name like that, could well have been the last entry in the Domesday Book). She hanged herself from a tree beside the river. Because she was a suicide she could not be buried in consecrated ground, so her grave was dug on the river bank and the stone became part of

The White Hart at Bailgate, with almost as many ghosts as customers.

The unseen guest at Ye Olde Ferryboat Inn, with a permanent place near the bar.

A jilted bride still awaits her wedding breakfast in the Castle Inn at Castleton.

the pub. Every March 17th, the anniversary of her death (it is known as precisely as that), her ghost rises from beneath the slab and floats down the river – but of course only while the customers' backs are turned.

Unrequited love is always a good ingredient in a ghost story. It crops up at the 17th century Castle Inn at **Castleton** in Derbyshire, under the shadow of the ruins of Peveril Castle – remember Scott's 'Peveril of the Peak'? This is a gripping tale too, of a young woman who was left at the altar and died of a broken heart. She lingers on at the Castle Inn, in the passage to the restaurant, waiting for the wedding breakfast that was never served. As if that were not enough, it is said that the body of another woman is buried at the entrance to the inn, following the pagan belief that this unattractive practice will bring good fortune to a new building. Nevertheless if you don't mind stepping across one of the ladies in the front doorway and dodging the other in the corridor, the restaurant supplies a very pleasant meal.

More heartbreak at the unromantically-named Pig and Whistle at **Littlehempston** in Devon. It was the scene of secret meetings between a local farm-girl and a monk from the original Buckfast Abbey. It was said that a tunnel led from a chapel at the abbey to the room where they met, so that his brothers at the abbey could assume he was at his devotions in the chapel while he was actually displaying his devotion in the pub. However, the Abbey was about six miles from the pub, so this seems a little unlikely – but they still maintain that Brother Freddie, as he is known locally, continues to roam the Pig and Whistle seeking his loved one.

Incidentally, this was not the Buckfast Abbey we know today, which was only completed 50 odd years ago and has hardly had

A monk still seeks a tryst with his loved one at the Pig and Whistle, Little-hempston.

time to produce a well-established ghost. Brother Freddie was a member of the medieval Cistercian monastery which stood on the same site and was pulled down after the Dissolution. But the French monks who built the new one would appreciate the romance of the story even if they would not dream of emulating it.

Many pubs relish a good slice of gruesome ghoulishness about their ghosts, rather than lovelorn ladies and frustrated monks. The Busby Stoop Inn at **Sandhutton** in North Yorkshire, much frequented by racegoers attending meetings at Thirsk just down the

road, is also frequented by Tom Busby, who was hanged and gibbeted there in 1702, on a gallows just opposite the inn. He attacked his father-in-law, Daniel Auty, with a hammer after an argument about money (could he have lost heavily at Thirsk?) and beat him to death. He still returns to the pub, stooping of course, with his head drooping and the noose round his neck. The landlord considerately keeps a chair empty for him in case he drops in.

The Birdcage Inn at **Thame** in Oxfordshire has a history which makes it a natural for a good haunt. During the Napoleonic Wars it

An empty chair is still kept for Tom Busby at the Busby Stoop Inn at Sandhutton.

was used to house French prisoners in conditions anything but luxurious. Earlier it was a staging post for criminals on their way to punishment. With such a wealth of potential misery, small wonder that strange bangings have been heard on the walls in the early hours of the morning. A seance was held in the hope of exorcising these unhappy souls – only to discover that another soul was responsible, a leper who had been kept in one of the upper rooms until he was stoned to death by an angry mob.

When a pub is called Trouble House you would expect it to be asking for it, and certainly the sign confirms it – a bloody hand and a hanging corpse between a Roundhead and a Cavalier, each in unfriendly mood. However, the history of the haunting of this establishment, at **Cherington** in Gloucestershire, is more recent than the Civil War. The first rattling chains, and icy blasts, and barred doors bursting open unaided, did not manifest themselves until about 1930, an unaccountable example of delayed-action haunting.

French prisoners, convicted criminals, a leper – do they still linger at the Birdcage Inn at Thame?

Trouble House, Cherington – but the trouble only started 60-odd years ago.

A case of halted haunting occurred at **Rugby** in Warwickshire. Before the Industrial Revolution turned it into a railway town the local squire used to drive around the place in a coach with six horses, causing considerable consternation to the inhabitants – particularly as he was dead at the time. A number of clergymen formed an exorcising consortium and managed to trap this troubled spirit in a bottle, which was sealed and thrown into a lake. The ghostly roadhog was effectively banned for the next hundred years or so, when someone fished out the bottle and returned the spirit of the squire to its home, Brownsover Hall, which is now a hotel. The last owner of the hotel, presumably not too happy about his permanent resident, cemented the bottle into a wall (he would not reveal where) to ensure the squire did not escape and resume his nocturnal travels. The roads of Rugby – and the hotel – have remained free of his presence ever since.

The Abbey Hotel at **Crowland** in Lincoln-shire also houses the spirit of an energetic traveller, but this one used his own feet. A local farmer, Henry Girdlestone, set out in 1844 to get into the Victorian equivalent of the Guinness Book of Records by walking one thousand miles in one thousand hours. He returned 49 days later, a total of 1,176 hours, having walked 1,025 miles 173 yards. According to the locals he can still be heard dragging his sore feet around the attic of the hotel.

Brownsover Hall, Rugby, home of a locally bottled spirit.

Henry Girdlestone, like Felix, keeps on walking at the Abbey Hotel, Crowland.

What goes up does not always come down – Charlie 'Spider' Marshall is still somewhere in the chimney of the Bear at Stock.

Mr Girdlestone attempted that feat for a bet. The same reason lay behind the curious exploit of Charlie 'Spider' Marshall, ostler at the Bear Hotel at **Stock** in Essex some time in the last century. He would make a few extra bob by crawling up the chimney in one bar and coming down the chimney in the other. If he was feeling coy he would stay up there until a fire was lit and forced him down. One Christmas Day, however, he performed his trick for the last time. He went up the chimney, and never came down. His remains are said to be still up there somewhere, well cured by now.

Some hauntings seem to have no particular story behind them. The Albion Hotel at **Longton** in Staffordshire looks as much like a haunted house as the local supermarket, yet it is said that the figures of a Cavalier and a serving maid have been seen floating along the bar and through the wall. More mysterious still is the ghost of the Black Horse at **Cirencester**, "a nasty old lady" as she was described by the landlord's niece who saw her, one August night in 1933. She has not been seen since, but she left behind, scratched upside down on one of the windows, the name 'James'. Was this another tale of unre-

Not the most likely of haunted pubs – the modern-style Albion at Longton has a ghostly Cavalier and a serving-maid among its clientele.

"James", the mysterious message left on the window at the Black Horse, Cirencester.

quited love – did James desert her before she became nasty and old? Was it another murder story – did she kill James or did James kill her? Or was she actually James – in drag? Such speculation is guaranteed to keep the bitter flowing.

The White Hart in **Chalfont St Peter** in Buckinghamshire, must be one of the few pubs to claim a musical ghost. Donald Ross was a landlord in the last century who used to entertain his customers on the violin. According to some, he still does.

Mysterious music at the White Hart, Chalfont St Peter – a ghostly landlord still serenades the guests.

The Old Silent Inn at **Stanbury** in West Yorkshire did not earn its name from its ghost. Bonnie Prince Charlie spent some time in hiding there (where did he not?) and relied on the silence of the locals for his safety. The Eagle became the Old Silent Inn as a result. Much later, in the last century, a landlady used to feed the stray cats that roamed wild on the moors that surround the pub. She summoned them by ringing a bell in the doorway. They say the bell can still be heard on a wild winter's night, and the landlord insists that he is pestered by an unconscionable number of cats . . .

The **Saltersgate** Inn, halfway between Pickering and Whitby in North Yorkshire, has maintained for two hundred years the tradition of never allowing the peat fire in the bar to go out – or if it did go out during closing hours, successive landlords have kept very quiet about it. The inn stands at the meeting place of several ancient tracks over the moors from Pickering to the sea, where packhorses used to carry fish and salt from the coast – thus Saltersgate, though it is better known locally as T'Gate. The inn itself was built in 1648, in an age when more valuable items than salt were being taken inland without the

The fire never goes out at the Saltersgate . . .

. . . the cats never come in at the Old Silent Inn.

knowledge of the Customs, and it is said the smugglers used the inn as a hide-out. There is a tiny window in what was once the kitchen where they are supposed to have placed a lantern as a warning that the Excise men were on the prowl.

The warning did not always work, and in one of the violent encounters which ensued a man was killed and reputedly buried under the hearth of the turf fire. It has been kept burning ever since to prevent his ghost escaping.

Alternatively you can accept the tale of the Owd Devil – nothing to do with the Devil's Elbow which is not too far away on the main road over the moors, but an old hermit who lived two hundred years ago in the nearby Hole of Horcum, the biggest hollow in Yorkshire. He is said to have told the landlord that if ever the peat fire went out, the building would be destroyed. His warning has been observed ever since, though these days the fire burns mainly wood. At night a few turves are laid on the embers to keep both the smuggler's ghost and the Owd Devil quiet.

Pubs like to preserve old traditions even if no specific ghost is involved. The Rose and Crown at **Hempstead** in Essex has a tradition attached to its fireplace. It bears the warning:

It is the landlord's great desire that no-one stands before the fire.

There was a time when no-one would have argued with the landlord about that or anything else, because this was the home of the infamous Dick Turpin, romantically described as a highwayman, but actually a robber and murderer. His father was landlord in the days when it was called the Bell Inn, and no doubt between them they kept the fireplace clear.

To be fair to Hempstead, it was also the home of a man whose discovery did much to counter the ill effects of Turpin and his kind.

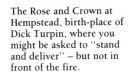

The Rose and Crown at Hempstead, birth-place of Dick Turpin, where you might be asked to "stand and deliver" – but not in front of the fire.

A pub with an irremovable Bible – the White Horse at Keswick (above) and a pub with irremovable coins – the Cross Keys at White Notley (below). Some of the coins hve been nailed up in the bar for two hundred years (below, right).

He was William Harvey, who in the 17th century took medical science a major step forward with the discovery of the circulation of the blood. There is a sculpture of him in the nearby church, just as there are many portrayals of Turpin and his exploits in the bar of the Rose and Crown.

The White Horse, just outside **Keswick** in Cumbria, has a more religious tradition. It cannot claim, like the Royal Oak in Keswick itself, to have been the haunt of Tennyson, Sir Walter Scott, Robert Louis Stevenson, Wordsworth, Southey and Coleridge (it must have reached the stage there where orders were only accepted in verse), but it does possess a Bible which is actually mentioned in the deeds of the property. According to those deeds it must never be allowed to cross the threshold.

Many pubs go in for quaint collections to decorate their bars, from beer mats to foreign currency, but these are comparatively modern traditions. A much earlier collection was started at the Cross Keys at **White Notley** in Essex. In the 18th century waggoners used to stop there overnight on their way with timber from Maldon to Braintree. Any newcomer making his first stopover had to buy everyone a drink (a custom common to many pubs) but he also had to pin a coin to the wall with a nail specially provided for the purpose by the village blacksmith (who no doubt shared in the free round). Some of the coins still remain around the front windows of the Cross Keys, a reminder of those tyro waggoners of two hundred years ago and a tribute to the sturdiness of the blacksmith's nails.

Come tip-toe through the tombstones

The most prominent building in the average English community – and in the average English guidebook – is the church. It is probably the biggest, the oldest and the most expensive pile of masonry in the place. It can also be – unless you are very devout or fascinated by rising damp – the most boring. One can always ponder of course on whether a wall is Early English or Decorated Gothic, on where the Saxons left off and the Normans began, or on why one window is wide and arched while another is narrow and comes to a point. But as someone who thought all churches were Perpendicular, otherwise they would fall down, I have never been clued up about clerestories or moved to passion by a piscina.

What does interest me about a church is an eccentric saint, or a curious carving, an unlikely effigy, a whimsical epitaph, a strange relic – any sort of ecclesiastical idiosyncrasy. So what I like about Ely Cathedral, for instance, more than its magnificent west tower and its famous lantern roof, is that the monks who built it paid for their materials in eels. In their day Ely really was very eel-y, and they had no problem paying four thousand eels a year for stone from Barnack Quarry. Today, alas, with three million pounds needed for restoration work, the cathedral authorities are not quite so well-eeled.

But if the eels have gone from Ely, I have located a number of unusual features which remain elsewhere, from the 108 cobbled steps to the Church of St Michael and All Angels at Macclesfield, which are said to grant any wish if you can run up them in one breath (more breath perhaps?), to the tombstones in Whalley churchyard in Lancashire which bear dates that never existed – April 31st 1752, February 30th 1819. A slip of the chisel? An April 1st joke? Or just the work of a Whalley wally . . .

I built it **my** way

Ask what **Ayot St Lawrence** is famous for, and nine out of ten people will say George Bernard Shaw. The tenth may mention Lady Hart Dyke's Lullington silkworms, producers of royal vestments. Mr Shaw's 44 years in this Hertfordshire village and to a lesser degree those hard-working worms have distracted attention from the feature which made it unique long before he was born – England's most extraordinary 18th century village church.

The Grecian takes over from the traditional at Ayot St Lawrence (top, left and above) while the Italianate takes over at Hoarwithy.

Do not seek here a tower or a spire or the odd flying buttress, unless it be among the ruins of the original church which still stands, where you would expect a village church to stand, opposite the village pub. This is more like a Greek temple, with a Doric portico and two colonnaded wings leading to pavilions on each side. The front is stuccoed, the back is plain brick. A columned screen separates the nave – which is rectangular – from the vestibule. And strangest of all, the altar is at the west end, not the east.

The story behind St Lawrence's church is as odd as the church itself. In the late 1700s Sir Lionel Lyte of Ayot House decided to build a new church for the village – but primarily for himself. One suspects he did not actually consult his fellow parishioners. Instead he consulted Nicholas Revett, designer of Sir Francis Dashwood's remarkable creations at West Wycombe and a well-known exponent of the Grecian style. While Mr Revett got to work with notebook and pencil, Sir Lionel got to work on the old 13th century village church and started knocking it down.

This did not go down too well with the Bishop, who stopped him in mid-hammerblow. The demolition work ceased, but the work on the new church kept going. The back of it was left undecorated, presumably because Sir Lionel could not see that side of it from his house. The altar was put at the wrong end, ecclesiastically, because it just happened to fit in better that way. And the pavilions on each side were put there specifically to contain the remains of Sir Lionel and his wife. It seemed Sir Lionel had his own back for what had not been the happiest of marriages. "Since the Church united us in life," he is quoted as saying, "she can make amends by separating us in death".

If Sir Lionel was gripped by the Grecian, the Vicar of **Hoarwithy** was entranced by the Italianate. Hoarwithy is a pleasant little village on a loop of the River Wye, halfway between Hereford and Ross and well away from the main A49 road that joins them. In the midst of this very English landscape is a very Italian church, complete with campanile. It was virtually the life's work of the Rev William Poole, who was vicar for nearly 50 years during the last century, and seemed to spend most of that time adding mosaics and

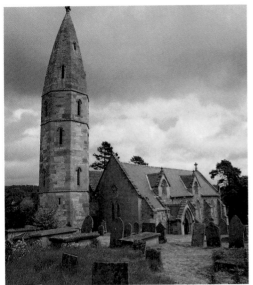

A sky-rocket designed by a 'sky-pilot' in Shropshire . . .

lapis lazuli and the sort of decorations that are more often found in an early Roman basilica than in an English parish church.

The Italian flavour of the church is reflected in some of the local families. Mr Poole brought a team of Italian workmen to Hoarwithy to work with local craftsmen in building it, and some of them stayed on and married local girls. He also brought pink-grey marble from Devon for the columns which support the choir dome, and marble from Ireland to adorn the chancel. Fortunately he did not have to rely on the average country parson's stipend – the church cost him a considerable fortune.

Not far away in Shropshire, in a very English village with a very Welsh name, another 19th century vicar also spent most of his time and money on converting the parish church to his own liking. The Rev John Parker, vicar of **Llanyblodwel** from 1845 to 1860, drew the plans and carried out the work himself. The result was neither Grecian nor Italianate, but neo-lunar. The tower and spire look exactly like a moon-rocket. They stand virtually detached from the church itself, octagonal in shape, over one hundred feet high, swelling slightly up to the halfway mark, with the spire continuing straight out of the tower without a break. It looks due for lift-off at any time.

Inside the church Mr Parker painted every available space with his favourite texts, to provide a little reading matter for the congregation if his sermons failed to grip. There are a few features of the original church left – the

. . . and if the sermons are too boring, the vicar has provided a little reading matter on the walls. The Rev John Parker's church at Llanyblodwel.

old south door and a 14th century tombstone in the porch – but the Normans who built the original church of St Michael and Archangel would get quite a jolt if they came back today.

In much more recent times a church has been built to the design of a vicar, inspired by his curate, which is also revolutionary but for a very practical purpose. In the early 1930s the Rev William Keble Martin was in charge of the new parish of **Milber**, near Newton Abbot in Devon, but he had no permanent church. He did however have a curate (it could not have happened in these more straitened times) who it seems had a dream one night in which he saw a church with three naves instead of one, all converging on the altar like darts converging on a bull's-eye. This had the great merit, he realised, of giving a much larger proportion of the congregation a clear view of what was going on.

The curate passed on this bright idea to the vicar, who passed it on to the architect, and Milber church was duly built with its three fan-like naves. It has been known as the Dream Church ever since.

There are four round churches still in use in England – the churches of the Holy Sepulchre in **Cambridge** and **Northampton**, which have always been parish churches; the Temple Church in **London** erected by the

The Dream Church at Milber (above) with three naves instead of one.

The Saxon church at Greensted-juxta-Ongar, the only one which still has its original walls of split oak logs.

Knights Templars; and St John the Baptist Church at **Little Maplestead** in Essex, which belonged to the Knights Hospitallers.

The Hospitallers – the Order of the Knights of St John of Jerusalem – were normally to be found looking after pilgrims on their way through the Holy Land to Jerusalem, which all seems a long way away from Little Maplestead. The village was actually given to them along with a lot of other property in the area, and they did very nicely out of it for three or four centuries, using it as a recruiting centre, collecting rents, and living in considerable comfort in the house they built there – the staff in 1338 included a steward, four clerks, a cook, a baker, a porter and assorted varlets.

They also built a church. The original 12th century one has now completely disappeared, but the present building dates back to 1335 and it retains its 'round' shape. The quotation marks are there because although it is rounded at both ends, one much larger than the other, it has a straight bit in the middle, rather like a lopsided dumb-bell or an old-fashioned barometer. But the overwhelming impression is of roundness, and 'The Round Church of Little Maplestead' will always be known that way.

There is just one Saxon church left in England which still has the original walls of split oak logs. It is the Church of St Andrew at **Greensted-juxta-Ongar** in Essex, where the body of King Edmund rested in 1013. He was an early Christian martyr killed by the Danes, and a carving in the church tells the story of how his severed head was guarded by a wolf until his followers discovered it. There is no other evidence for the story, but historians are in no doubt that they brought the body here, one hopes with the head, on their way to bury St Edmund at Bury St Edmunds.

Greensted's little Saxon church has been much restored over the years. Happily the oak walls have been left intact, but there is now a brick sill and plinth, instead of the old wooden one, and a wooden tower, dormer windows, a porch and a chancel have been added. There is even a 20th century lectern to bring it right up to date.

The oldest unaltered Saxon church in England was rediscovered by accident after being lost to sight for hundreds of years. In 1857 the vicar of **Bradford-on-Avon** in Wiltshire was looking down on his parish from a hill above the town when he spotted a stone roof, amid the jumble of buildings, in the

shape of a cross. He found that the people living in the houses all around and against it had long since forgotten its original use. The surrounding area was cleared, and although it has been left plain and unadorned, except for two 10th century angels flying towards each other on a collision course over the chancel, St Lawrence is now a church once again.

The nave of St Lawrence is only 26 feet long, which puts it in the running for the smallest complete church in England as well as the oldest, but **Culbone** Church in Somerset, 33 feet 10 inches from end to end, lays claim to that title. It is not an easy church to reach – having driven the five miles from Porlock there is a long scramble for half a mile down a steep combe which can be very treacherous in wet weather. But the effort is worth it. The church stands in a glade beside

The oldest unaltered Saxon church in England, rediscovered at Bradford-on-Avon when the vicar spotted its cross-shaped roof.

The smallest and the biggest parish churches in England? Culbone (above) and Great Yarmouth (right).

a little stream with the steep sides of the combe rising above it. Its nave is only twelve feet wide, its chancel ten feet. The spire is tiny too, but it only dates from the last century. According to legend – a comparatively recent one as legends go – it was originally the spire of Porlock Church, but because of the misdoings of the parishioners St Michael removed it, with the assistance of a well-placed bolt of lightning, and gave it to Culbone instead.

The largest parish church, incidentally, is claimed by **Great Yarmouth**. St Nicholas' was bombed in 1942 but has been restored to its original splendour and its original size. It is in the shape of a cross, 236 feet long, 112 feet wide, and it covers an area of more than 23,000 square feet. Apart from its central tower and spire it has a mass of gable roofs and turrets, each with its own little spire. Before the Reformation it was bigger still – the aisles were widened before that to accommodate about 20 chapels. The Reformation not only saw the demolition of the chapels, it caused the brasses to be melted down for use as weights and measures for the town, and the gravestones were turned into millstones. Since then however an enormous pulpit has been provided, as big as a small room and a fair claimant for the biggest in the country, twelve feet long and four feet wide. There is enough room on the panels around it for the feeding of the five thousand, Christ blessing little children, the miraculous draught of little fishes and John the Baptist preaching, without any of them looking too overcrowded.

The church can claim another minor record. Edward Lupson was parish clerk for 45 years, and acted as witness to more than twelve thousand weddings, which works out at five or six a week for nearly half a century – a test of stamina for which Mr Lupson deserves congratulations as well as those twelve thousand couples – let alone the vicar.

While Culbone may be the smallest parish church, there are plenty of smaller chapels – and very strange some of them are too. At **Mugginton** in Derbyshire is the Halter-Devil Chapel, attached to a local farmhouse. It is said to have been built in 1723 by a local toper after he had been afforded a remarkable revelation which changed his drunken ways. One night in his cups Francis Brown vowed that he would ride to Derby, seven miles away, even if he had to 'halter the Devil'. He blundered out into the darkness to find his horse, and when he tried to put on the bridle was disconcerted to discover it had horns. Such was the shock and remorse this produced that he gave up drinking, and in order to ensure that he had no further encounters with the Devil he built the chapel. One wonders if anyone eventually got around to telling him that the animal was actually a cow.

Drink was the reason for another chapel being built at **Halstead** in Essex, but in rather different circumstances. It was kindly provided by the management of Fremlin's Brewery, within their premises.

A chapel for brewery workers at Fremlin's Brewery, Halstead . . .

. . . and a chapel which owes its existence to drink, the Halter-Devil Chapel at Mugginton.

The mortuary chapel at **Compton** in Surrey is an early example of do-it-yourself, inspired by Mrs Mary Watts, who was married to the Victorian painter and sculptor George Frederic Watts. She was a talented painter herself, and also went in for clay modelling. Combining these two talents, she designed a chapel for the new burial ground when the churchyard became full. Her clay modelling pupils from the village turned their hands to bricks instead of models, and built the chapel to her design. The result from outside is not too enchanting, but Mrs Watts made sure the interior was elaborately decorated with distinctive intaglio and relief work. The Watts Mortuary Chapel, as it is officially known, is something of a Watts Memorial Chapel too.

The parish churches of **Reepham**, **Whitwell** and **Hackford** have the curious distinction of being built in the same Norfolk churchyard. Hackford church was burnt down in 1543 and only an arch remains, but the other two still stand there, joined by a common vestry. This unusual illustration of ecclesiastical togetherness – or was it independence? – occurred in more prosperous days when the three adjoining villages were each determined to have their own church. It did them little good, now they have been merged into the market town of Reepham. Reepham's church is the larger and grander of

Watts Mortuary Chapel, built by amateurs but decorated by an expert (above and above, left).

Sharing the same churchyard – Reepham and Whitwell churches. There used to be a third one there as well.

A church which looks like a rotunda and a house which looks like a church – the Roman Catholic church at Lulworth Castle (left) and the Tattingstone Wonder in Suffolk (below).

the two now remaining, but Whitwell's has the more handsome pulpit, a splendid example of Jacobean woodwork which must be the envy of its senior partner next door.

The little church near **Lulworth Castle** in Dorset owes its existence to the fact that it does not look like a church at all. It was the first Roman Catholic church in England for which royal permission was given after the Reformation. George III agreed it should be built in 1786 on condition that it did not look like one. So Thomas Weld, who owned the castle, built it to look like a rotunda instead. It has fared rather better than the castle itself, which was gutted by fire in 1929.

Incidentally, at the other extreme to a church built to look like something else, at **Tattingstone** in Suffolk there is something else built to look like a church. It even deceived our photographer with its medieval tower and high nave – but it is in fact the Tattingstone Wonder, built in the 18th century by the local landowner who wanted a view of a church from his house in Tattingstone Place. The existing one was out of sight – so he built this imitation, just to look at. It is now a private house.

St Giles' church at **Holme** in Nottinghamshire survives from an era which has very scanty representation among our village churches. We have Saxon, Norman, then a bit of a gap. St Giles' is almost completely Tudor.

The Tudor church at Holme (left) built by a prosperous wool merchant – "the shepe hath payed for all". In it is 'Nanny Scott's Chamber', (right) so named because she took refuge here with a stockpile of food during the plague of 1666. From this window she watched the funerals of all her friends. Unfortunately her supply of food ran out. On finding only one survivor she returned to her chamber till her death.

The church that decided for itself where to be built – on God's Hill.

It was rebuilt by a prosperous wool merchant, John Barton, who occupies a corner of it himself under a rather morbid monument featuring a rotting corpse. The church still has its original screens and poppy-head benches, the walls still lean a bit, and there is still medieval glass in the east window, including John Barton's memorial glass. Mr Barton expressed his thanks for his prosperity in other ways too. On a window at his house was said to be inscribed:

I thanke God and ever shall. It is the shepe hath payed for all . . .

There is nothing especially distinctive about the church at **Godshill** on the Isle of Wight except that it decided for itself where it was going to be built. The builders' idea was to erect it at the foot of the hill in the village, which stands on the main road from Shanklin to Newport. They accordingly dug the foundations there and put down the foundation stones. The church itself apparently had other ideas. Two guards were disturbed at midnight by a rumbling sound which must have been the stones climbing the hill, because next morning they were at the top. The builders took the hint and built the church there, on God's Hill.

I name this church . . .

The choice of a name for a church must have caused as much heart-searching in days gone by as choosing the name of a baby does now. There must have been great debates over which saint should have the dedication. If anyone has worked out a church league table for saints, as those faithful correspondents of 'The Times' and the 'Daily Telegraph' do each year with the births announcements, I suspect Mary would be at the top, though the apostles and the archangels must have a lot of nominations for second place. (James and John must be the front runners, just as they still are among the births.)

They were chosen for particular churches for all manner of reasons – sometimes a local connection, sometimes because one was in fashion at the time, sometimes I am sure because – as with babies – they just liked the sound of the name. And if all else failed they had the option which is denied to parents; they could just call the church All Saints.

The Cornish churches had quite a different field to draw on, all those Celtic saints whose names rarely crop up anywhere else. St Cleer, St Cubert, St Clether, St Merryn, St Mawgan, St Kew – how they roll off the tongue. Some of them have been imported from Wales. There is St Keyne, a Welsh saint of the 5th century who is said to have turned off the main road from Liskeard to Looe and cast a spell on the **St Keyne** Holy Well, so that if two newly-weds drank from it, whoever drank first "the mastery gains". The water is now stagnant and the well almost invisible under a hedge, but St Keyne village is still there and if in any married couple there is a particularly bossy partner, this may still be the explanation.

St Nonna (or St Non) was another saintly Welsh immigrant, the most illustrious of them all – she was the mother of St David of Wales. She also provided the inspiration for a very illustrious church, known as the Cathedral of the Moors because of its size, and it has Cornwall's largest parish. This is at **Altarnun**, a moorland village above a stream on the edge of Bodmin Moor, some eight miles from Launceston. The church itself is comparatively recent but there is a Celtic cross in the churchyard which must date from Nonna's time, and of course there is a well.

This had rather different properties from St

St Nonna's Church and the well which was supposed to cure madness.

Keyne's. It was believed to cure madness; lunatics would be plunged in the well, then taken into the church for masses to be sung over them. If they regained their wits, there would be prayers of thanksgiving to St Nonna. If they did not, then they used her alternative name and it became a Non-event.

St Endellion was also a Welsh wanderer who made her home in Cornwall and offered the locals a chance to choose a distinctive name for their church. She was the daughter of a 6th century Welsh King, but she lived like a hermit in the Cornish countryside inland from Port Isaac, existing only on the milk from her cow. Unhappily the cow wandered on to the property of a local landlord who felt so strongly about it that he killed its unfortunate owner. Before she died she asked that her body be put on a cart and the young cattle which drew it should be allowed to wander where they liked. She wished to be buried wherever they stopped. **St Endellion** Church was built on that spot, from granite shipped from Lundy Island, and her body is said to be under the carved slate altar-tomb which was placed there eight hundred years later.

The Church of St Endellion and her altar tomb. She was killed by an irate landowner when her cow wandered on to his property.

Strangely the same last wish about a burial location was expressed by another saint with an unusual name, hundreds of miles away on the opposite side of England. St Walstan also lived frugally in the village of Taverham in Norfolk, but he was a native Norfolkman, not a Welsh wanderer, and he died more peacefully. He worked as a farm labourer all his life, finding God among the furrows, and became the patron saint of all who till the soil. In 1016 he died at work in a hayfield, having instructed that his body be drawn in a cart by the two oxen his master had given him, and he should be buried wherever they stopped.

The instructions were not quite followed to the letter, because the oxen first stopped in nearby Costessey Wood, perhaps not the ideal spot for a funeral. However they paused only long enough for a spring to gush from the ground, then wandered off to **Bawburgh**, which by a happy chance was where St Walstan was born. They stopped not far from his old home, and the locals buried him there and built a shrine. Inevitably, another spring gushed up there too.

The Church of St Wandrede – Wandregesilus to be formal, Wando to his friends. Bixley in Norfolk claims to have the only church dedicated to him.

He was not allowed to rest in peace. In one of Henry VIII's more destructive periods the shrine was razed and the saint's bones were burned and scattered. But his well is still there in a nearby orchard, and his name lives on as one of the patron saints of Bawburgh Church.

There can be very few churches dedicated to St Walstan; it is claimed there is only one dedicated to St Wandregesilus – Wandrede for short, or even Wando to his friends. This too is in Norfolk, in the tiny village of **Bixley**, a few miles outside Norwich. Wando's connection with Bixley is a little obscure; in the 7th century he started his career as a wealthy courtier in what is now France, then left the palace to become a monk. This irked the king, who demanded his return. On his way back through the streets of Metz he stopped to help a carter drag his horse out of the mud, and arrived at the palace in a distinctly messy state. The king was impressed by his kindly action and sent him speedily on his way – if only to avoid any more mud on the carpet.

Wando made a pilgrimage to Rome, spent ten years in the Jura mountains, took a turn around Rouen and finally founded a settlement for three hundred monks at Fontonelles, five miles outside the city. He governed the monastery for 20 years until his death in 667.

Where little Bixley comes into all this the chroniclers do not mention, but there is no doubt that in the Middle Ages pilgrimages were made to St Wandrede of Byskely, who we are assured is the same chap. As the little church has few other claims to fame except for a memorial to the prolific Ward family – father, mother, nine sons, three daughters – it would be a shame to explode the legend.

I would hesitate to claim any more 'one-off' dedications, but I feel safe in saying there are only two churches dedicated to St Bega, since her movements are fairly well chronicled and she did not stray far from either church. One of them, the Church of St Mary and St Bega, is confusingly in the little Cumbrian coastal resort of **St Bees**. There is actually a St Bees church as well (the only one? I doubt it). St Bega's church originally belonged to a Benedictine priory of the 12th century. Before the priory there was a nunnery, which was founded by St Bega.

She came across from Ireland in about 650, and having founded the priory it is said she headed inland through Ennerdale (where

St Bridget's and St Bega's Church by Bassenthwaite Lake. Churches are rich in Bridgets, but Begas are meagre.

there is a chapel associated with the priory) and on into the wilds of the Lake District, finishing up at a remote spot on the banks of **Bassenthwaite Lake**. There stands the little church of St Bridget and St Bega (she never managed to get a church dedication all to herself) and since there is no community nearby to justify a parish church, that explanation seems as good as any. It is a lonely but lovely spot – Tennyson spent sometime in those parts, and had St Bega's in mind when he wrote 'Morte d'Arthur':

The bold Sir Bedivere uplifted him,
Sir Bedivere the last of all his knights,
And bore him to a chapel in the fields,
A broken chancel with a broken cross,
That stood on a dark strait of barren land
On one side lay the Ocean, and on one
Lay a great water, and the moon was full

A church dedicated to The Beheading of St John the Baptist. The church itself was in effect 'beheaded' – its original tower was struck by lightning and destroyed (left). St Mungo's Church at Simonburn (below) where the nave has quite a pronounced gradient.

Also in the far north of England is the Church of St Mungo, in the quiet village of **Simonburn** in Northumberland. St Mungo was the illegitimate son of a Pictish princess, but he survived the scandal and finished up as Bishop of Strathclyde. Most of his activities were presumably north of the border, but Simonburn selected him as their patron saint and built a church to him. Their selection of a site was not quite so fortunate. They built it on a steep slope and did not manage to adjust the floor level accordingly. There is therefore quite a gradient, which can turn a stately procession down the aisle into quite a scramble if it is allowed to gather momentum – urged on perhaps by a saintly exhortation, "Go Mun-Go"!

There are Doddingtons and Dodingtons all over England, from Northumberland to Somerset and from Cheshire to Avon, but **Doddington** in Kent has singled itself out from the rest by selecting a most unusual dedication for its church. When it was founded around 1150 it was dedicated not just to St John, nor to St John the Baptist, like so many other parish churches, but to 'The Beheading of St John the Baptist'. The church has not fared too happily over the years – the tower was destroyed by lightning in the 17th century and a weatherboard substitute was put up instead.

Is it a man in a robe or a woman with a beard? Paintings said to be of St Uncumber in Worstead Church, Norfolk. She grew a beard to avoid being forced into marriage, and suffered crucifixion instead.

The strangest named saint with perhaps the strangest legend attached to her is, I think, St Uncumber, a princess who it is said miraculously grew a beard when her father tried to force her into matrimony. Thus Uncumber remained unencumbered, but it did her little good. In his rage her father crucified her. Now it is thought she has the power of ridding women of unwanted husbands. Since most churches are run mainly by men, this is perhaps why I know of no church where she has been chosen as patron saint. Some churches, like **Worstead** in Norfolk, claim to have paintings or statues of her, but I imagine it is difficult to distinguish between a woman with a beard and a bearded man in a long robe . . .

Through a glass colourfully

The glory of many a parish church which is otherwise undistinguished is its stained glass windows. The man we can thank for that idea is thought to be Benedict Biscop, who lived in Northumbria in the 7th century. Benedict was a travelling man – he made five journeys to Rome, he spent some time as a monk in Gaul, moved on to Canterbury and eventually returned to Northumbria to found monasteries at Wearmouth and Jarrow. But his most notable contribution was to introduce ideas from Rome and the Continent into English churches and monasteries. He is said to have built the earliest stone churches to replace the simple wooden ones, and in these churches he placed the earliest stained glass windows.

Benedict's significance in the development of Christianity in England is rather overshadowed by that of his pupil, the notable historian now known to us all as the Vener-

able Bede, who translated the Bible into the Saxon tongue, along with a great deal more. The snag was that not a lot of Saxons could read in those days, and to them Benedict's windows, telling Bible stories in pictures, were much more use than Bede's books. So, while not neglecting the veneration of Bede the Book, let us also remember the fenestration of Benedict the Window.

The art of 'painting in light' developed from his primitive efforts. The discovery in the 14th century that certain silver salts fired on white glass gave a rich orange stain opened up a vast new range of rich and brilliant colours, and medieval windows like those in King's College Chapel, **Cambridge** are still unequalled. Indeed many of the secrets of those early glaziers died with them. But modern artists still produce some fine masterpieces, and just like Benedict they seek not just to decorate but to tell a story.

The Bible stories are told again and again in church windows throughout the country – no need to direct you to any of them. But there are lesser known stories I find fascinating, such as the story of St Neot in one of the marvellous windows at **St Neot** church in Cornwall. Little Neot must have been the smallest saint in the business; he was 15 inches high. In spite of being so tiny – or perhaps because he could address them at their own level – he is said to have had the power to make crows obey him, long before Alfred Hitchcock got around to it. At the other extreme he also had the ability to plough with stags, which came in very handy when a thief stole his oxen. At some stage his remains were taken to a Benedictine monastery in Cambridgeshire, which is how the town of St Neots got its name, but Cornwall has the prior claim on the little fellow, and St Neot's Holy Well is still believed in the West Country to strengthen delicate children. A window in the north aisle tells the whole story.

A window in the church of **Minster-in-Thanet** in Kent tells the tale of Princess Ermenburga and her uncle King Egbert, a tale which is as delightful as their names. Traditionally this is where the Anglo-Saxons first landed in England, which must have been a little frustrating since it used to be separated from the mainland by the Wantsum Channel,

A big window for a little saint – the story of St Neot, who was only 15 inches high, told in stained glass at St Neot's Church in Corwall.

so they still had some more sailing to do. But in the 7th century it was established as one of the first nunneries in the country, thanks to Ermenburga and Uncle Egbert.

It seems that the princess's two brothers were murdered by Egbert's thane, Thunor, and as compensation Egbert offered her as much land as her pet hind could encompass in one non-stop run. The hind went off at such a lick that Thunor the Thane decided it would mean far too much land for Ermenburga and forthwith got up to more skullduggery. He tried to stop the hind from going any further, but failed to look where he was going himself and he and his horse fell into a ditch and were drowned. The hind kept going on this first-ever sponsored run, and Ermenburga finished up with one thousand acres of her uncle's land. It is all depicted in the window of St Mary's.

The tradition of telling stories in stained glass has continued into modern times. In the little Warwickshire village of **Binton**, not far from Stratford-upon-Avon, a set of windows in the Victorian church of St Peter's illustrate

The story of Captain Scott's last expedition to the South Pole, told in the windows of Binton Church, Warwickshire, where his brother-in-law was Rector.

Princess Ermenburga and her sponsored stag at Minster-in-Thanet – her uncle gave her as much land as the hind could encompass in a single run. It worked out at a thousand acres, a useful start for Ermenburga's nunnery.

Captain Scott's ill-fated expedition to the South Pole in 1912; the story in words is told beneath. One of the most striking pictures is the departure of Captain Oates:

here, unwilling to be a burden to his companions, (he) leaves them and the shelter of the tent, to die

The link between Robert Scott and Binton was his brother-in-law, the Rev Lloyd Bruce, who was rector of the parish. Scott visited him there to say goodbye before he set out for the Antarctic.

A story of a very different kind is illustrated in a window of All Saints' Church, **Daresbury** in Cheshire. There is a cheerful looking fellow with a big hat, a cat with a big smile, a queen with a big heart . . . This is the memorial window to the Rev Charles Lutwidge Dodgson, who as Lewis Carroll was creator of

A Wonderland in stained glass – Lewis Carroll's memorial window at Daresbury, where he spent his childhood.

There is more to Stoke Poges Church than memories of Thomas Gray and his Elegy. It has a naked cyclist in one window . . .

. . . and two windows, hand-painted not stained, depicting a little girl's flight to Heaven after her death at the age of nine.

the Mad Hatter, the Cheshire Cat, the Queen of Hearts and many more in his tales of Alice in Wonderland. He was the son of the village parson and spent his early years there. The parsonage has been demolished but the window lives on, erected with subscriptions from all over the world to mark the centenary of his birth in 1932.

If you are ever among the charabanc-loads who make the pilgrimage to **Stoke Poges** in Buckinghamshire, spare a moment if you can bear it from all the memorabilia of Thomas Gray and his Elegy. Things have changed a lot in that area since those days – the ploughman homeward plodding his weary way today would probably be mown down by the rush hour traffic from Slough, and the lowing herd winding slowly o'er the lea would probably find itself in an industrial estate – but one feature of the church has not changed since long before he wrote all that. Pass the Gray monument outside and the Gray altar tomb inside and you will find a very odd stained glass window, depicting the nearest an early artist ever got to Mr Norman Tebbit's catch-phrase, "Get on your bike".

The window came from a nearby manor house which fell empty and was in danger of being vandalised. It depicts a young man astride what looks very like a bicycle. The front wheel is very clearly depicted; we do not see much of the back one because when he got that far the artist ran out of window. There are no handlebars, just a curved projection like a ship's prow, but this does not seem to worry the rider, since both his hands are occupied with the long horn he is blowing (could it be a raspberry, Mr Tebbit's critics might suggest). There also seems to be no saddle, so he has to perch on the square-cut crossbar – a painful position, one imagines, since the young man is completely naked.

Stoke Poges also has two painted windows – yes, hand-painted, not stained. They tell the story of a little girl who died at the age of nine; in one window she is being parted from her earthly mother, in the other she is safely in the care of a winged mother in Heaven. That at least is what the guide book says. There is another version that the mother died in child-birth. The 'winged mother' is actually an angel taking the child to Heaven to be re-united, and the 'parting' window is really a re-union. Either way, they are very striking paintings.

While it is nice to have a break from

Thomas Gray at Stoke Poges, it is even nicer to get away from the prison at Princetown, as no doubt the prisoners would testify. When you have had your morbid fill of gazing at the prison itself, have a look in **Princetown** church at the American window. It is a reminder of the prison's earlier days, when it was built to house French and American prisoners-of-war. That was the idea of a rich friend of the Prince Regent, Sir Thomas Tyrwhitt, who needed cheap labour to build a splendid house on the moor, realised that nobody came cheaper than POWs, and built the prison to house them while they worked for him. They built the church too, and it contains a commemorative window presented by an Americans Women's Organisation.

A much later war is recalled in **Yalding** church in Kent, in a small window in the south wall of the chancel. It commemorates Edmund Blunden, the 'poet of peace and war' who was brought up in Yalding. After his death in 1974 the window was engraved by his friend Laurence Whistler. It combines the two themes of Blunden's work, with a bomb exploding into bloom like a tree and a briar coiled up to look like barbed wire.

The American Window at Princetown Church, in memory of some of the earliest residents in what is now Dartmoor Prison.

Laurence Whistler's windows at Yalding in memory of his friend Edmund Blunden, illustrating the two themes of "the poet of peace and war".

Chagall's window (right) in Tudeley Church (above), one of the finest modern windows in an English village church.

Perhaps the finest modern window in an English village church is also in Kent, at **Tudeley**. It is a splendid work by Marc Chagall, the only one of its kind in England. It was dedicated in 1967 when Chagall was 81. In it he commemorates the young daughter of Sir Henry d'Avignon-Goldsmith, who was drowned in 1963. It shows a Crucifixion scene floating above water, a red horse representing happiness, and a ladder leading up to the heavens.

No modern artist has matched the gimmick of John Prudde, who was responsible for the stained glass windows in the Beauchamp Chapel in **Warwick** Church. The entire chapel, burial place of the Earl of Warwick who was involved in the burning of Joan of Arc, is enormously impressive – his tomb is said to be one of the most beautiful in Europe – but the windows have a special glamour. When Mr Prudde came to illustrate the jewels in the robes of his subjects, he used the real thing!

I ought also to mention a remarkable example of murals, another form of church decoration which goes back for many centuries, but which in recent years has been mainly limited to texts. It has been revived by Stanley

Sandham Memorial Chapel at Burghclere where Stanley Spencer painted the murals.

Examples of Stanley
Spencer's murals in
Sandham Memorial
Chapel, depicting the life
of a soldier in wartime. He
too looked beyond the
obvious – he painted, not
great battles, but everyday
scenes of the unglamorous
side of Army life. The
exception is his final
painting at the east end,
his own version of the
Resurrection (opposite
page).

Spencer in the Sandham Memorial Chapel at
Burghclere in Hampshire. The chapel was
built in 1926 by Mr and Mrs J L Behrend to
commemorate a relation who died in the first
World War, and Spencer, who served in the
war himself as a hospital orderly and was
much influenced by what he saw, painted a
series of 19 murals illustrating the day-to-day
life of a soldier in wartime. This is not the
inspirational material to be found on so many
war memorials, but a down-to-earth picture
of the unglamorous side of army life. Only at
the east end does the theme change; he has
drawn the Resurrection, with a heap of
wooden crosses in the foreground, handed in
by the soldiers. It is a striking modern successor to those illustrative windows of Benedict
Biscop, 13 centuries before.

Now let's come to the point

The famous twisted spire at Chesterfield (above and right) in Derbyshire . . .

The most quoted spires in England are probably those at Oxford, "city of dreaming spires" – though I prefer Frederick Raphael's version, "Cambridge, city of perspiring dreams". But for oddness the most obvious choice is Chesterfield's crooked spire, which suffered from the effect of changing temperatures on the lead covering the frame, and now appears to be nearly falling over in its efforts

to emulate a corkscrew. But since it *is* so obvious, let us look beyond it to another spire which is contorted in much the same way but is much less widely known. It is hundreds of miles away from Derbyshire, in Devon.

The spire of **Ermington** Parish Church, overlooking the peaceful Erme Valley, does not have the height of Chesterfield's but it certainly has the twist. It was built in the 13th century, and like Chesterfield's leans noticeably, as if about to fall. Again like Chesterfield's, we are assured it won't.

For sheer ostentation it is difficult to beat the monstrous ball that surmounts the church of St Lawrence at **West Wycombe**. Like the other eccentricities which changed the character of this otherwise attractive Buckinghamshire village it is the product of the slightly overheated imagination of Sir Francis Dashwood, one of our more eccentric Chancellors of the Exchequer. Sir Francis rebuilt West Wycombe House, put up a Temple of Music and various other fancy structures, and made use of the caves under his land as a headquarters for his notorious Hell Fire Club.

For a bit of extra excitement the Club is said to have held card parties inside this

. . . and the not-so-famous but just as twisted spire at Ermington in Devon.

West Wycombe Church, where the tower is topped by an 'orb' instead of a 'sceptre'. Sir Francis Dashwood put the golden ball there in place of a spire, some say to use as a globular gaming-room.

golden ball, which is big enough to seat eight people and a pack of cards. They are also supposed to have met in a room inside the tower, which seems rather more likely and certainly more comfortable. The Club now consists only of waxwork figures in various stages of debauchery providing amusement for tourists in the caves, but the golden ball is still poised over the village, six hundred feet above sea level, a reminder of Sir Francis's funny little ways.

A more macabre tale is attached to the unfinished spire of All Saints' Church at **Beeby** in Leicestershire, known locally as Beeby's Tub. It is said to be responsible for three deaths. Two brothers working on it had a quarrel in which one was pushed off and fell to his death. The other, filled with remorse, followed suit. The third fatality is supposed to be the principal builder of the spire himself, who hoped that he could match the height of Queniborough spire in the next village, found that he couldn't, and jumped off. The drop was presumably not as far as he would have liked, but it was far enough.

'Beeby's Tub' – the unfinished spire on Beeby Church, the scene of unhappy building disputes which proved fatal.

The twin towers of Wymondham Abbey, now the parish church of **Wymondham** in Norfolk, were the subject of much unseemly controversy for years, but happily without the fatal consequences of the Beeby brothers. It was between the monks and the citizenry, over whose bells should go in which tower. It is a complicated tale, involving the monks blocking off the central arch so the church was divided in two and the parishioners could not see the high altar. The monks built the octagonal tower which is at the east end of the church (though at that time it was at the centre – I told you it was complicated)

Wymondham Abbey where the monks and the citizens tried to outdo each other in tower building.

and they hung their bells there. The parishioners wanted their own bells in their own belltower, and rioted mightily until they got them. They built a tower at the west end of the church which was going to be bigger and better than the monks' at the other end. They got as far as 142 feet, then somehow reached an agreement with the monks and never bothered to go any higher. Both towers have plain tops and give the impression of needing some finishing touches, but everyone seems quite happy to leave it at that.

Wymondham is in the midst of Norfolk's six hundred fine medieval churches, and nearly all of them have towers which are traditional in style. A notable exception is the tower of **Burgh St Peter**, which looks out across the Waveney Valley towards Oulton Broad. It is built up in a series of decreasing squares, like a heap of outsize toy bricks, and it is nearer a pyramid than a tower. It is the work of some 17th century individualist who had perhaps wearied of all those square or circular towers everywhere else. The rest of the church is a lot more traditional and a lot more attractive, with a thatched roof and porch. The Boycott family must have liked it, in spite of that tower – they were rectors without a break for 135 years.

The Church of Burgh St Peter, with its building-brick tower.

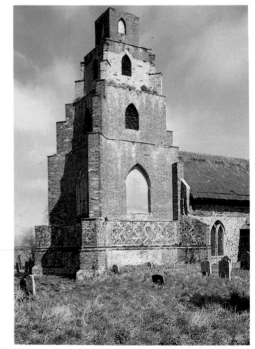

The smallest round tower in England? St Swithin's Church at Ashmanaugh in Norfolk. It also has the tomb of a 16th century bride who died on her wedding eve.

Incidentally the smallest round tower in England is probably the one at **Ashmanaugh** – it is certainly the smallest in Norfolk. St Swithin's church has only one other distinction, apart from being dedicated to a saintly meteorologist; it has the tomb of Honor Bacon, a bride who died tragically on the eve of her wedding day in 1591.

Round towers, square towers, a building-brick tower – how about a triangular tower? The only one in the country, they say, is at **Maldon**, on the banks of the Blackwater in Essex. It was put there in the 13th century, surmounted by a hexagonal spire. This makes it clearly distinguishable from the 'church' just down the road, which turns out to be the public library.

The village of **Lamarsh** in Suffolk can offer another striking combination on its church, a round Norman tower topped by a pointed Gothic turret, straight out of the Rhineland and looking a little out of character by the water meadows of the Stour Valley.

Tamworth's church tower in Staffordshire is also distinctive, some say unique. It is square with a spire on each corner, which is fairly standard, but in one corner also is a

The triangular tower of Maldon Church, a change from the square and the circular.

Tamworth's four-spired tower, with its double-spiral staircase.

double-spiral staircase. One stairway starts from an entrance in the churchyard, the other from inside the tower, and they are so skilfully intertwined, with the floor of one forming the roof of the other, that people climbing up one will never see people climbing down the other. Curiously, one staircase has 106 steps, the other only 101, providing a sort of two-speed gear change for climbers – those with longer legs should take the 101 . . .

From miles away across the Plain of York you can see the tower and spire of St Mary's Church, **Hemingbrough** – the tower is only 60 feet high but the spire rises for another 120. The tower is worth a much closer look. In the tower moulding you will find carved a row of washing tubs, or tuns, an unlikely feature for a church. It is a medieval rebus, a pictorial pun. The tower was built by Prior Washington, and whether it was he or one of his masons who had the brainwave, his name was immortalised in the washing tuns.

The best equivalent in towers of the tilting spires of Chesterfield and Ermington is probably at **Little Puxton**, in Avon. The tower of Holy Saviour church looks in danger of parting company from the main body of the building – but like Chesterfield and Ermington, it is not expected to, just yet.

In a great many cases, of course, the architects fully intended the tower to be separate from the church. These are the campaniles, the belltowers which were usually built at the same time as the church and make an obvious pair – St Nicholas Parish Church in

The Leaning Tower of Little Puxton.

The 'washing tuns' on Hemingbrough Church tower, a reminder of its builder, Prior Washington.

Dereham, where my elder son was christened to become a true Norfolkman, is an outstanding example. But it has not always worked quite like that.

The present parish church of **Middleton-in-Teesdale**, in County Durham, is only one hundred years old – it was completely rebuilt in the 1870s. But its stubby stone belltower is more than three hundred years older and still retains its three original bells, which can all be rung by one person, using two hands and a foot. **Yarpole**, midway between Leominster and Ludlow, also has a belltower much older than its church – it goes back to the 13th century.

Brookland in Kent has a very odd belltower alongside the church of St Augustine. It is shaped more like a Christmas tree than a belfry, with three cones sitting on top of each other, biggest at the bottom, smallest at the top, all made of weatherboarding. It dates from the 13th century, the same period as the church, and originally stood as an open framework, but the ringers must have found this singularly draughty and it has been covered in for the last few hundred years. The medieval architect who designed it used much the same principle as a modern electricity pylon with four massive canted beams able to support a heavy moving load – these days the swinging cables, in his case the swinging bells.

The original timber was said to have been gathered from wrecks on the coast, though another school of thought says the belfry originally stood at Lydd and was moved to Brookland, for reasons too obscure to have survived, by Cardinal Wolsey. Much more enterprising is the theory that the belltower originally stood above the church, but was twice blown down and nobody thought it worth putting up for a third time.

But the most attractive story is that it leapt off the church of its own volition, in sheer amazement, when an aged virgin came to the church to be married.

Strangest belfry of them all must be at **East Bergholt** in Suffolk. It is not so much a belltower as a bellcage, a low wooden building with a high roof which was built as a temporary measure in 1531. Cardinal Wolsey had given a number of donations towards the building of a belltower over the previous five years, but then came his downfall and it became apparent that there would be no further aid from that quarter. The bells were

Examples of an old belltower with a not-so-old church – at Middleton-in-Teesdale in County Durham . . .

. . . and at Yarpole in Shropshire.

Brookland's 'Christmas Tree' belltower – did it leap off the church?

A spire without a church –
all that remains of St
Andrew's, Worcester.

already available but the belltower was incomplete, so this wooden cage was built until a new benefactor was forthcoming. They are waiting still.

The bells are mounted on heavy wooden stocks and are rung upright by swinging the stocks by hand. It is no mean feat; this is the heaviest set of five bells currently in use in England, weighing altogether over three tons. If they ever get around to finishing the belltower, it will need to be pretty sturdy. But it seems unlikely; the bellcage was restored in 1972, with an eye to having an indefinite future.

Buried near the bellcage are the parents of East Bergholt's most famous son, John Constable. The bells may well have tolled at their funerals.

One imagines there are good reasons for housing bells separately from the main body of the church. It is more difficult to imagine a good reason for having a separate spire. And indeed it has only happened by some strange quirk of fate. There is for instance the spire of St Helen's Church at **Burton Joyce** in Nottinghamshire. The top section was struck by lightning in 1890 and fell to the ground. After nearly a century nobody has tried to replace it – advisedly, perhaps, in view of its rather decrepit condition – and it stands a little forlornly in the south porch of the church.

There is a detached spire at St Andrew's church in **Worcester**, but it is detached for a rather different reason. The rest of the church has been demolished and only the spire remains.

Another free-standing spire stands all on its own in a meadow at **Remenham** in Berkshire, at the end of a track off the Marlow-Henley road. It is about 30 feet high, attractively fluted with a little carved figure on top, the whole thing neatly mounted on a plinth. It turns out to be the spire from St Bride's Church in the City of London, which was acquired by a Mr Fuller Maitland in 1837 and brought 30-odd miles out into the Thames Valley for reasons only Mr Maitland could have explained.

Perhaps the strangest church spire of them all, which never stood on or anywhere near a church, was the creation of one of the great eccentrics of all time, 'Mad Jack' Fuller of **Brightling** in East Sussex. He went in for all manner of odd obelisks and rum rotundas, but his 'spire' must be the most entertaining. It was the result of boasting to his guests about the splendid views from his home at Brightling Park. He assured them that it was possible to see the spire of Dallington church. Some of those present thought he was pushing it a bit, since Dallington lies in a dip in the Downs, and they told him so. Since it was dark at the time it could not be proved either way, but Mad Jack stuck to his guns and happily accepted bets on it.

Early next morning, so the story goes, he looked out of his window towards Dallington, and indeed no spire could be seen. But by the time his guests awoke he had put the matter right. They were clearly able to see the cone-shaped spire in the middle distance. They paid up without bothering to investigate any further. Had they done so they would have found that it had been hastily constructed out of stones and mud at a point visible from the house. These days it is known as the Sugar Loaf, but I still prefer to think of it fulfilling its original purpose, as the doppelganger of Dallington church spire.

The fake spire at Brightling, built because of a bet.

The transplanted spire at Remenham, moved because – who knows?

The permanent congregations

The practice in past centuries of erecting elaborate effigies of deceased dignitaries in their local parish churches has always struck me as – literally – a monumental waste of money. It could have been much better spent on a modest plaque and a substantial contribution to the church restoration fund. How many churches do you know which boast a magnificently decorated tomb underneath a leaking roof, or an impressive statue alongside an equally impressive display of rising damp?

Did the occupants of these tombs and the originals of these statues demand this expensive form of recognition, or was it lavished on them by their relatives to preserve their importance for posterity – and outdo the neigh-bours in the next tomb? Were all those armoured knights lying on their stone slabs quite so heroic, were all those horizontal husbands quite so faithful?

Whatever the logic or the justification we have some magnificent sculptures and carvings to thank them for – and some very odd ones as well, which the deceased could hardly have visualised. Lady Warburton of **Chester**, for example, would no doubt be gratified to know her memorial was by Edward Pierce, who worked for the likes of Christopher Wren, but would she have relished the upright figure of a skeleton he carved on her tomb, holding its shroud open to display the details of her demise? And would Sir Marmaduke Constable, a member of one of the major families of **Flamborough** in Humberside, who died in 1520, enjoy worshippers being treated to the sight of his bared heart being eaten by a toad. On his tomb in St Oswald's Church is the upper section of a skeleton, and inside the rib-cage is the heart with a lump on it which is supposed to portray the toad. It is said Sir Marmaduke inadvertently swallowed it while having a drink of water – presumably one expected to find a little contamination in the water supply in those days, and the occasional lump, even a live lump, passed unnoticed.

The toad, however, declined to be passed any further. It remained inside Sir Marmaduke and ate away at his heart until he died. One fervently hopes this was not the origin of toad-in-the-hole . . .

There is a gruesome monument in **Broad Hinton** church, Wiltshire, which illustrates another sobering story. Sir Thomas Wroughton came home from hunting to find his wife Anne reading the Bible instead of preparing his supper. He seized the Bible from her and flung it in the fire, but she managed to retrieve it, badly burning her hands in the process. Because of his blasphemous behaviour Sir Thomas's hands withered away too and, less understandably, so did those of

Lady Warburton's gruesome tomb at Chester. The toad features in an even more grisly memorial.

Memorials to the handless – the family tomb of Sir Thomas Wroughton at Broad Hinton (above) and that of Dorothy Paunceforte at Hasfield (left).

his four children. The monument is to the entire family, all handless. A Bible with a corner burnt off is shown too.

A severed hand features in the story of Dorothy Paunceforte, whose tomb is in **Hasfield** Church, near Tewkesbury. Dorothy's lover Julian was captured by pirates and fell into the clutches of a female Captain Bluebeard who wanted him to marry her. Julian gamely declined, saying there was a maid back home who would give her right hand to have him back. He must have wished he hadn't because his captor seized upon his suggestion and said she would swap him for Dorothy's hand. Amazingly, Dorothy came up trumps, and as a result Julian returned home and married her, no doubt promising to be a little more judicious in his statements in the

future. In the 19th century Dorothy's tomb was investigated and from the remains that were uncovered it seems the story could well be true.

As with Mrs Paunceforte, it is the contents of the tomb rather than the tomb itself which singles out one of the effigies in **Danbury** Church in Essex, but the effigy itself is quite impressive – a wooden figure of a Crusader knight dating back to the 1300s, one of three in the church, each one carved with a different posture and expression. In 1779 one of these effigies was lifted, and in the coffin underneath was found the knight's body, still perfectly preserved in pickle after four hundred years. It is said that somebody actually sampled the pickle and said it tasted of catsup and Spanish olives. Even if he said it tasted of ambrosia I doubt that many others would have fancied it.

A knight in a pickle at Danbury . . .

. . . knights in profusion at Aldworth.

There are knights in profusion in **Aldworth** church, near Goring in Berkshire, but preserved rather more attractively. However large they were in life, their effigies are larger still. These are the 'Aldworth Giants', Sir Philip de la Beche, who was Sheriff of Berkshire and Oxfordshire in the 1300s, and eight of his relatives. Unfortunately nobody knows which is which; it is said that the Earl of Leicester took down the tablet bearing their names to show to Elizabeth I when she visited the church and forgot to put it back. Three of them however were known as John Strong (that was Sir Philip), John Long and John Never-Afraid, who is said to have promised his soul to the Devil if he were buried either inside or outside the church, but avoided paying up by being buried in the wall.

Some of the figures were badly mutilated in Cromwell's time but they still make an impressive group, some lying on their backs, one couple lying on their sides, and a nonchalant knight leaning languidly on an elbow, a position rarely assumed in such circumstances.

There is another rarity in effigies at **Stow Bardolph** in Norfolk. While such monuments are usually carved in stone or depicted in brass, Sarah Hare is commemorated in wax. Mistress Hare was a member of the family

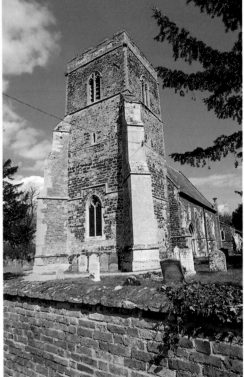

Sarah Hare, still alarmingly lifelike after two hundred years – the wax effigy in Stow Bardolph Church.

HERE · LYETH · THE · BODY · OF · SARAH · HARE · YOUNGEST DAUGHTER · OF · Sᵗ · THOˢ · HARE · BARᵗ · AND · DAME · ELIZABᵗʰ HIS · WIFE · AND · SISTER · TO · THE · PRESENT · Sᵗ · THOˢ · HARE WHO · DEPARTED · THIS · LIFE · THE · IX · DAY · OF · APRᵗ · MDCCXLIV AND · ORDERED · THIS · EFFIGIES · TO · BE · PLACED · HERE

A tennis fatality commemorated at Elford Church in Staffordshire. The boy was apparently hit on the head by the ball.

who were lords of the manor for four hundred years, living there through 17 reigns, and a good many of them are represented in Stow Bardolph church by orthodox marble figures. But in the Hare Chapel, which is actually bigger than the chancel and accommodates the squire's pew as well as his ancestors, the wax figure of Sarah is preserved in an oak case, dressed in the clothes which she herself requested before her death, and still looking almost alarmingly life-like after more than two hundred years. This strange form of preservation may have something to do with the way she died. It is said that while sewing on a Sunday, a wildly sacrilegious practice in the 1700s, she pricked her finger with the needle and died as a result.

Another unexpected death from an unlikely cause is illustrated in St Peter's Church at **Elford** in Staffordshire. The church is mainly renowned for its remarkable collection of heraldic shields, all in excellent condition, but it also contains the memorial to the grandson of Sir John Stanley, who died not in battle but in a game of tennis. The boy is depicted holding the offending ball in one hand, and pointing ruefully at his head with the other. The date was 1460, when presumably tennis balls were a lot harder than they are now.

Elford Church

A plaque in the wall of **Bampton** Church in Devon, a few miles north of Tiverton, tells how another child met an equally unfortunate accident in 1776, though the wording is somewhat facetious. One assumes the lad must have died from an icicle falling on his head, because the verse reads:

"Bless my i i i i i i" (yes, eyes),
"Here he lies,
In a sad pickle,
Killed by icicle."

One wonders if the boy's father, who was Parish Clerk, found this terribly amusing, but his successors obviously thought it worth preserving because when the original plaque became too worn to be legible they replaced it with this present one.

Having complained about the extravagance of some early effigies I am happy to record an instance of admirable economy in the use of church memorials, where brasses originally used on earlier occasions have been turned over and used again. There are two of them in **Halvergate** Church in Norfolk. They were both first used in the mid-1400s, then one hundred years later were re-used, perhaps by the same frugal metalworker.

Another unusual fatality – but a much more bizarre memorial. This boy also died from a blow to the head, not from a ball but an icicle. The writer of his epitaph at Bampton seemed to find it good for a chuckle.

One originally had the head of a monk on one side, shaven and with serious face, then it was used again as a memorial to Robert and Alice Swane, and bears on the reverse side a small half-figure wearing a headdress, with hands clasped in prayer. The second brass is believed to have come originally from Blackborough Priory, because it bears an inscription to Elizabeth, wife of Lord Scales, and most of the Scales were buried there. A

Praying not to be used again? The two-sided brass at Halvergate Church.

century later it was inscribed on the back to Robert Golward and his wife. There must be other two-sided brasses but not on the same Scale.

Finally, a memorial richly deserved, in the parish church of **Bingham** in Nottinghamshire. There is a modest floorstone to Sir Thomas Rempstone, who as 'John Ramston' had the obscure distinction of being mentioned by Shakespeare as a member of the assembled company when John of Gaunt declaimed "This royal throne of Kings, this sceptred Isle". He was actually a distinguished warrior himself, but it is not his memorial I commend, but the figure of Ann Harrison, a simple fish-seller who worshipped at the church throughout her 99 years, and put every other half-crown she earned into the collection. Her contributions paid for the Book of Honour to the Fallen, a fitting memorial in itself. But if the parishioners felt she deserved another, who can carp at that?

Memorials to a remarkable benefactor in Bingham Church. Ann Harrison gave half of what she earned as a fish seller to the church. She made a special effort to provide the Book of Honour (below).

This Roll of Honour was, for the most part, obtained through the exertions of **Ann Harrison** who was born on 20th September 1829, and died on 14th January 1928. Her method was to visit all her friends and neighbours in the parish with a large fish-basket which she filled with their household refuse, such as potato parings. This refuse she sold for feeding pigs, and all the money she obtained from this source she gave towards providing the Church with this Book. At the time she was 88 years of age, and her sole means of support was an old age pension of 7s.6d. a week.

To commemorate both her and this act of self-sacrifice, some of her friends have given the memorial to her which is placed on the south pillar of the Chancel arch.

Church memorabilia – relics to relish

Could this hand at Marlow have come from St James the Apostle? Certainly Preston's mosaic and lamp came from his part of the world.

The early Church was a great collector of sacred memorabilia. No doubt assuming that the world was full of doubting Thomases who would only believe in what they could touch, monks and priests liked to acquire actual evidence of long-deceased martyrs and long-gone events. There was always a demand for a piece of a saint's clothing, or better still, a piece of a saint, such as the mummified hand in St Peter's Church, **Marlow**, believed to have belonged to St James the Apostle.

When the supply of personal relics ran out, churches went in for anything even obscurely associated with holy places and the Holy Land. The village church of **Preston** in Leicestershire has perhaps the most extensive collection. It has lamps and candlesticks from Damascus, floor mosaic from Constantinople, an almsbox from a church in Asia Minor, and yew trees which are said to have been brought from the Garden of Gethsemane.

As the centuries passed the Church broadened its collection to include an even wider range of items and organs, but it still attached importance to supplying evidence of early events, so if the events became forgotten or over-embroidered by succeeding generations, at least the evidence remained unchanged. Which is why there is a bandaged heart entombed in a pillar at St Mary's Church, **Woodford** in Northamptonshire, not of a saint but of a sinning vicar.

John Styles lost his parish in the 16th century because of his Catholic beliefs and fled to Belgium, taking with him a valuable chalice from the church. It proved of little use to him – he died soon afterwards. His successor, Andrew Powlet, located the chalice and the body some years later. Presumably as evidence of his death, he brought back to Woodford not only the chalice but John Styles' heart. Strangely, both these trophies were mislaid in later years, until a 19th century vicar claimed he saw Powlet's ghost in the parsonage, hovering near a panel in the

The heart of an errant vicar at Woodford Church (above and right). The communion table of an heroic vicar at Stowbridge

wall. Inside a secret cavity was the chalice, and in the best tradition of treasure hunts it also contained the next clue. It was a letter, saying the heart was inside the pillar, where it still rests, visible these days through a glass panel.

A very different relic of a very different vicar is retained in the church at **Stowbridge**, a tiny village on the west bank of the River Ouse, on the Norfolk border. It is a simple wooden communion table, which was used during the British Army campaign in Afghanistan in the 1870s by the Rev James William Adams, the first army chaplain to be awarded the Victoria Cross. He was on the staff of Lord Roberts and had a number of mentions in despatches before his major act of heroism, when he saved one cavalryman under the guns of the Afghan Army, and rescued two more who were trapped under their horses. As a civilian he was ineligible for the VC, but Roberts twisted the rules on his behalf.

James Adams settled in Norfolk and accepted the living of Stow Bardolph, where he was almost as energetic as he had been in Afghanistan. Even in his 60s he held five services and preached three sermons every Sunday, and for those in the outlying area of his parish at Stow Bridge he would conduct services in the schoolroom there, using the same wooden communion table he had taken on active service.

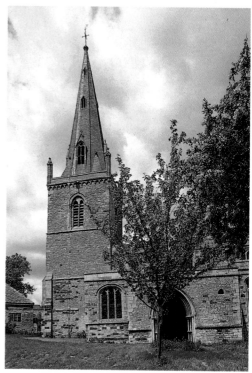

Other churches have retained relics from earlier days because of the stories attached to them – or just because nobody ever thought of throwing them away, like the collecting shoes in another Norfolk church at **Bressingham**, which were used in the 1600s to collect offerings before the introduction of plates and bags. They are rare enough to be of interest in their own right, but a medieval chest at **Lower Peover** in Cheshire would be just another chest without the story that goes with it. It was used as a test of strength for young girls who were to marry into farming families, to see if they could cope with the farm chores. They had to open the lid with one hand – and since the lid is extremely heavy there must have been some very strong girls in Peover, or some very frustrated farmers.

If those who failed the test had lived at **Abbotts Ann** in Hampshire they might have qualified for one of the garlands which are hung in the parish church. These are 'Maidens' Garlands', memorials to virgins of either sex who died within the parish. They are made of white paper or linen, in the shape of a bishop's mitre. Often there are paper gauntlets attached to them, a challenge to anyone who casts aspersions on the deceased's virginity. The custom started before the Reformation and continued until

Collecting shoes at
Bressingham in Norfolk.

Maidens' garlands at
Abbots Ann (above).

some 30 years ago. Among the 40-odd garlands still hanging there are some more than
250 years old.

Some churches have reminders of less
tolerant times, in particular the hagioscope,
or leper's squint, the nearest these unfortu-
nates were allowed to get to the rest of the
congregation. **Bolton-by-Bowland** church in
Lancashire has one. But it is believed there is
only one surviving example of another nasty
little ecclesiastical device, a finger pillory. It
consisted of two grooved beams which were
fastened on the fingers of anyone who misbehaved in church. It is kept – for show only –
in St Helen's Church, **Ashby-de-la-Zouch** in
Leicestershire.

A leper's squint carved
out of one piece of stone
at Bolton-by-Bowland
(left).

The finger pillory at
Ashby-de-la-Zouch, a
punishment for those who
misbehaved in church.

A considerable number of stocks have finished up in and around village churches, but I know of only one which has acquired the door of the local jail. The Church of St Andrew at **Stratton**, two miles from Bude on the north Cornish coast, has it in its south porch. The door is only five-and-a-half feet high and two-and-a-half feet wide, studded with 240 square-headed nails, some of which form the word 'Clink', which really sounds a little too good to be genuine. The original 'Clink' was a prison in Southwark, and it seems remarkable the slang word should have travelled all the way from London to the Cornish coast, and even more remarkable it should have been inscribed on the prison door. But I gather it has other meanings too in the West Country.

Another unusual word in an unusual setting crops up at **Eyke**, a little Suffolk hamlet ten miles from Ipswich. The wrought-iron key to the parish church is cut to represent the letters IKE, which was the local spelling for the village's name. No doubt the locksmith also found it simpler to incorporate three letters instead of four. It now hangs on the wall of the church, retired from active service.

The door of a 'clink' at Stratton Church – the key with an 'IKE' at Eyke.

Great Ponton's wrought-iron relic is on the church roof. It is a weathervane in the shape of a violin. In the 17th century the parishioners of this Lincolnshire village were so impressed by the talents of a local fiddler that they had a whip-round to pay his fare to America (or did they just want a little peace?). Happily he made his fortune, and in gratitude provided a fiddle-shaped vane for the church, of which the present one is a replica.

While Great Ponton has a fiddle on the roof, **Wimborne St Giles** in Dorset has a robin by the altar. It is permanently perched on a plaque recalling the slightly eerie events in which two families of robins were involved. The first family nested near the altar while the roof was off for repairs in 1887. Robins were thought of as sacred birds in England, with the blood of Christ on their breasts, and their arrival was considered a very favourable omen. The workmen kept clear of the robins until the fledglings had hatched out and the family had flown away. Then they put the nest in a jar and built it into the wall, with an account of what had occurred.

Here while the respond to the arcade of A.D. 1887 was building a robin nested & again during the building of the new arcade after the fire of 1908

Reminders of a lucky fiddler at Great Ponton (top) and of a lucky robin at Wimborne St Giles Church (above and left).

The eerie part of the story came 20 years later, when the church was extensively damaged by fire and again the interior was open to the skies. Again a pair of robins arrived and nested in almost the identical spot. When the eggs had hatched and the robins had left the nest was again built into the wall. Some accounts say it was only at this stage that the first nest was discovered and the story of the first robins revealed. On the other hand, as only 20 years had elapsed and the second architect had actually worked for the first one, it seems more likely the tale had been handed down, and the second workmen knew where to look in the wall. But that does not account for the second robins choosing the same nesting place as their predecessors; or do robins hand down these stories too?

Incidentally **Gloucester** Cathedral has the tale of a real robin that lived close to the High Altar in the mid-18th century. A woman who had lost her favourite daughter was convinced that her soul had been transferred into a robin. Rather surprisingly she was given permission to keep robins in the cathedral in return for contributing to its upkeep, and an elaborate gilt birdcage was installed by the altar with matching seed and water troughs and curtain. It was an unorthodox form of church ornament unlikely for all manner of reasons to be repeated today.

The most common form of church ornament is a wood carving, and it is a modest church indeed which cannot boast an unusual bench end or a decorated pulpit or an imposing door. But medieval wood carvers were an imaginative and energetic lot, always ready to illustrate an old legend or invent a new animal, and one or two examples stand out.

Are you familiar, for example, with the manticore, the sciapod or the woodwose? These are mythical creatures which gave the carvers plenty of scope for creating something really unpleasant. One of them can be seen, but not too clearly on the outside of the otherwise very attractive village church at **North Cerney**, just off the Cheltenham to Cirencester road in Gloucestershire. It is the manticore, a beast which was half-lion and half-man. There is also a leopard trying to look fierce, but it appears almost benevolent by comparison.

The High Altar in Gloucester Cathedral where a woman was permitted to keep a robin in a cage because she thought it possessed the soul of her dead daughter.

Strange church beasts: the manticore at North Cerney . . .

. . . the woodwose about to meet a dragon at Peasenhall . . .

The woodwose was another half-human creature of the forest. There is one climbing over the porch of St Michael's Church, **Peasenhall** in Suffolk, en route for a show-down with the dragon which is climbing up the other side. And also in Suffolk, in St Mary's Church, **Dennington**, is the sciapod, a desert creature with a foot so large that it could be used as a sunshade. The Dennington sciapod is lying on its back, doing just that, the only such carving in the country. It is on a bench-end (the sixth on the right in the central aisle, to be exact) along with a fair assortment of other unlikely creatures.

. . . and the sciapod at Dennington, with its built in sunshade.

One of the odd bench ends at Horning.

Dragons of course are regularly featured in churches, mostly being done a mischief by St George, but they have had a variety of other opponents, all of which seem to have got the better of them. At **Crowcombe** in Somerset, for example, among a number of 16th century bench ends which mostly seem to symbolise fertility, there is a dragon fighting with two naked men, for no obvious reason. But there is a reason behind the carving of a dog fighting a dragon which is in the church at **West Clandon**, in Surrey, a village mainly famous for its Palladian mansion with the Capability Brown garden. Long before Mr Brown was capable of anything, an army deserter passing through the village was promised a pardon if he rid the village of a marauding dragon. The soldier duly despatched it with the help of his dog, which did the really dirty work – it grabbed the dragon's head while the soldier hacked it off. The carving is a modern replica – the original disappeared many years ago.

Dragon versus men at Crowcombe – dragon versus dog at Clandon.

A rare instance of a dragon actually having an ally is depicted on a bench-end at **Horning** in Norfolk – it shows a man being pushed into a dragon's mouth by the Devil.

A more romantic tale, but with a sadder ending, is recalled at **Zennor** Church in Cornwall by the carving on a chair in the chancel of a mermaid, who it is said was lured there by the melodious singing of the squire's son. She did a little luring herself and the lad went off with her, never to return.

There are much jollier carvings in **Cirencester**, where among the fine brasses in the Lady Chapel commemorating prosperous wine and wool merchants there is a representation of a cat chasing a mouse, and in **Cranleigh** Church in Surrey, where a grinning cat's-head on one of the arches could well have inspired Lewis Carroll. But the jolliest carver of all must surely be the Anglo-Saxon stonemason who worked on the font at **Melbury Bubb** Church in Dorset. It has a fine assortment of wolves, stags, lions and horses – all upside-down. Was it a well-planned joke or had he been too long at the mead? To do him justice, there are other explanations. Some say the font was once part of a cross which had to be turned over for its new use, others that there was a belief that such inverted carvings would put an end to cruelty 'through the influence of Christ'.

The Zennor mermaid, who lured away the squire's son to a watery end.

What does the Cranleigh cat find so funny? (left). Perhaps the upside down animals at Melbury Bubb (right).

Without this man, this section could have been much longer – the Laxfield memorial to William Dowsing, destroyer of church treasures.

Ploughers and planters at Burnham Deepdale (left); just one Reaper at Little Barningham (below).

A great many churches have carvings portraying the Seven Deadly Sins – early carvers seemed to relish illustrating them as vividly as possible, particularly Lust. But there is a more tranquil and less common sequence of carvings round the Norman font at **Burnham Deepdale** in Norfolk. It shows the twelve 'Labours of the Month' and must be one of the earliest gardening guides in existence. The figures seem to be engaged in much the same tedious chores that are inflicted upon us today – digging, weeding, and the like. There is no indication that the Normans had yet invented my own favourite gardening implement, the deckchair.

Also in Norfolk, but of a much later era, is a macabre wooden carving of a shrouded skeleton, standing on the corner post of a pew in **Little Barningham** Church, together with the cheering inscription:

As you are now, even so was I, Remember death for ye must dye . . .

The pew is intended only for 'couples in wedlock', though the message would seem to be universal.

Finally I must mention a relic to the man who, if he had fully achieved his purpose, would have ensured that we inherited no relics at all. William Dowsing was appointed under Cromwell to destroy 'superstitious pictures' in England's churches. Mr Dowsing took that to cover just about everything from stained-glass windows to screens, and from crucifixes to carvings. In his heyday he was destroying church ornaments at the rate of one thousand a day. But the Restoration came before he could wipe out the Church's heritage entirely, and he retired, no doubt breathing heavily, to his native village of **Laxfield** in Suffolk. There it seems all was forgiven, and in the village church of All Saints he has a commemorative tablet which will no doubt be preserved safely for posterity unless – heaven forbid – another William Dowsing comes along.

Churches with time on their (south) side

The Church used to be obsessed with Time. It started in the monasteries, where the monks liked to conduct their monastic offices at specific times. During the day they could manage with a sundial; during the night they had to invent an alarm clock which would wake up the watchman, who in turn would wake up them. So sundials and clocks and bells became an integral part of the Church's life, and although the original purpose for them has long since passed, nearly all our churches have one or the other or all three.

I will not trouble you too much with bells, which are generally pretty inaccessible and when you have seen one bell, unless you are a bell buff, you have seen them all. There are just two or three instances where they have sufficient significance to warrant being able to boast that you have been there.

It is worth mentioning **Queen Camel** in Somerset just for the sake of its name, but it has another distinction too. The church bells are said to be the heaviest six in the world. This is a much more impressive claim than

Queen Camel Church – that sturdy tower needs all its strength – it contains the heaviest peal of six bells, so it is said, in the world. One more might well break the Queen Camel's back . . .

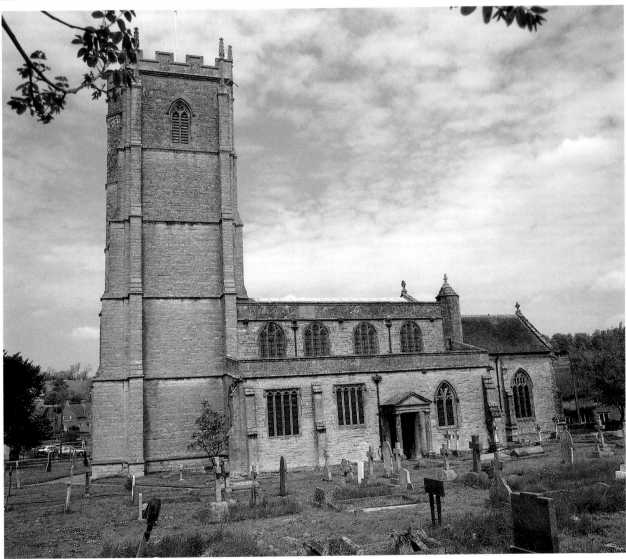

East Bergholt's bell-cage, with the heaviest five bells in England – and perhaps the most accessible.

Stoke d'Abernon bell-tower, not so accessible, but with the first feminist bell in England.

those at **East Bergholt** in Suffolk, which are supposed to be the heaviest five in England. But while those at East Bergholt are at ground level in a bell cage in the churchyard, you have to work a bit harder to reach those at Queen Camel, which are in a more orthodox position. They have been in that position for many centuries; as long ago as the 1500s the village was famous "for its fine peel of bells and for the fine sort of brown thread called nun's thread." There is not much thread-making today, but the bells ring on.

From the heaviest to the oldest. This is claimed by a Lancashire village, so watch out for a counter-claim from Yorkshire. **Claughton**, which has been pronounced in various ways but prefers 'Claffton', believes that the bell in its little church is the oldest working bell in the country. It bears the date 1296, and goes back to the original Church of St Chad built in 1100. It now hangs in the rebuilt church of 1815. They were very strong on re-building in Claughton – the 17th-century mansion Claughton Hall was moved from its original site almost in its entirety so the occupants could have a better view.

The other bell I would commend to you looks indeed like just another bell, but it could well be a rare example of early Women's Lib. **Stoke d'Abernon** Church in Surrey has a bell cast some five hundred years ago by one Joanna Sturdy of Croydon. This is a difficult one to accept. Bell foundries are still very much a man's world, if only because of the manual effort involved, and if Joanna was able to cope with all that metal as well as all that medieval male prejudice she must have been very sturdy indeed. It is also difficult to visualise Croydon as a centre for an industrial sex revolution. But that is the story, and let us hope that it is not just due to someone in the last five hundred years slipping up over the spelling of Joanna.

The manufacture of sundials was rather simpler. They have been around since the Ancient Egyptians wanted a way of making sure the workers clocked in on time at the Pyramids, and erected tall obelisks in the town centres which cast a shadow – literally and figuratively – over the populace. Woe betide the workers if they failed to keep up with the shadow. Then came the garden-size version, and so to the church wall.

Sundials have a fairly basic design, a circle showing the hours and an arm sticking up in the middle called a gnomon. There could not be much variation of the arm design – most people were content with a common or garden gnomon – but there were some very ingenious substitutions for the numbers. The trick was to find an appropriate phrase with twelve letters, which could be put where the hours ought to be.

The most popular, which appears on church clocks and sundials from West Acre in Norfolk to Burgh le Marsh in Lincolnshire, is WATCH AND PRAY. **Burgh le Marsh** actually goes the whole hog and has the complete quotation printed over the clock on its tower:

> *Watch and Pray, for ye know not when the time comes.*

Just as a reminder of when the time for curfew comes, they still ring the church bell at eight o'clock each weeknight from Michaelmas to Lady Day, long enough to recite Psalm 130, then it rings the day of the month, which must be quite hard work when it nears the thirties.

At **Buckland-in-the-Moor** on Dartmoor a devoted son used the twelve-letter dedication, MY DEAR MOTHER, and a loyal restorer at **Baslow** in Derbyshire plumped for VICTORIA 1897, but my favourite is at **Castle Bytham**, another Lincolnshire village which preferred letters to figures, and puns to texts. The 18th century sundial on the tower is inscribed, BEE IN THYME – and who cares if there are only ten letters there instead of twelve?

WATCH AND PRAY was a popular phrase to use in place of numbers on church clocks. Burgh le Marsh (above) kindly provided the complete quotation.
Alternative offerings: VICTORIA 1897 at Baslow (far left) and BEE IN THYME at Castle Bytham (left).

At **Eyam** in Derbyshire there is a much more elaborate sundial also erected in the 18th century, perhaps to distract parishioners from memories that this was the famous plague village, where one hundred years earlier the rector persuaded the inhabitants to isolate themselves when the plague came, to save neighbouring communities. Eighty per cent of them died, including his wife. Near her grave is Eyam's remarkable sundial, which tells the time throughout the world by means of a curved graph.

For sheer sundial saturation there is **Seaton Ross**, in Yorkshire, not far from Market Weighton. A local enthusiast called William Watson went in for sundials in a big way. One old cottage in the village supports one of his massive products, twelve feet in diameter. He put another on his farm and a third on the church. He died in 1857 at the age of 73, and on his tombstone appears the epitaph he wrote himself:

At this church I so often with pleasure did call, That I made a sundial Upon the church wall.

For church clocks there is none to beat the one in **Wells Cathedral**, made by a monk

Eyam Church and its sundial, giving vast information . . .

. . . and the cottage sundial at Seaton Ross, vast in itself.

from Glastonbury, Peter Lightfoot, six hundred years ago, complete with a moving star to tell the hour on an outer circle and a smaller speedier star to mark the minutes on the inner one, plus four mounted knights who meet for a contest at noon and a little 'clock-jack' who strikes the hour with his feet on two bells.

Clock-jacks, or 'Jacks-o'-the-Clock' were very popular on the Continent but comparatively rare in England. One of the few remaining, apart from Mr Lightfoot's, is in the massive Church of the Holy Trinity at **Blythburgh** in Suffolk, three miles from Southwold on the A12. The church has been compared to Ely Cathedral in the way it towers over its flat and marshy surroundings, but it lost its spire in a storm in 1577, and as trade declined and the channels silted up the town and the church fell on hard times. So did its 'Jack-o'-the-Clock', which has long since ceased to strike the hours, but he will still strike the bell with his hammer if you pull the cord – and give you a nod of acknowledgement too.

More Seaton Ross memorials to sundial enthusiast William Watson – the church sundial (below) and his grave (left).

'Jacks-o'-the Clock' at Blythburgh and Wells.

The Daddies of them all – the clocks at Wells (right and left).

Telling the time with one hand tied behind its back – or somewhere. The world's biggest one-handed clock, at Coningsby in Lincolnshire.

In contrast to Peter Lightfoot's complex creation at Wells and a similar one at Wimborne Minster in Dorset, made about 1320, the Church of St Michael at **Coningsby** in Lincolnshire satisfied itself with just a one-handed clock – but it is the biggest one-handed clock in the world. The dial is 16½ feet across, so that even with just one hand it is possible to tell the time within five minutes. The pendulum is so long that it takes two seconds to complete a single swing, and the weights are made out of blocks of stone.

Coningsby's other claim to fame, incidentally, is having a rector who was made Poet Laureate for writing possibly the worst poetry of the 18th century. His couplet dedicated to

Jack Spratt may eat no fat, but he was very handy with scraps. He made the church clock at Wootton Rivers from odd bits and pieces, and had enough left over for apt letters instead of numbers on the clockface.

George II on his Coronation was a fair example:

Thy virtues shine peculiarly nice,
Ungloomed with a confinity to vice . . .

Finally, perhaps the cheapest church clock in the country. The villagers of **Wootton Rivers** in Wiltshire needed one to complete the restoration of St Andrew's Church and to celebrate George V's Coronation, but the funds had run out. They contributed instead whatever spare parts they could find – old bicycles, bedsteads, farming implements and other mechanical left-overs. Out of this a Mr Jack Spratt constructed a church clock, and even had enough ingenuity left to incorporate one of those twelve-letter phrases into the dial instead of numbers:

GLORY BE TO GOD.

What lies beyond the graves

While churchyards are primarily places of rest for the deceased, quite an assortment of extraneous material has crept into some of them over the centuries, from stocks to pesthouses, and monuments which seem to have little connection with departed souls.

A churchyard was a logical place to build a pesthouse, since it could be easily isolated and the occupants rarely survived. There is one in the grounds of the old parish church at **Odiham** in Hampshire. Sufferers from the plague were incarcerated there, lasting out as long as they could on whatever food was left for them by the more generous townsfolk.

At Odiham the old stocks and whipping post are outside the churchyard, but at **Colne** in Lancashire they stand inside, under a tiled roof, and at **St Feock** in Cornwall they are actually in the church porch. The Colne stocks are a luxury model, mounted on wheels and with a hinged oak backrest on the same principle as the driving seat of a car, with holes for the feet instead of pedals. The stocks would accommodate three people, in considerable discomfort in spite of the refinements.

The one at St Feock would apparently accommodate three-and-a-half – there are seven holes for the feet. One wonders if the carpenter who made it had taken as much ale as the drunks who had to sit in it . . .

Stocks for all seasons. A luxury model at Colne with reclining back rest (above) and making the punishment fit the crime – well, nearly – at St Feock.

Not every churchyard cross is a memorial or a grave. The tall stone cross at **Ampney Crucis** near Cirencester in Gloucestershire is actually a weeping stone. More ostentatious penitents would go to it to bemoan their shortcomings. It was missing for some years, probably hidden to save it from the Puritans, so sinners had to repent in private.

The meaning of four stone carvings in the churchyard of St Andrew's, **Dacre**, a few miles away from Penrith in Cumbria, is much more obscure. They depict four stages in an encounter between a bearlike creature and a cat. In the first, the bear is asleep; in the second, it is woken up by the cat; in the third, it grabs the cat; and in the fourth, it eats it. No one seems quite sure why a cat-eating bear should deserve such an elaborate memorial, and in a churchyard at that. Perhaps it just points to a moral – let sleeping bears lie.

The weeping stone at Ampney Crucis – not for remembrance but for penance.

St Andrew's Church, Dacre (above) and its strange story in stone (left, below and right).

The story of another cat featured in a churchyard monument at **Fairford** in Gloucestershire is much better documented, since it is less than 20 years old. Amid all the tombstones commemorating the human departed there sits the stone effigy of "Tiddles the Church Cat, 1963–80". Tiddles was a tabby who lived in the church for 15 years, attending the services and killing the mice. She was looked after and fed by the verger, and when she died he commissioned a stonemason to carve the memorial. He defended her inclusion in the churchyard very simply:

> She spent more time in the church than anyone else and she deserved a plot of her own.

Tiddles' tombstone is no stranger than some of those which mark human graves. There is a pack-shaped stone in the churchyard of St Cuthbert's at **Bellingham** in Northumberland which recalls the Legend of the

Tiddles the church cat remembered at Fairford (left) and a much more sinister figure remembered at Bellingham (below).

Long Pack, a tale of skullduggery that went wrong. It is said that a pedlar called at a local mansion, Lee Hall, and asked for a night's lodging. The maid refused, but let him leave his long pack in the kitchen. Sometime later she saw the pack move. Much disconcerted, she called in a ploughboy, who took no chances and fired a shot into the pack. Blood poured out, and they found inside the body of a young man, obviously smuggled into the house for a nefarious purpose. A silver horn was in the pack with him, which they shrewdly deduced was a method of summoning his confederates once he had opened a way in. They summoned more help, blew the horn and were waiting for the robbers when they came. The young man was never identified; his body lies beneath the stone pack.

Another miscreant is buried in a corner of the churchyard at **Odstock**, not far from Salisbury in Wiltshire, whose influence still hangs over the church. A gypsy called Joshua Scamp was hanged for horse-stealing in 1801.

Not for miniature croquet or for turning into a cloche – the protective hoops in Warden churchyard.

The ever-open door of Odstock Church – not just welcoming, basically a precaution.

He protested his innocence, and his family did too. Each year they assembled round his grave on the anniversary of his death, and other gypsies came along with them. The route to the churchyard lay past the Yew Tree Inn, and by the time they had refreshed themselves the wake developed into the sort of party which might well have waked the dead.

Eventually the Rector and his churchwardens could stand this annual invasion no longer. They locked the church door and pulled up a briar rose which the gypsies had planted by the grave. This annoyed them considerably. Inspired by an extra glass or two at the Yew Tree, the gypsy 'queen' pronounced a mortal curse on anyone who locked the church door again. And, indeed, it worked. The churchwardens and the parish constable all came to untimely deaths. To save further casualties the Rector threw the key into the River Ebble, so the door could never be locked again – though some reports say that he too met an unpleasant death.

The headstone has now split but remains to tell the tale, and a new briar rose was planted by the grave. The Yew Tree Inn also continues to flourish.

Back in Northumberland, in the churchyard at **Warden**, are three graves covered with wrought-iron hoops. They are the graves of the rector and his wife and child. They were placed there at his request to foil body-snatchers — though anyone prepared to dig down six feet for a body would probably have made short shrift of an iron hoop.

Churchyards on the coast inevitably have reminders of those who made their living, and in some cases met their deaths at sea. The coast of Cornwall can be the most hazardous of all, and the graves of shipwreck victims abound. One of the most dramatic is in the churchyard at **Morwenstow**, a mass grave for 40 of the crew of the Caledonia, an Arbroath ship which was wrecked in 1843.

The Vicar of Morwenstow at that time was the Rev Robert Stephen Hawker, whose remarkable taste in vicarage chimneys is mentioned elsewhere. Mr Hawker had many unusual qualities. As a young man he married a woman old enough to be his mother – a teacher at the village school which he had built. After she died he married for a second time, to a woman young enough to be his daughter.

He also originated the harvest festival, an idea which his fellow clergy deprecated but it caught on nonetheless. And he had a pet pig which he took on his parish rounds . . .

It was his idea to place over the mass grave the figurehead of the Caledonia, which had been washed ashore with the bodies of the crew. It represented a Scot brandishing a sword, and this has given rise to yet another story about the impact Mr Hawker had on the lives of his parishioners. They claimed that if they walked too near the figurehead at midnight, the sword would descend and decapitate them. Presumably nobody did, since Mr Hawker did not record having to preside over any resultant funerals.

There is a happier story attached to another grave linked with the sea at **Henbury**, near Bristol. The tombstone has two black boys portrayed on it, with the inscription:

Born a Pagan and a Slave, now sweetly sleep a Christian in my Grave.

Morwenstow Church with its strange Scot (above and left), and Henbury churchyard with its sleeping slaves.

A happy couple at Ashby St Mary (above). An outsize couple at Hale (above, right) and Stamford (right).

In **Ashby St Mary**, another Norfolk churchyard, stand two tombstones which clearly illustrate the occupations of those beneath them, a 19th century rural Darby and Joan. Ann Basey was the first to die, at the age of 71, and her tombstone shows her in bonnet and apron, with stick, bag and basket, feeding her geese in the farmyard – the archetypal Norfolk farmer's wife. The thatched farmhouse is there too, and her husband is leaning on the fence watching her at work (the archetypal Norfolk farmer?). He followed her when he was 82, and his stone balances the picture – it shows him working too, scattering corn to his turkeys. Mrs Basey was buried with a grandson Joseph, Mr Basey with two more; they all died in infancy.

There are some graves which must have caused the diggers a particular problem. In the Cheshire village of **Hale** they could not have relished catering for John Middleton, the Childe of Hale, who was over nine feet tall with muscles to match – he wrestled at the court of James I and is given a mention by Samuel Pepys. They were also kept busy at **Stamford** in Lincolnshire to accommodate Daniel Lambert in the churchyard of St Martin's. He weighed 52 stone, measured 92 inches round the waist and was said to be the fattest Englishman of all time. Robert Hales, the Norfolk Giant, also rated a super-grave in **West Somerton** churchyard to take his eight-feet-tall frame and his 32 stone. Fortunately he made enough money touring America for his widow to erect a suitably large memorial.

There is another sizeable grave at **Hathersage** in Derbyshire, reputed to be the last resting place of Robin Hood's hefty hench-

man, Little John. He was said to have loosed an arrow to mark the spot where he wished to be buried. The grave was opened in the 18th century and a 32-inch thigh bone was discovered, confirming that if it was not actually Little John's, it was someone fairly substantial. The headstone firmly attributes it to him, and the grave is still tended by the Ancient Order of Foresters.

More problems for the grave diggers. The last resting places of Robert Hales, the Norfolk Giant (left) and – possibly – of Robin Hood's henchman Little John (below).

Bowes churchyard – last resting place of Charles Dickens' Smike.

The home of Jeffrey Hudson (below), so small he was used as a pie filling, before he became the answer to a gravediggers prayer.

At the other extreme the diggers were let off lightly by Jeffrey Hudson of **Oakham** in Leicestershire, who achieved the distinction of being served up to Charles I in a cold pie. Apart from this curious culinary experience he led an eventful life, being captured by pirates twice, and sold into slavery – though he could hardly have been a bargain as slaves go. When he died back at Oakham at the age of 63 he was still only three feet six inches tall, claimant for the title of world's smallest man.

George Taylor of **Bowes** in County Durham may not have been the thinnest, but there must have been very little of him when he was buried at the age of 19, poor chap, because he was said to be the inspiration for Dickens' sickly character Smike in Nicholas Nickleby. One of the houses in the village was used as a school called Shaw's Academy, on which Dickens based Dotheboys Hall. William Shaw, the real-life equivalent of Wackford Squeers, is also buried in the churchyard not far from his unhappy pupil.

Just a few last words

The modern epitaph is generally convention-al and brief. It is no longer fashionable to leaven such farewells with a little gentle whimsy, as our ancestors loved to do. In any case the high cost of letter-carving discour-ages any superfluous observations. For many a gravestone the name, the date, and RIP are sufficient. But as an epitaph to this chapter on churches, here are some of the more original valedictory comments of our forefathers, either in the form of a tribute to the deceased or as a mournful message from the grave.

Some epitaph-writers took a pride in suit-ing the wording to the trade or the calling of the departed one. George Routleigh, local watchmaker, lies in St Petrocks churchyard at **Lydford** in Devon:

> *. . . wound up in hopes of being taken in hand by his Maker and of being thoroughly cleaned, repaired and set a-going in the world to come . . .*

And at **Bromsgrove** in Worcestershire two engine-drivers who died in a railway accident share the same inscription:

> *My engine now is cold and still,*
> *No water does my boiler fill,*
> *My coke affords its flames no more,*
> *My days of usefulness are o'er.*

Much more pithy is the epitaph to a coro-ner at St Margaret's Church, **Cley** in Norfolk:

> *He lived and died, by suicide.*

Punsters occasionally ran riot among the gravestones. Two of the worst examples come from Suffolk. A memorial to a lady called Lettice at **Stowlangtoft** in Suffolk reads:

> *Grim death, to please his liquorish palate,*
> *Has taken my Lettice to put in his sallat.*

And if you find that difficult to swallow, there was reputed to be at **Bury St Edmunds** the epitaph:

> *Here lies Jonathan Yeast – pardon him for not rising.*

Trade testaments: to a clock-maker at Lydford (far left) and to engine drivers at Bromsgrove (above).

Not every East Anglian farewell was facetious. Some spared no expense to tell the full sad story of how the death occurred. The parents of a little girl at **Buxton** in Norfolk who died after an inoculation, one of the earlier attempts to provide protection from smallpox, were particularly bitter about medical science. On the wall of the chancel is a plaque:

To Mary Ann Kent, who died under inoculation on the tenth day of March 1773 in the fourth year of her age. This much lamented child was in the highest state of health and her mental powers began to open and promise fairest fame, when her fond parents deluded by prevalent custom suffered the rough officious hand of art to wound the flourishing root of nature and rob the little innocent of the gracious gift of life.

Death from over-eating at Woodditton – a cheerful farewell.

In Cambridgeshire William Symons of **Woodditton**, near Newmarket, left his own account of his demise, but in much more frivolous vein. On a gravestone a barely visible iron dish, behind iron bars, is the inscription:

Here lies my corpse, who was the man,
That loved a sop in the dripping pan.
But now believe me I am dead,
See here the pan stands at my head.
Still for sops till the last I cried,
But could not eat and so I died.
My neighbours they perhaps will laugh,
When they do read my epitaph.

Or was it the neighbours who wrote it?

Messages attributed to the mouth of the dear departed were not always so good-humoured. At **South Lopham** is the sour farewell:

At three score winters' end I died,
A cheerless being, sole and sad.
The nuptial knot I never tied – and wish
my father never had.

And comments about the deceased are not always too kindly either. In **Woodton** burial ground, also in Norfolk:

Here lies John Rackett in his wooden jacket,
He kept neither horses nor mules.
He lived like a hog and died like a dog,
And left all his money to fools.

I must turn to Norfolk also for an epitaph which I consider unsurpassed for aptness and brevity. It conveys its message in just two words, half the number in that famous crisp tribute in Westminster Abbey:

O Rare Ben Johnson.

At All Saints church, **Walsoken**, the epitaph to one Charles Knight simply says:

Good Knight.

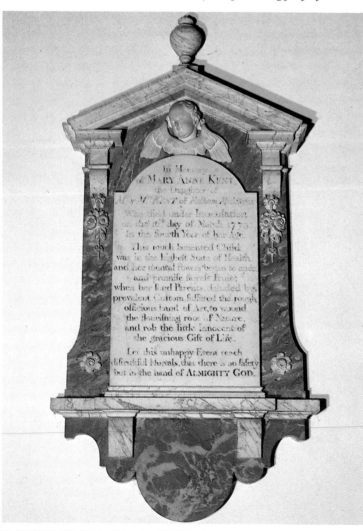

Death from trial vaccination at Buxton – a bitter valediction.

The rest of Timpson's England – A Timpson Tour

So far I have been looking beyond the obvious at items which fall into convenient categories. There are however several which fall into no category at all. Others I have saved up because they have some special quality which merits an individual mention. And there are a few, I confess, which I could not think what the devil to do with, so I put them aside for just such a chapter as this.

Rather than merely empty this collection of assorted oddities over your head, I have arranged them geographically, to take you from one side of England to the other via all manner of curiosities, some natural, some man-made. If you complete the entire tour you need to be very curious yourself, in every sense of the word, but you may like to join the route for a short stretch or just visit one or two of the more convenient locations.

If you prefer to follow it from the comfort of your armchair, I shall quite understand.

Kick off from the Cape

Let me start you off at the far south-western tip of England. No, not Land's End, that most over-publicised and over-run of tourist attractions, but a few miles up the coast to a headland which is not only spectacular in its own right but was given a unique distinction by some early English geographer. **Cape Cornwall** is the only 'cape' in England. We have all manner of 'heads' and 'points' and even 'bills', but it seems the map-makers decided that the coast of England was, well, incapable – with this one exception.

Cape Cornwall – the only 'cape' on the English coast. It now meanz beanz.

It is not quite on the same scale as some of the world's other famous capes, but there was much rejoicing when a benevolent baked-bean manufacturer bought it for the nation and presented it to the National Trust. It qualifies for all the top awards in the conservation honours list – it is designated as Heritage Coast, as an Area of Outstanding Natural Beauty, and as a Site of Special Scientific Interest.

It was owned by a descendant of Francis Oates of St Just, who made his fortune in South Africa in the last century and became the first chairman of de Beers, the mining company. The National Trust negotiated for four years to save it from development before Heinz came along with its million-pound sponsorship of the World Wildlife Fund UK conservation project, and Cape Cornwall was transferred from de Beers to de Beans.

It still has its other mining connection. In the 18th and 19th centuries it was a notable centre for the tin and copper industry, and it is still surmounted by an old chimney stack. The Trust plans to restore many of its industrial architecture features. But there are also two-hundred-foot granite cliffs, said to be the finest in Britain, a medieval landing place called Priest's Cove, still used for fishing, and acres of grassland on the promontory with rare flowers which are to be treasured for their names alone – the upright chickweed, the lanceolate spleenwort, the prostrate dyers' greenweed and the autumn squill.

I see they have called Cape Cornwall "the connoisseur's Land's End". I only wish I had thought of it first. From every point of view – its spectacular beauty, its unusual history, its debt to baked beans, and its unique title – it is an appropriate starting point for Timpson's Tour.

Twenty-odd miles from Cape Cornwall, still in Cornish tin-mining country, there are the twin towns of **Camborne** and **Redruth**. The Camborne School of Mines (which according to the Post Office is in Redruth, but actually is midway between the two) is one of the oldest mining schools in the world. It actually has a tin mine underneath it. These days it specialises in a very different kind of underground resource, one of the newest sources of energy. I was going to say that the variety of 'hot rock' to be found at Camborne (or is it Redruth?) has nothing to do with music, but come to think of it, the other variety has little to do with it either.

It is not the hot rock I would commend to you at Redruth (or is it Camborne?) but a curious aftermath of those earlier mines in the 18th century. At **Gwennap Pit**, part of the workings collapsed, causing land subsidence which created a shallow saucer-shaped depression of some considerable size. It was found to possess the same remarkable acoustics as the old Greek amphitheatres, and when Wesley came upon it during his mission to the Cornish tinners he could not resist having a preach there.

He visited this natural auditorium at least 15 times, and in due course it was lined with 13 circles of grass seats. The Wesleyan tradition has been preserved, and every Whit Monday it resounds to the stirring words and

music of his favourite hymns. If you are there on a Whit Monday you can join in; any other day, why not try out the acoustics on your own? I am sure the locals are quite resigned to it by now.

Head another 30-odd miles north-eastwards along the A30 trunk road, and beyond Bodmin turn right to the little village of **Warleggan**, where another memorable cleric used to preach, in very different but just as unusual circumstances. The Rev Frederick Densham came to the parish in 1931 and made an immediate impact, not with his preaching but with his precautions. He erected barbed-wire around his property and kept fierce dogs as an added deterrent. He also put locks and bolts on the church doors and windows.

One gathers this did not endear him too greatly to his parishioners. Church attend-

Gwennap Pit – Cornwall's natural amphitheatre. Wesley spoke here – so could you!

ances slumped. But Mr Densham took precautions against that too. He cut out cards and sat them in the pews instead of people. One cannot report on the quality or substance of his sermons; one can only record, with some confidence, that none of the congregation ever walked out. In his own way, Mr Densham must have been quite a card himself.

He and his silent flock are long since gone – he died in the 1950s – but you may still find it a little eerie to sit in his church where in his day you would only have had cards for company.

Now a longer run to the next stop – eastward to Wiltshire.

Great Wishford, a few miles north-west of Salisbury, has the good fortune to be just off the A36 trunk road, unlike **Little Wishford**, which is actually on it, thus experiencing all the heavy traffic between Salisbury and Warminster, with the longer-distance lorries from Southampton to Bristol for good measure. Both villages are in the valley of the Wylye river, and in the past villagers of Great Wishford have proved quite wylye as well. When the Earl of Pembroke tried to close Grovely Wood, on the hill above Great Wishford, so

he could create a park, they stood by their ancient rights and successfully established that they could still cut and gather wood there, as indeed they still do on Oakapple Day, May 29th. They use the green branches to decorate their homes and their church. I gather there are also quite a few new runner bean sticks in position on May 30th.

It is not the woodgathering ceremony, known as the Grovely Festival, which I have in mind – Oakapple Day has become an occasion for all manner of rural festivities, and Wishford's is but one of them. More unusual and worth your inspection are the plaques set in the south-east corner of the wall surrounding St Giles's Church. They record how the price of bread has varied over the last 150 years – and the record is kept in 'gallons'. There seems little reason to preserve such information in this way, in gallons or any other measure, unless some local statistician wished to draw attention to the rising cost of living and devised this early version of the retail price index. As for the actual figures, like any other statistics they can be made to prove almost anything . . .

Eastward again now, to Sussex.

Warleggan Church, where the parson had cards instead of a congregation – and no doubt gave them a good deal.

I am anxious to get your opinion about those two long poles which are being held so firmly by the Long Man of Windover Hill. To reach it from the West Country, though, it is difficult not to pass near **Brighton**, and there is one feature of Brighton which may not be as familiar to you as the Royal Pavilion or the Lanes or the Conference Centre, and which is worth a minor diversion. It is the grave of Phoebe Hessel at St Nicholas Church, which has been there since the days when Brighthelmstone was just a fishing village. The village has long since disappeared and the church was largely rebuilt in the last century, but the grave remains.

Phoebe was born in 1713, and at the age of 15 fell in love with a soldier, to such a degree that she disguised herself as a young man and joined the army herself. We are assured that she served for many years without her sex being discovered, a tribute either to her skills of deception or the singular stupidity of the 18th century British Army. She came back home, apparently unscathed and undiscovered – and, it would seem, unmarried. Her military experiences must have kept her singularly fit, because she lived to the age of 108, enjoying a certain amount of fame once the story came out, but little else.

Now, back to that other imitation man, the Long Man of Windover Hill, some 15 miles away at **Wilmington**, on the South Downs. You probably know of it already, and may well have seen it. Indeed for many miles around it is impossible not to see it. It has been said many times, and I have not heard it

Surprising statistics: bread in gallons at Great Wishford (below, left), a woman in an all-male army at Brighton (below).

Squire May's fruitless Folly among the fruitfields of Kent.

The Long Man of Windover Hill – what is he doing with those sticks?

contradicted, that it is the largest representation of a human figure in the world – 226 feet from head to toe, cut into the turf on the white chalk. What I have heard contested is its origin, and, in particular, what is it doing with those sticks?

The first time it is mentioned in any records is 1779, but some say it was put there by the Saxons, others by the Vikings. The version I prefer is that it was created by sun worshippers, and the 'sticks' represent the doors of Heaven being opened after the demons of darkness had been overcome.

Or was he just going ski-ing?

I vowed earlier not to include any purpose-built Follies, partly because I felt I would be posthumously pandering to the conceit of the egotists who built them, and partly because my aim is to look beyond the obvious, and most Follies are very obvious indeed. But there are one or two which are worth reconsidering because of the unusual story that lies behind them – and May's Folly, at **Hadlow** in Kent, a few miles outside Tonbridge, is an example.

It was built in 1840 by Squire May, as part of his pseudo-Gothic castle, with a particular purpose in mind. Or rather, three particular purposes, depending on which authority you quote.

The most popular story is that Mr May wanted to obtain an uninterrupted view of the English Channel. His problem was that the Weald lies in between, and short of hiring a helicopter there was no way he could achieve this. Presumably he did not realise this until the tower had reached a height of some 170 feet, at which stage he called a halt and devised (or later chroniclers devised) another purpose for it.

His wife, it seems, had deserted him for a local farmer, and it has been suggested that the tower served as a reminder to her of his existence, wherever she might take refuge in a wide area around. It seems unlikely though that this would have particularly bothered her. He is also quoted as saying that when he died, he wished to be buried "above ground, high enough to be able to keep an eye over all my demesnes". But unlike the Stevenage grocer who asked for his coffin to be placed in the roof of his barn to foil the bodysnatchers, there is no evidence that his wish was complied with.

The rest of the castle has been demolished and the stables and outbuildings converted into homes, but the octagonal tower with the circular turret attached to its side still looms over the hopfields, not just a Folly but a Failure, since none of Squire May's purposes, it seems, was ever achieved.

Time to alter course now and turn back westward, skirting London on the A25.

The building of the M25 must have been a great relief to the villagers of **Abinger Hammer** in Surrey. They endured all the heavy traffic that used the A25 trunk road between Guildford and Dorking. Drivers who pass that way now should have a better opportunity to enjoy the scenery, and in particular notice the details of the clock which juts out across the road in the middle of the village.

It bears the figure of a blacksmith which strikes the hours on a bell. His hammer is a reminder of the village's name and its origin; it lies in what used to be a notable iron-forging area.

The inscription on the clock,

> *By me you know how fast to go*

is presumably intended just as a gentle reminder, not to encourage speeding.

An Abinger of Doom? The clock-watching blacksmith urges on the motorists at Abinger Hammer – but not too fast, please . . .

At some stage before Guildford turn north, and if you can pick your way through the stockbroker belt hinterland of Woking, Staines and Egham (I would not attempt to direct you, but unless you live in Woking, Staines or Egham, I would not recommend you linger) you will eventually emerge into the daylight somewhere near **Runnymede**.

There can be few places in England with a more significant role in English history than **Runnymede**. Here on the banks of the Thames, or on an island in the middle of it (historians are uncertain), the triumphant barons established themselves after taking control of London, and summoned King John from his castle at Windsor for a parely. The charter he signed with them on June 15th, 1215, the Magna Carta, became the foundation stone on which English liberties are built. It was based in turn on Henry I's charter, which in its turn promised to observe "the good laws of Edward the Confessor".

At Runnymede, a very English historic occasion commemorated by an American memorial.

Yet with all this very English background, in these very English surroundings, the memorial you will find there was put up by the Americans! There was no memorial at all for over seven hundred years – somehow nobody got around to it, or perhaps it was just assumed, in our lofty English way, that everybody knew about it anyway. Within the last 30 years the American Bar Association decided to do something about it, if only as a guide for American tourists. They put up a pillar protected by a star-spangled dome (mercifully, no stripes) standing on eight stone pillars. They also chose the inscription:

To commemorate the Magna Carta,
symbol of freedom under law.

At least the pillar itself is of English granite . . .

Not long after, England was able to return this generous gesture. Opposite Magna Carta Island are three acres of land which were presented to the United States, and there

stands a memorial to John F. Kennedy, the American president assassinated in 1963. A block of Portland stone is inscribed with a quotation from the speech he made at his inauguration – a re-affirmation of the principles embodied in Magna Carta.

It would be nice now to say "Follow the river to Reading", but this is a little impractical unless you have a boat. The roads nearby let you catch sight of the river. If you are eager to get on, then just follow the M4 to Reading.

Looking at **Reading's** giant office blocks and factories, and its army of commuters heading for their daily battle for a seat on the fast trains to Paddington, you may find it difficult to appreciate that this is the town where Henry I is buried, where John of Gaunt was married, where Jane Austen went to school and Oscar Wilde went to jail. But there is still a very substantial reminder of one chapter in its past – the Forbury Gardens Lopsided Lion.

Reading was the headquarters of the 2nd Battalion the 66th (Berkshire) Regiment, later the Royal Berkshires, which was massacred during the Afghan Campaign of 1880. Incidentally that was the last time the British army carried colours in battle – it was seen to cause needless loss of life. An eminent local sculptor, George Simonds, was invited to design an appropriate memorial. He chose a lion – not just an average lion, but an enormous beast, three times life-size and weighing 16 tons, the largest cast-iron lion at that time in the world.

We are told Mr Simonds went to London Zoo to study the animal's correct proportions. What he could not have studied very closely was the way a lion walks. When his creation was unveiled it was seen to have both its right legs forward, and both its left legs back. I am told that horses can be trained to walk in this way, but one suspects that if the Forbury Lion were a real one it might well overbalance sideways. Then again, if it were a real one,

The Forbury Lion: "You put your right legs in . . ." Why doesn't it fall over?

judging by the menacing expression on its face I would run first and see if it fell over later . . .

Better still, get back on the M4 and head for Gloucestershire and the Vale of Berkeley, alongside the Severn Estuary.

Berkeley must possess one of the few temples dedicated to a disease; certainly it is the only one dedicated to cowpox. It is called the Temple of Vaccinia, which sounds a lot more elegant than the Cowpox Temple, but that is what vaccinia means, and the temple stands in the garden of the home in Berkeley of Edward Jenner, the discoverer of vaccination.

Mr Jenner was born at the vicarage in 1749 and after his medical training spent much of his life in the town, devoting himself to the study of smallpox. There was a tradition in Gloucestershire that people who had caught cowpox while they were milking were immune to smallpox. Jenner achieved great fame – and government grants of £30,000, which today would be quite a chunk out of the NHS budget – by discovering the technique of vaccination.

My congratulations however go to a lad called James Phipps, who acted as the guineapig for his experiments. Jenner inoculated him with matter from a cowpox sore on

The Cowpox Temple – sorry, the Temple of Vaccinia, in memory of Edward Jenner of Berkeley – but don't forget little James Phipps, the first vaccination guinea pig.

a milkmaid's hands, then six weeks later he crossed his fingers and inoculated him with smallpox. Happily young James survived, and Jenner's fame was assured. Small wonder the doctor had a Temple of Vaccinia in his back garden, and there is a rose window dedicated to him in the church and a sculpture of him actually vaccinating a very small and completely bewildered James Phipps. One wonders what public reaction would be to his experiment today. Would he be condemned for illegal experiments on a human being, or would people just admire his initiative and regard him as a Berkeley card?

I hesitate to direct you to **Chedworth**, because what really qualifies it for this tour is a cottage which is no longer there. But it is a delightful spot anyway, a cluster of stone cottages (the ones that are left) around a little stream which flows eventually into the Coln, set in the Cotswold hills west of the old Fosse Way, now the A429. It is so attractive, in fact, that in the 1930s it caught the eye of Mr Henry Ford, the American car magnate and collector extraordinary.

He took such a shine to Chedworth that no doubt he would have liked to acquire the whole village, but he settled for just one of the cottages, Rose Cottage. He had it taken to pieces, shipped to the States and re-assembled in the English-style village he created at Greenfield, complete with English dovecote, English flowers, and even English sheep.

Rose Cottage formerly of Chedworth, Gloucestershire (above), now of Greenfield, U.S.A. (below).

Chedworth has other attractions still to offer which Mr Ford kindly left behind – the remains of a Roman villa considered to be the most comprehensive of their kind in the country, a fine village church, and a wineglass pulpit. But if you do not have time for them all, skip the wineglass pulpit, because I have another one for you, with a strange tale attached to it, later on the tour.

Meanwhile, head eastward again through Oxfordshire and into Buckinghamshire.

Tucked away along winding lanes to the south of Buckingham are the Claydon family – Botolph Claydon, East Claydon, Middle Claydon and Steeple Claydon – a group of thatched and timbered villages dominated at **Middle Claydon** by Claydon House.

The house itself is remarkable enough – a grand stairway inlaid with ebony and ivory, fine fireplaces, a picture gallery, and a Chinese room smothered in rococo decorations which include a Chinese family taking tea round a table with a fringed tablecloth, all of them waving cheerfully at the passers-by, who these days are customers of the National Trust.

It is one of the past occupants of Claydon House, however, who took my fancy. It has been the home for centuries of the Verneys,

and a sister-in-law of Sir Harry Verney (who must have been quite a character himself, he was an MP for 50 years) was Florence Nightingale, who had a suite of rooms there and is said to have brought back from the Crimea the seeds from which grew the cedars and the cypress trees in the park. However it is not Miss Nightingale nor the immovable Sir Harry I have in mind, but a much earlier Verney, Sir Edmund, who was King's Standard Bearer at the Battle of Edgehill.

Sir Edmund, it seems, was given to rash statements, but had the courage to stand by them. As the battle commenced he cried, "He who takes this banner from my hand must first hew my hand from my body!" Alas, somebody did. He left his severed hand on the battlefield, still grasping the standard.

You may remember earlier on this tour the Forbury Lion at Reading, which commemorated the last occasion at which colours were carried into battle; the practice was stopped because of needless loss of life. The story of the gallant Sir Edmund illustrates how it caused needless loss of hands as well.

Only a dozen miles from the Claydons, but in the rather less attractive surroundings of **Wing**, which has expanded greatly in recent years along with its near neighbour Leighton

A bodiless hand remembered at Middle Claydon, and a topiary hand still working at Wing.

Buzzard, is another fine house with another unusual distinction. Ascott House, built in 1606 on the site of the old manor house, has a Chinese flavour too – it has an outstanding collection of Oriental porcelain – but it is the garden which I commend. It has perhaps the only topiary sundial in the country.

The Roman numerals around the dial are made from box hedges and the hand, or gnomon, is a yew tree. To make it really distinctive it could do with a gnome sitting in the yew tree, to make it the only known gnomon with a gnome on . . .

Incidentally Wing's other claim to fame is its Saxon church, which was standing there a century before the nearby Norman castle, now nothing more than a mound. But I shall remember it for being the only church I have come across where a former incumbent, one William Dodd, was hanged at Tyburn for forgery.

A longer haul now, to the environs of Ipswich, avoiding Luton and Stevenage if you can – nice people, terrible roads. Happily the A12 now takes you safely round Colchester.

Freston Tower, just south of the Ipswich bypass, is another Folly which has slipped past my guard, partly because of the reason it was built, partly because it is reckoned to be the oldest Folly in the country, thus setting a rather bad example which was followed in succeeding years by other landowners who also had more money than taste.

It was built in the middle of the 16th century by Lord Freston on the banks of the River Orwell, a brick tower six storeys high with a parapet and a lantern on top. Appropriately for a Folly it is best seen from the side most difficult to get at – the estuary itself. Photographers have been seriously advised that their best plan is to hire a boat and use a telephoto lens.

A logical explanation for the Folly – which is a contradiction in terms anyway – is that it was built as a lookout tower for invaders coming up the river. Much less logical and therefore far more likely is the story that Lord Freston built it as a personal one-girl training college for his daughter Ellen. Each floor was equipped to provide her with a different virtue or skill, for each day of the week.

On Monday she was on the ground floor, practising the virtues of charity – presumably handing out goodies to passers-by. In view of the tower's isolated position this would not

Lord Freston's one-girl training college, where his daughter learned the skills and the virtues of the 16th century – from charity on the ground floor to astronomy on the roof.

have been too arduous. On Tuesday she moved to the first floor to weave tapestry; on Wednesday, on the second floor, she studied music; on Thursday, on the third floor, she read the classics; on Friday, on the fourth, she read English writers; on Saturday, on the fifth, she did a little painting; and finally on Sunday, having reached the top floor, she studied the stars.

We are not advised whether this resulted in Ellen turning into a genius or a lighthouse keeper, but happily Lord Freston's education system did not catch on. Unhappily, Follies did.

Turn westward again, back past Cambridge and across the M11. There is a pleasant back road to St Neots, and on it are the Gransdens.

Great Gransden's eerie post-mill . . .

Great Gransden is still an attractive little village and the Rev Barnabas Oley must have thought so too back in the 17th century – he spent 53 years as vicar, apart from a period when, as an ardent Royalist, he had to go into hiding. He left two tangible reminders of his sojourn there – the almshouses, which have been in use ever since, and the church pulpit, to which of course the same applies.

That cannot be said, however, for the feature which brings us here, the old wooden postmill which stands about half-a-mile outside the village. It looks a little eerie even now, a box-like structure on high legs, rather like an elevated cricket scorebox with sails; and there is an eerie chapter in its history.

In the 1860s the man who owned it, one William Webb, while sifting through the be-

. . . and Rushton's Triangular Lodge.

longings of his deceased brother, came upon a book called "The Infidel's Bible", which turned out to be all about black magic, a sort of witch's handbook. Alarmed or perhaps fascinated by his discovery, he hid it away from his household in the mill – which promptly stopped working. It stayed that way for three years, until the book was removed and burnt. At that moment, so the story goes, the sails started turning again . . .

On past St Neots now, and if you cannot find a more peaceful route the hard-pressed A45 will take you to Higham Ferrers and Rushden in Northamptonshire. Take the A6 and about 4 miles after you have passed through Kettering take the turning to Rushton.

The Triangular Lodge at **Rushton** is not so much a Folly as an Obsession. It was built not long after the Freston Tower, before the end of the 16th century, by Sir Thomas Tresham of Rushton Hall, a Roman Catholic convert who went to prison many times for his faith. His son Francis, incidentally, was the man who betrayed Guy Fawkes and his Gunpowder Plot. Sir Thomas manifestly felt deeply about his religion, but he was particularly obsessed with the Trinity. The figure three became an almost sacred emblem, and in the grounds of Rushton House is lasting evidence of this, the Triangular Lodge

Each of its three sides is thirty-three feet three inches long. It has three floors, and each floor has three triangular windows in each of its three walls, with three triangular gables to each side and three pinnacles above. There are three-times-three gargoyles and inscribed on the front wall (if a triangle can have a front) are the figures three and nine. All the Latin inscriptions on the building are in double-three couplets and each line has thirty-three letters.

Only one feature of the Triangular Lodge escaped this obsession with threes. The builder refused to use triangular bricks . . .

Now return to the A6 and it will take you to Market Harborough. From there journey down the A427, pick up the A426 to Rugby, just the other side of the M1. Wind your way through Rugby towards Southam. Between there and Leamington Spa is Chesterton Green.

If your mental image of a windmill is the traditional cone-shaped tower with four great sails that you see in Holland or along the Norfolk coast, then **Chesterton** Windmill will give you a shock. The only feature you will recognise is the sails. The body of the mill is a circular domed building standing on great stone legs forming six open arches. It looks like an ungainly six-legged tortoise with sails instead of a head.

The man responsible was Sir Edward Peyto, of the family which occupied the manor house at Chesterton for centuries. He was the Parliamentarian governor of Warwick Castle who held it against the Royalists. Inigo Jones has been given the credit – if that is the word – for designing the windmill, and to be fair it has been suggested that it was originally intended as an observatory and the inappropriate sails were added later. In reality it seems

Chesterton's weird windmill – could it be an observatory with sails?

Kenilworth Castle – knocked about a bit by Cromwell, but once the scene of great parties. One lasted 18 days and cost £1000 a day – at 1575 prices!

The guest of honour was invariably the Queen.

It was this period of lavish entertainment which for me singles out Kenilworth from all the other castles. One of Dudley's parties for the Queen in July 1575 went on for 18 days and cost him one thousand pounds a day, which in modern terms is a substantial fortune.

One can understand, however, this generosity. Apart from the fact he was her lover, she had given him the castle in the first place. She may well have financed the parties too. It was all to no purpose; she still declined to marry him. When he died the parties ended and Kenilworth started going downhill. Cromwell gave it the final shove.

If you can skirt the southern environs of Birmingham without getting too confused, and too depressed, you will find Stourport-

unlikely that the illustrious Inigo would have bothered himself with such a modest structure anyway. His name is linked with it because he was also said to have designed the manor house, but there is no longer any evidence of that because the house was demolished in 1802.

The windmill must have been much admired over the years because Benedict Arnold, who was born in nearby Leamington, is said to have copied the design for the Old Stone Mill he built at Newport, Rhode Island. And indeed there are those who love it still – it has been restored in recent years. But if you prefer the more traditional approach there is a watermill not far away which you may find more pleasing, if less striking.

Just beyond Leamington Spa is Kenilworth.

Kenilworth Castle is one of the ruins that Cromwell knocked about more than a bit. It has been called the grandest fortress ruin in England, and Cromwell's demolition experts must have worked quite hard to get it that way. But in its prime it was the home of John of Gaunt and his son Henry IV, and in 1563 it came into the hands of Robert Dudley, favourite of Elizabeth I.

Before John of Gaunt's day it was a fortress. John turned it into a castle. Robert turned it into a setting for the most lavish country house parties of the 16th century. He converted all the old apartments, built a range of new buildings to accommodate more guests, and added the Long Barn and the Great Gatehouse.

The Gothic clocktower at Abberley – an example of the Joneses keeping up with somebody else.

England's best answer to the Leaning Tower of Pisa – the Leaning Tower of Bridgnorth, which leans at three times the angle but is still – they assure us! – perfectly safe.

on-Severn, gamely holding its own against the larger presence of Kidderminster, further along the Stour.

Between the Abberley and Woodbury Hills, some five miles from Stourport, is **Abberley** Gothic clock tower which is remarkable, not merely because it has 20 bells which can play over 40 different tunes, but also because instead of somebody keeping up with the Joneses, it demonstrates how the Joneses will sometimes go to great lengths to keep up with somebody else.

The clock tower was erected in 1883 by John Jones, occupant of Abberley Hall, ostensibly in memory of his father Joseph, but there was widespread belief that he did it just to impress the rather more blue-blooded residents of Witley Court, the other big house in the neighbourhood, which was built by the first Lord Foley in the 18th century – one hundred years before Abberley Hall – and included among its residents the Earl of Dudley and Queen Adelaide.

It is not recorded whether the occupants of Witley Court were duly impressed, or merely irritated by having tunes played at them every hour. As it turned out, the clock tower (which Mr Jones would be very irked to know is now called Jones's Folly) survived both families. Witley Court was burned down in 1937, Abberley Hall is now a school.

Again it would be nice to say, "Follow the river to Bridgnorth", and indeed on this stretch of the Severn you can do it by train as well as by boat, because the railway hugs the river all the way. The road, alas, is not so obliging, but it gets there eventually.

England's equivalent of the Leaning Tower of Pisa, only more so, is at **Bridgnorth** in Shropshire, that remarkable town which, unlike any other in England, is split in two by a red sandstone cliff, so that High Town and Low Town have to be linked by several flights of steps and a railway with the steepest gradient in the country. For those who did not fancy living in either, there are caves carved out of the sandstone which were used as homes until about a hundred years ago. The caves were probably there long before any houses – one of them, known as the

Much Wenlock's Guildhall, built with much haste. It was completed in two days.

Big game hunting in Staffordshire: 'Giffard's Cross', which marked a successful panther shoot at Brewood. The original has been moved into the grounds of Chillington Hall.

Hermitage, is said to have housed Ethelred, the brother of King Athelstan, in the 10th century.

The Leaning Tower belonged to the old castle which was another victim of Cromwell's personal leaning towards knocking down old castles. The Parliamentarians destroyed most of it in 1646, but they did not quite succeed with the tower of the keep. About 30 feet of it remained standing in spite of all their efforts – but it stands at 17 degrees to the vertical, more than three times the angle of the Leaning Tower of Pisa, which by comparison is almost upright. It has stayed that way for over three hundred years, and since the area around it is now a public park, everyone assumes it will continue to do so.

Only a few miles from Bridgnorth, the Guildhall at **Much Wenlock** looks the sort of place you would expect in a medieval market town – half-timbered, with oak arches supporting it above the old butter market and still housing a court and a council chamber. What is remarkable about it is the speed with which it was built. According to the records it was put up in 1577 in just two days. The workmen must have been sound as well as speedy – but would they be surprised to know that it is still standing after four hundred years?

A slight zig-zag now to avoid Telford, but you can use the M54 for a stretch, which is quite a treat, because not many people do – it is Telford's private motorway. You can almost see Brewood from it, but it involves quite a long detour via the next junction to reach it.

Brewood is one of Staffordshire's more attractive villages "but visitors are surprisingly rare", says one guidebook – perhaps because it is called "Brood" locally and strangers asking for "Breewood" could well be ignored. If they do find their way there the first thing to strike them would probably be Speedwell House, an 18th century Gothic house in the main street which has one modest claim to fame – it was named after a horse. A local apothecary backed Speedwell at such excellent odds that he was able to build the house with the proceeds.

It is however another animal that interests me about Brewood, rather more unlikely, which is commemorated by a cross instead of a house, a little way south-west of the village. "Giffard's Cross" is named after Sir John Giffard of nearby Chillington Hall, an ancestor of the Giffards who sheltered the future Charles II at their hunting lodge, Boscobel House. Does that name ring a bell, or shake a branch? It was indeed the Boscobel Oak that Charles sheltered in when the enemy got too close. A descendant of that oak still stands there.

Sir John though was around Chillington a century and a half earlier, and while out hunting with his crossbow he shot an animal described as a 'panther'. This seems a little unlikely, since not too many panthers roamed the Staffordshire forests in 1513, though one explanation is that it had escaped from a menagerie at Chillington Hall. Sir John was proud enough of his feat to have the spot marked with a cross. The original cross has been restored and moved into the grounds of the house; a 20th century successor now stands in its place.

Now northwards in the general direction of Cumbria, but a diversion across the Pennines first to Halifax. I would not normally direct you into a town of this size, because the delights of unusual discoveries are generally tempered by the tedium of the traffic. But this may solve a little mystery for you as well as offer a curious glimpse of the past.

"From Hull, Hell and Halifax, good Lord deliver us", went the Beggars' Litany, and in Gibbet Street, **Halifax** is one of the reasons why. Halifax folk used to feel very strongly about the value of their cloth; it was the foundation of the town's prosperity and the Piece Hall, where weavers displayed their wares to the merchants, piece by piece, is still a dominant building. Long before the Piece Hall was built, until the middle of the 17th century, Halifax had a law under which anyone who stole a piece of cloth worth more than 13 pence was beheaded. Unlucky indeed for some . . .

Fifty thieves were despatched in this way on the Halifax guillotine before the practice ended in 1650. The blade used on the final victim is still preserved in the Industrial Museum in Piece Hall, and Gibbet Street has a replica of the guillotine, which is now called the Halifax Gibbet, perhaps since the French Revolution gave guillotining a bad name.

We shall be returning to less populated parts of Yorkshire later but we are back on track for Cumbria now, and in particular that droopy bit on the map which hangs down below the Lake District into Morecambe Bay. On its far tip is Barrow-in-Furness.

"From Hull, Hell and Halifax, good Lord deliver us" – particularly from Halifax, where a guillotine awaited petty thieves.

The monks' castle on Piel Island. The island's pub can bestow the title of Knight of Piel Island on its customers.

You will not want to linger too long in the industrial areas or the ship-building yards, which are as lacking in charm as most such places, and suggest the town might better have been called Barrow-in-Furnace. But **Furness** itself is an attractive area of what used to be Lancashire until the great re-shuffle of 1974, and now forms part of the Lake District of Cumbria. It used to be ruled by the Abbot of Furness Abbey, the ruins of which lie in a pleasant wooded valley north-east of the town. But come the Dissolution and there was an even bigger shake-up than in 1974.

The monks of Furness built themselves a castle on Piel Island to take refuge from Scottish raiders, and it is this island which brings us to Barrow – it is in fact within the town boundaries, along with Foulney, Walney and Roa, which sound like a firm of slightly suspect solicitors, but are actually three more islands sheltering the Barrow dockyards.

Piel Island still has the ruins of the monks' castle, but of more pressing interest, if you are thirsty by now, is the island's pub, because here you can acquire a drink, and a title as well. The landlord is 'King' of this little domain, and he is entitled to bestow the title of Knight of Piel Island on his customers. Surely no other pub in England can claim to have such a beknighted clientele.

Arise, Sir Reader. We have more travelling to do . . .

If you head northwards through the Lake District via the **Kirkstone Pass** you may spot Hartsop Hall, a 16th century manor house which is now a farm. Spare a thought for its present owners. At some stage in its history the house was extended, inadvertently spanning an ancient right of way. There was a time when local folk took a delight in exercising their right to take a Sunday morning stroll through the new wing. It is not a practice which I – or the owners – would encourage. Why should the sins of the father's architect be visited on the sons? So spare a thought – but nothing more!

Hartsop Hall straddles an ancient right of way – but don't blame the present owners!

Keep going north until you are some-where between Carlisle Airport and Had-rian's Wall. If you find yourself hacking your way through the Kielder Forest you have gone too far. They are very strong on castles in these parts, for reasons which will become apparent in a moment – Thirlwall Castle, Naworth Castle, Featherstone Castle, and so on. But we are not in search of a castle but a priory.

The remarkable thing about **Lanercost Priory** is that it is there at all. When it was founded in the 12th century by Augustinian monks they decided upon one of the most impressive and delightful areas of Cumbria – but whoever persuaded them to go there in the best tradition of property agents, omitted to mention a certain disadvantage. It was on the direct route of the raiders who regularly came down from Scotland to disport them-selves in the English countryside. William de Vaux, the benefactor who selected the site, had made a Vaux pas.

The priory was built around 1144. By the end of the century it had been ransacked, rebuilt and ransacked again. That went on well into the 13th century, but the monks stuck to their spiritual guns and their tempor-al building equipment, and eventually the raiders must have given up. Much of the monks' work still stands, and indeed in the last century the nave and north aisle were put into use again as the parish church.

This is our northernmost point. Head south-east now, crossing the Pennines by whatever route you fancy, and aim for North Yorkshire and Masham Moor.

Mention **Masham** to a beer drinker and he will know there is something peculiar about it. It is in fact the home of Theakston's Old Peculier beer, a powerful brew which earned its name, not because of a particular peculiar-ity but because the Peculier (note the slightly different spelling) was a medieval official in Masham, and the brewers adopted his ancient title.

That is not to say however that Masham does not have a peculiarity. The site of Nutwith Cote Farm was once a stop-over for monks travelling between the two great abbeys of Rievaulx and Fountains, and it still has some unusual features. There is supposed to be a tunnel which the monks dug so they could pass underneath the river, though it seems an unnecessarily ambitious project just to avoid a river crossing.

Lanercost Priory – a sturdy shelter for monks.

Nutwith Cote Farm , a sturdy shelter for bees.

What does remain is an outbuilding which has niches in its base for beeboles.

It is said to be one of only two such arrangements in the country, though I know of another at Fletcher Christian's cottage at **Eaglesfield**, near Cockermouth, and there may be a few more. So it is not peculiar to Masham, but it is still, well, peculiar.

Across the North Yorkshire moors – and here, any route is a delight – until you hit the sea between Whitby and Scarborough.

One might think there could be no weirder building in the vicinity of Robin's Hood Bay than those monstrous golfballs which adorn Fylingdales Moor, but long before modern technology devised this strange variety of globular architecture, Squire Barry was introducing some distinctly odd architecture in the grounds of Fyling Hall near **Fylingthorpe**, now a private school.

In the 1880s Squire Barry decided to erect a pigsty. It took the form of a Grecian Temple, with portico and pillars, Egyptian-style windows and a fluted frieze. Even the drainpipes were ornate. It follows no particular architectural style; according to one of the men who built it the squire had no particular style in mind, he was inclined to make it up as he went along. One would not like to say he made a pig's-ear of it, but even the pigs must have been a little startled by their new home. Personally I rate it an excellent example of piggery-jokery . . .

We are heading south now, and our final objective is still within sight of the North Sea; but en route, turn inland around Bridlington and between there and Great Driffield is the legend-laden village of Harpham.

Harpham was the scene of a brutal attack on the youngest daughter of Sir Henry Griffith, who built the magnificent Elizabethan mansion at nearby Burton Agnes. A gang of ruffians set upon her and inflicted fatal wounds. On her deathbed she asked that her head should remain in the mansion where she had always lived, but her wish was disregarded and she was buried, in one piece, in the churchyard.

Strange manifestations took place at her grave, and it became clear she would not rest in peace. The coffin was brought out, and it was found that her head had been separated from her body. The family took the hint, and the head was reburied in the house. There were later attempts to return it to consecrated

The Grecian Temple for pigs at Fyling Hall (above) – did Squire Barry go crackers over crackling?

ground but each time there were further disturbances. The head is back in the mansion again, though nobody is quite sure where.

We do however know the location of another Harpham legend, involving another violent death. This is the Drumming Well, where it is said that a member of the St Quintin family, the lords of the manor at the time, drowned an inoffensive drummer boy. The mother, understandably annoyed, put a curse on the St Quintins and forecast that her son would drum them to their deaths. If you hear the sound of ghostly drumming coming from the well, you will know another St Quintin is about to meet his Maker . . .

Not satisfied with one weird well, Harpham actually has two. The other has a more benign history. It is dedicated to St John of Beverley, another local boy, and it is said that its waters have a soothing effect on wild animals. Since wild animals are rare in this part of Yorkshire it has not recently been put to the test, but one never knows when it may come in handy.

Now we make our final leap, over the Humber Bridge and down through Lincolnshire until we join one of those appallingly inadequate roads that leads the more determined traveller from the world of motorways and Inter-City 125s into that very different world to the east of King's Lynn.

Some of the ingredients of the Harpham legends – one of the many St Quintin family tombs (opposite, below), the St Quintin family vault (above), the Drumming Well (left) and the well of St John of Beverley (right).

South Creake is one of the many peaceful villages in North Norfolk just far enough away from the coast to be off the standard tourist routes, though it sometimes gets an overspill of pilgrims from Walsingham, a few miles away. It has a quiet stream running alongside its main street, and most of the cottages are in pleasant Norfolk flint, but to show I am not completely blind to Norfolk's failings let me point out quite the most hideous building in the village, and probably in the county.

It is a ramshackle factory-like building which towers over the cottages in the centre of the village, deserted for many a year. But indeed it was once a factory, and of all unlikely products for an isolated little village it made razorblades. These were the Ace works, home of the 'Ace of Blades'.

George Theophilus Money was a Londoner who came to South Creake in the 1920s after marrying a local girl and set up his razorblade factory, making most of the machinery himself. He did not however believe in the law of built-in obsolescence. Instead of relying on his customers to throw away a blade after a few shaves and buy a new one, he actually offered to sharpen the old ones. Sales inevitably slumped and the enterprise folded. Since then the building has seen other products come and go, from bread to ginger beer. At

The two faces of North Norfolk. One of its ugliest buildings – the old razor blade factory at South Creake – and one of its finest assets, the 15th century wineglass pulpit at Burnham Norton (above).

the last sighting it was for sale again. One can only hope a demolition firm will snap it up.

Having displayed the unattractive face of North Norfolk I hasten to redress the balance. head for the Burnhams, not to wallow in the memory of their most famous son (though you will find it difficult to avoid all the pubs called Lord Nelson or simply The Hero), but to the church of St Margaret's, **Burnham Norton**. Even here you cannot escape the Nelson connection – his father was Rector here as well as at Burnham Thorpe, where the family was based, and so was his brother Suckling – a name, one imagines, not easy to live with. But it is the pulpit from which they preached that took me there.

This is a wineglass pulpit, claimed to be the finest example in the country. It stands on a slender stem, and its panels show the four Doctors of the Church, looking suitably learned as they read a scroll, or write, or contemplate their pens. It was donated in 1450 by John Goldale and his wife, perhaps as a sort of penance, because four years earlier he was prosecuted for entering the salt marshes by night and stealing oysters. This act of contrition may or may not have worked for Mr Goldale, but it still affords pleasure to those who see it, though it is no longer actually used.

I have another reason for bringing you to St Margaret's. It stands on a hill – oh yes, Norfolk does have hills – and from it you can look across the fields to the great sweep of the salt marshes and the empty sands and the sea beyond. Over it all there is that vast Norfolk sky.

It is not by accident that I have ended this tour, and this book, in such a place. To me Norfolk epitomises what 'Timpson's England' is all about. It is nowhere near the top of the tourist league, it is not on a main route to anywhere. It does not have the grandeur of the Lake District, or the wild beauty of the Yorkshire moors, or the black-and-white prettiness of the villages in Somerset and Devon. But it does have a very special character of its own.

To find the real Norfolk, you must look beyond the flat fenlands, and the overcrowded Broads, and the holiday camps and caravan sites that pepper the coast from Yarmouth to Cromer. You must look, in fact, beyond the obvious. And as I hope you have found with this book, you will not be disappointed.

Maps

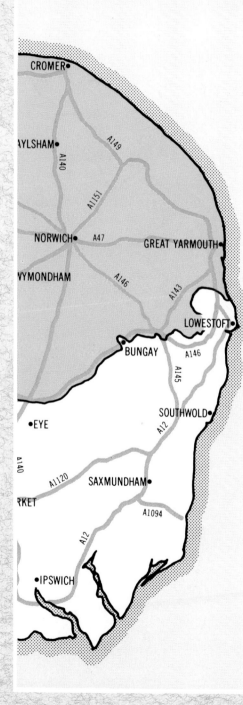

1

Cleveland
Cumbria
Durham
Tyne & Wear

CROWN COPYRIGHT RESERVED

KEY TO SYMBOLS

- Odd buildings and features
- ≋ Water-related objects
- ↝ Roadside oddities
- Stately homes
- Castles
- ✝ Churches
- Stones
- Public Houses
- Trees
- Villages
- Miscellaneous

The maps provided are for general reference as to the position of a particular object of interest only. They are not recommended as route maps. The use of your regular route planner is therefore advisable.

BERWICK-ON-TWEED ● ≋ 39
🏚 128
🏰 ≋ 37
🏯 95

● WOOLER

ALNWICK ●

AMBLE ●

● ROTHBURY

🏚 114

🏯 19

N O R T H U M B E R L A N D

113 🏚

A696

BEDLINGTON ●

98 🏰

✝ 167
✝ 210
● HALTWHISTLE   ● HEXHAM

AY ●

EAR ●
NDERLAND ●

HAM

HARTLEPOOL ●

BILLINGHAM ●   REDCAR ●

C L E V E L A N D   ● GUISBOROUGH

113	🏚	Ashington
39	≋	Berwick-upon-Tweed
128	🏚	Berwick-upon-Tweed (mid-February to mid-September)
114	🏚	Blakehopeburnhaugh
37	🏰	Coldstream
37	≋	Coldstream
19	🏯	Otterburn
98	🏰	Seaton Delavel Hall, the garden
167	✝	Simonburn, St Mungo Church
95	🏯	Twizel Castle, by Twizel Bridge
210	✝	Warden, churchyard

2
Northumberland

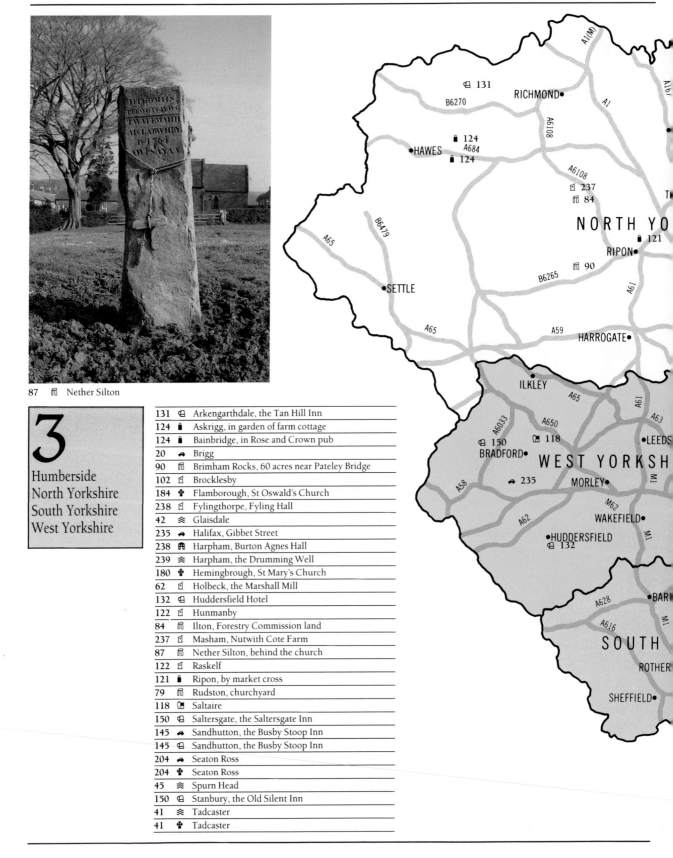

87 Nether Silton

3

Humberside
North Yorkshire
South Yorkshire
West Yorkshire

131	Arkengarthdale, the Tan Hill Inn
124	Askrigg, in garden of farm cottage
124	Bainbridge, in Rose and Crown pub
20	Brigg
90	Brimham Rocks, 60 acres near Pateley Bridge
102	Brocklesby
184	Flamborough, St Oswald's Church
238	Fylingthorpe, Fyling Hall
42	Glaisdale
235	Halifax, Gibbet Street
238	Harpham, Burton Agnes Hall
239	Harpham, the Drumming Well
180	Hemingbrough, St Mary's Church
62	Holbeck, the Marshall Mill
132	Huddersfield Hotel
122	Hunmanby
84	Ilton, Forestry Commission land
237	Masham, Nutwith Cote Farm
87	Nether Silton, behind the church
122	Raskelf
121	Ripon, by market cross
79	Rudston, churchyard
118	Saltaire
150	Saltersgate, the Saltersgate Inn
145	Sandhutton, the Busby Stoop Inn
145	Sandhutton, the Busby Stoop Inn
204	Seaton Ross
204	Seaton Ross
45	Spurn Head
150	Stanbury, the Old Silent Inn
41	Tadcaster
41	Tadcaster

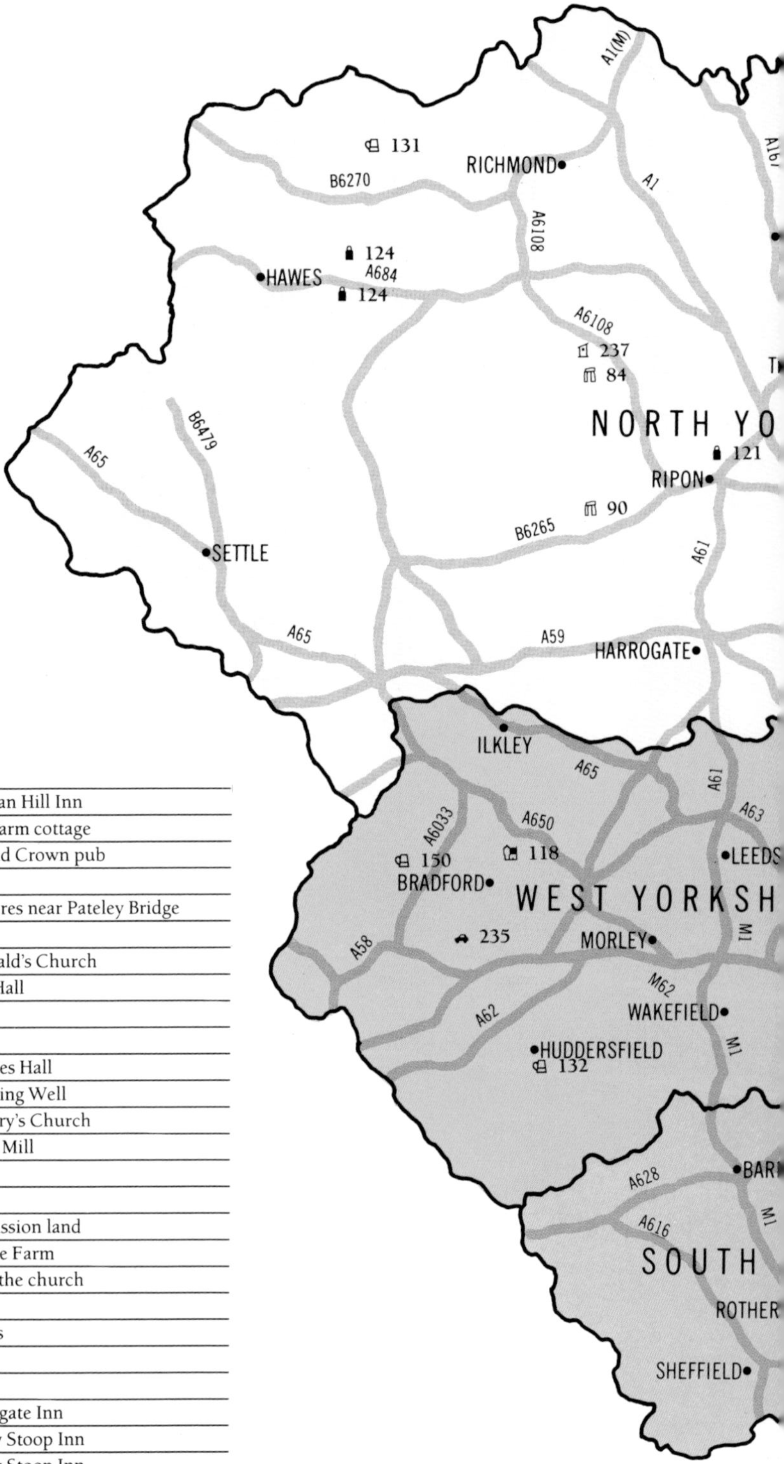
131
RICHMOND
B6270
A1(M)
A1
A6108
124
HAWES
A684
124
A6108
237
84
NORTH YO
B6479
A65
121
RIPON
90
B6265
SETTLE
A61
A65
A59
HARROGATE
ILKLEY
A65
A61
A63
A6033
A650
150
118
LEEDS
BRADFORD
WEST YORKSH
235
MORLEY
A58
M1
M62
WAKEFIELD
A62
HUDDERSFIELD
132
M1
A628
BAR
A616
M1
SOUTH
ROTHER
SHEFFIELD

KEY TO SYMBOLS

- ⌂ Odd buildings and features
- ≋ Water-related objects
- ⚲ Roadside oddities
- ⌘ Stately homes
- ♜ Castles
- ✚ Churches
- ⌺ Stones
- ⌸ Public Houses
- ⚘ Trees
- ⌖ Villages
- ⏚ Miscellaneous

STOKESLEY

WHITBY

≋ 42

239 ⌂

A171

⌂ 87

B1257

TON

A169

⌂ 150

A171

SCARBOROUGH

A170

A170

PICKERING

A165

IRE

B1257

A64

⌂ 122

A19

MALTON

B1248

⌺ 79

✚ 184

BRIDLINGTON

A166

A166

⌘ 238

≋ 239

A64

A19

STAMFORD BRIDGE

GREAT DRIFFIELD

59

A1079

A163

A165

YORK

HORNSEA

≋ ✚ 41

A19

⚲ ✚ 204

MARKET WEIGHTON

A614

H U M B E R S I D E

SELBY

A63

180

A63

A1041

KINGSTON UPON HULL

A1033

A15

HOWDEN

M62

≋ 45

THORNE

M180

A1

20 ⚲

102 ⌂

GRIMSBY

A18

SCUNTHORPE

BRIGG

A46

A16

635

A161

ONCASTER

M18

SHIRE

631

62

4

Cheshire
Greater Manchester
Lancashire
Merseyside

82	Anwick, by churchyard
143	Bailgate, White Hart Hotel
203	Baslow Church
190	Bingham Church
77	Blidworth
203	Burgh Le Marsh Church
182	Burton Joyce, St Helen's Church
127	Calverton
203	Castle Bytham, church tower
128	Castleton
144	Castleton, Castle Inn
176	Chesterfield Church
206	Coningsby, St Michael's Church
41	Cromford, on bridge
34	Crowland
147	Crowland, The Abbey Hotel

68	Darley Dale, churchyard
117	Edensor, Chatsworth Estate
124	Eyam
204	Eyam, churchyard
138	Gotham, the Cuckoo Bush
141	Grantham, three Inns
195	Great Ponton Church
98	Hardwick Hall, along the roof tops
212	Hathersage
162	Holme, St Giles' Church
24	Londonthorpe
158	Mugginton, attached to farmhouse
102	Newstead Abbey
24	Scarrington
212	Stamford, St Martin's churchyard

5

Derbyshire
Lincolnshire
Nottinghamshire

KEY TO SYMBOLS

- Odd buildings and features
- ≋ Water-related objects
- ↝ Roadside oddities
- 🏛 Stately homes
- 🏰 Castles
- ✝ Churches
- 🗿 Stones
- 🍺 Public Houses
- 🌳 Trees
- 🏘 Villages
- ⬮ Miscellaneous

6

Hereford
& Worcester
Leicestershire
Shropshire
Staffordshire
Warwickshire
West Midlands

233	🏛	Abberley
193	✟	Ashby-de-la-Zouch, St Helen's Church
73	🌳	Aston-on-Clun, the Arbor Tree
177	✟	Beeby, All Saints' Church
100	🏠	Benthall Hall, in the porchway
20	🚗	Bilstone, outskirts of village
170	✟	Binton, St Peter's Church
72	🌳	Boscobel House grounds
234	🏛	Brewood, Speedwell House and Giffard's Cross
233	🏰	Bridgnorth
215	✟	Bromsgrove, churchyard
127	🏘	Broseley
231	🏛	Chesterton Green, Windmill
39	≋	Coalbrookdale
80	🗿	Colwall, centre of village
60	🏠	Compton Wynyates
17	🚗	Craven Arms, junction of A49 and B4368
71	🌳	Cropthorne, in the village
188	✟	Elford, St Peter's Church
112	🏘	Flash
25	🚗	Hallaton, Market Square
98	🏠	Hanbury Hall
106	🏠	Harvington Hall
107	🏠	Hindlip Hall
154	✟	Hoarwithy Church
232	🏰	Kenilworth Castle
84	🗿	Kingstone
155	✟	Llanyblodwel Church
148	🍺	Longton, the Albion Hotel
104	🚗	Lugwardine, Longworth Hall Hotel
133	🍺	Leamington Spa, the Regent Hotel
14	🚗	Meriden, Cyclists Memorial
69	🌳	Much Marcle, churchyard
97	🏠	Much Marcle, on a window of Hellen's House
234	🏛	Much Wenlock, Guildhall
51	🏛	Newton Linford, Folly
214	✟	Oakham, churchyard
191	✟	Preston Church
146	🏛	Rugby, Brownsover Hall
135	🍺	Stretton, the Ram Jam Inn and the Jackson Stops
179	✟	Tamworth Church
174	✟	Warwick Church
136	🍺	Welford-on-Avon, the Four Alls pub
84	🗿	Weston Rhyn
91	🗿	Wolverhampton, St Peter's Collegiate churchyard
182	✟	Worcester, St Andrew's Church
181	✟	Yarpole Church

KEY TO SYMBOLS

🏛 Odd buildings and features
≋ Water-related objects
🚗 Roadside oddities
🏠 Stately homes
🏰 Castles
✟ Churches
🗿 Stones
🍺 Public Houses
🌳 Trees
🏘 Villages
🔒 Miscellaneous

STAFFORDSHIRE

LEEK

STOKE ON TRENT

STONE

STAFFORD

BURTON UPON TRENT

CANNOK

LICHFIELD

WALSALL

DUDLEY

SUTTON COLDFIELD

WEST BROMWICH

BIRMINGHAM

WEST MIDLANDS

KIDDERMINSTER

SOLIHULL

COVENTRY

RUGBY

NUNEATON

BEDWORTH

KENILWORTH

REDDITCH

WARWICK

WARWICKSHIRE

WORCESTER

ORCESTER

CESTER

EVESHAM

STRATFORD UPON AVON

LEICESTERSHIRE

SHEPSHED

LOUGHBOROUGH

MELTON MOWBRAY

COALVILLE

OAKHAM

LEICESTER

UPPINGHAM

HINKLEY

MARKET HARBOROUGH

69 Much Marcle

7

Avon
Berkshire
Buckinghamshire
Gloucestershire
Hampshire
Isle of Wight
Oxfordshire
Wiltshire

KEY TO SYMBOLS

🏛 Odd buildings and features
≋ Water-related objects
🛣 Roadside oddities
🏚 Stately homes
🏰 Castles
✠ Churches
🗿 Stones
🍺 Public Houses
🌳 Trees
🏘 Villages
⬤ Miscellaneous

227 ⌂ Berkeley

8

Bedfordshire
Cambridgeshire
Essex
Greater London
Hertfordshire
Northamptonshire

118	🏘	Ardeley
67	⚘	Aynho, cottages
154	✝	Ayot St Lawrence
110	🏛	Barnwell Abbey House
141	🍺	Birchanger, the Three Willows pub
122	⚘	Brent Pelham, village green
156	✝	Cambridge, church of the Holy Sepulchre
169	✝	Cambridge, King's College Chapel
16	⚘	Cambridge, Trinity Milestones, on A10
20	⚘	Caxton
49	≋	Chelmsford
117	🏘	Chippenham, near Newmarket
49	≋	Colchester
186	✝	Danbury Church
37	≋	Ely
49	≋	Epping High Street
67	🏰	Fotherinhay
36	≋	Godmanchester
230	⚘	Great Gransden, postmill
157	✝	Greensted-juxta-Ongar, St Andrew Church
159	✝	Halstead, Fremlin's Brewery
72	⚘	Hatfield House, grounds
151	🍺	Hempstead, The Rose and Crown
15	⚘	Holme Fen, Whittlesey Mere
143	🍺	Holywell, Ye Olde Ferryboat Inn
36	≋	Huntingdon
157	✝	Little Maplestead, St John the Baptist Church
156	✝	London, Temple Church, off the Embankment
179	✝	Maldon, river bank
107	🏛	Markyate Cell
78	🏛	Marston Moretaine, tower of St Mary the Virgin
15	⚘	Norman Cross, outside the village
156	✝	Northampton, church of the Holy Sepulchre
14	⚘	Ruislip, Polish War Memorial
231	🏛	Rushton, Triangular Lodge
130	🍺	St Albans, Ye Olde Fighting Cocks pub
35	≋	St Ives
35	✝	St Ives
58	✝	Stevenage
148	🍺	Stock, the Bear Hotel
49	≋	Stoke Newington, North London
74	✝	Tewin, churchyard
74	⚘	Tewin, churchyard
42	≋	Wansford
47	✝	Weldon, on tower of village church
152	🍺	White Notley, the Cross Keys
102	🏛	Woburn Abbey, grounds
216	✝	Woodditton, churchyard
191	✝	Woodford, St Mary's Church

KEY TO SYMBOLS

- 🏛 Odd buildings and features
- ≋ Water-related objects
- ⚘ Roadside oddities
- 🏛 Stately homes
- 🏰 Castles
- ✝ Churches
- 🏛 Stones
- 🍺 Public Houses
- ⚘ Trees
- 🏘 Villages
- 🛈 Miscellaneous

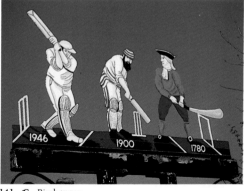

141 🍺 Birchanger

WISBECH

A47

≋ 42

PETERBOROUGH ● MARCH

🐎 15

OUNDLE 🐎 15

A10

A1

RAMSEY

A142

ELY ☩ ≋ 37

🏰 110

A141

≋ 36 C A M B R I D G E S H I R E 117

HUNTINGDON ≋ 36 ☩ 35

🏠 143

A604

🐎 20

ST NEOTS CAMBRIDGE ● ☩ 156
169

🐎 230 216 ☩

A428 A14 M11 A11

SANDY 🐎 16

BIGGLESWADE

A1

ORDSHIRE ROYSTON

SAFFRON WALDEN ●
🏠 151

A131

BALDOCK 157 ☩

A12

A6 🐎 122 159 ☩ HALSTEAD A120

BUZZARD 🏠 118 A604

58 ☩ STEVENAGE COLCHESTER ● 49

UTON ● A120 🏠 141 A120 ≋ 49

H E R T F O R D S H I R E A131 BRAINTREE ● A133

☩ 154 🏠 152 A12 CLACTON-ON-
SEA

107 🐎 74 E S S E X

HARPENDEN ● WARE

A1(M) 🐎 72

MPSTEAD 130 🏠 A41 CHELMSFORD ● ≋ 49 ☩ 186

ST ALBANS 179 ☩

M25 49 ≋ ☩ 157

POTTERS BAR EPPING

M11

W25 M25 148 🏠

A12 A130

WATFORD ENFIELD A127

M1 A10 191 ☩

HARROW ● ROMFORD ● BASILDON ●

M40 🐎 14 HAMPSTEAD ≋ 49 A13

☩ 156 DAGENHAM ●

A13 SOUTHEND ON SEA ●

M4 G R E A T E R   L O N D O N A2

BRENTFORD ●

M3 M20

SIDCUP ●
WIMBLEDON ● SIDCUP

CROYDON ●

M23

16 🐎 Cambridge

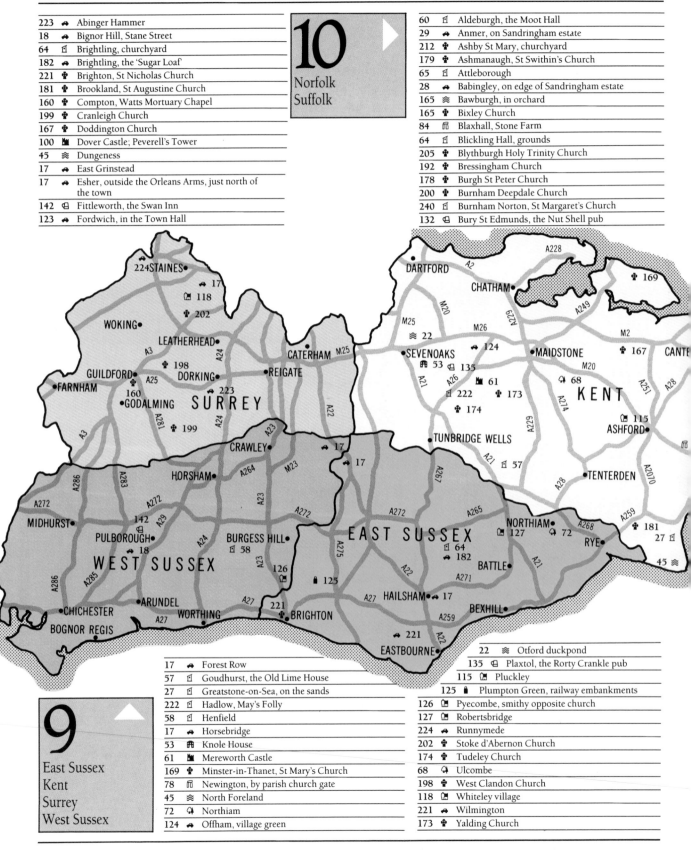

Map labels:

200 — 240 — 215 — CROMER
240 — 59 — A148 — A149
FAKENHAM — 117 — 29 — 28
A148 — 134 — AYLSHAM — 25 — 64 — 168 — 212 — 54
KING'S LYNN — A17 — 160 — 216 — 179 — A1151 — 199
124 — A1065 — A47 — 30 — NORFOLK — A140
216 — 192 — 187 — SWAFFHAM — 29 — EAST DEREHAM — 30 — 181 — 131 — NORWICH — 165 — 30 — GREAT YARMOUTH
DOWNHAM MARKET — 107 — 30 — 178 — WYMONDHAM — 165 — 212 — 189 — 158
A10 — A134 — ATTLEBOROUGH — 65 — 216 — 30 — 178 — LOWESTOFT
A11 — BUNGAY — A146
45 — THETFORD — A1066 — 216 — 192 — SOUTHWOLD — 205
RAMSGATE — A1065 — A143 — EYE — 200 — 197 — 57 — A12
123 — A256 — A134 — 197 — SAXMUNDHAM — 50
DOVER — 100 — 13 — 215 — A45 — STOWMARKET — 84 — 60
NEWMARKET — 132 — BURY ST EDMUNDS — A45 — SUFFOLK — 194
A134 — A1120 — A12
HAVERHILL — A1141 — HADLEIGH — IPSWICH — 161
SUDBURY — 179 — A12 — 229
202

KEY TO SYMBOLS

⚏ Odd buildings and features
≋ Water-related objects
⌂ Roadside oddities
⚏ Stately homes
▲ Castles
♠ Churches
⚏ Stones
⚏ Public Houses
♣ Trees
⚏ Villages
▮ Miscellaneous

11

Cornwall
Devon
Dorset
Somerset

157 ✝
MINEHEAD
≋ 22
A396
A358
A361
⛫ 33
≋ 33
198 BRIDGEWATER
🏠 120
A361
TAUNTON
✝ 189
M5
TIVERTON
≋ 76
A3072
HONITON
A30
A35
EXETER
⛫ 90
✝ 156
A380
46 ≋
A3022
TORQUAY
74
69
A385
55
DARTMOUTH
47
≋

92 ⛫
≋ 48
≋ 46
M5
✝ 204
GLASTONBURY
67
FROME
A361
A37
SOMERSET
A359
A303
✝ 201
⛫ 122
SHAFTSBURY
YEOVIL
● SHERBORNE
A30
A30
11
🏠 94
≋ 38
A350
23
A354
✝ 199
A37
DORSET
116
A31 ✝ 195
132
A348
BRIDPORT
A35
BOURNEMOUTH
DORCHESTER
A352
A354
63
89
161
A351
WEYMOUTH
120
86

Legend (centre columns):

173 ✝ Princetown Church
201 ✝ Queen Camel Church
22 ≋ St Audries, on a farm
164 ✝ St Endellion Church
207 ☛ St Feock, church porch
163 ≋ St Keyne
169 ≋ St Neot, Cornwall
169 ✝ St Neot, Cornwall
40 ≋ Saltash, the Royal Albert bridge
79 ⛫ Shebbear, in the village
94 🏰 Sherborne, Old and New castles
69 🌳 Stoke Gabriel, churchyard
194 ⬙ Stratton, St Andrew Church
38 ≋ Sturminster Newton
86 ⛫ Swanage, on Tilly Whim
46 ≋ Teignmouth
126 🏘 Totnes
120 🏘 Tyneham
53 🏘 Veryan, round houses at each end and middle
219 ✝ Warleggan Church
204 ✝ Wells Cathedral
195 ✝ Wimborne St Giles Church
33 ⛫ Winsford Hill, the Caratacus Stone, off B3358
199 ✝ Zennor Church

199 ✝ Melbury Bubb Church
82 ⛫ Men-an-Tol
156 ✝ Milber Church
116 🏘 Milton Abbas
90 ⛫ Moretonhampstead, the Bowerman's Nose
211 ✝ Morwenstow, churchyard
61 ⬙ Morwenstow, the Vicarage
23 ☛ Okeford Fitzpaine
82 ⛫ Pelynt
140 ⬙ Phillack, the Bucket of Blood pub
140 ≋ Phillack, the Bucket of Blood pub
105 ☛ Plymouth, overlooking the Sound
63 ⬙ Portesham, on the Black Downs
88 ⛫ Porthcurno, the Logan Stone on headland

KEY TO SYMBOLS

⬙ Odd buildings and features
≋ Water-related objects
☛ Roadside oddities
🏠 Stately homes
🏰 Castles
✝ Churches
⛫ Stones
⬙ Public Houses
🌳 Trees
🏘 Villages
⬙ Miscellaneous

Index

Clocks/Clock Towers

Cottages

Effigies

Ghosts

Gibbets/Gallows/Stocks

Lakes/Ponds

Lighthouses

Location	Page	Map
Burnham-on-Sea 12 miles south of Weston-super-Mare	46	11
Dungeness 6 miles south of New Romney	45	9
Froward Point Near Kingswear, by mouth of River Dart	47	11
Kilmersdon Near village, 10 miles north-east of Wells on B3139	48	11
North Foreland 4 miles north of Ramsgate	45	9
St Catherine's Down above St Catherine's Point	44	7 IoW
St Catherine's Point The Point	44	7 IoW
Spurn Head Mouth of the Humber	45	3
Teignmouth Southern end of promenade	46	11
Ulverston Summit of Hoad Hill, near town	48	1
Weldon Tower of village church, 2 miles north of Corby on A43	47	8

Lock-ups

Location	Page	Map
Bradford-on-Avon The chapel on the Oratory Bridge	36	7
Hunmanby 3 miles south of Filey off A165	122	3
Kingsbury Episcopi 2 miles north-west of Martock off B3165	122	11
Raskelf 9 miles north of Shipton off A19	122	3
Wheatley 3 miles east of Oxford on A40	66	7

Memorials/Monuments

Location	Page	Map
Abbotts Ann The church, 3 miles south-west of Andover off A343	192	7
Bampton The church, 6 miles north of Tiverton off A361	189	11
Barwick Park 1 mile south of Yeovil, just off A37	11	11
Berkeley The church, 12 miles south-west of Gloucester off A38	227	7
Bingham The parish church, 6 miles east of Nottingham off A52	190	5
Blockley Fish Cottage, 3 miles west of Moreton-in-Marsh off A44	105	7
Bodmin Car park of town	24	11
Brewood Giffard's Cross, south-west of village 3 miles north of M54, 12 miles east of Telford	235	6
Broad Hinton The church, 5 miles south-west of Swindon off A361	184	7
Brocklesby 8 miles west of Grimsby off B1210	103	3
Burghclere Sandham Memorial Chapel, 6 miles south of Newbury off A34	175	7
Elford St Peter's Church, 5 miles north of Tamworth off A513	188	6
Halvergate The church, 8 miles west of Great Yarmouth off A47	189	10
Hempstead The Rose and Crown, 6 miles east of Saffron Walden on B1053	151	8
Henley Beside main road to Henley on A423	24	7
Holcombe Moor near Rossendale Way, Lancashire	13	4
Holme Fen 3 miles south-east of Norman Cross	15	8
Kentford 8 miles west of Bury St Edmunds	13	10
Laxfield All Saints Church, 7 miles south-west of Halesworth off B1117	200	10
Lugwardine Longworth Hall Hotel, 1 mile east of Hereford off A438	104	6
Meriden The Cyclists Memorial, off A45 Coventry to Birmingham road	14	6
Newstead Abbey 6 miles north of Nottingham off A60	102	5
Norman Cross 2 miles north of Stilton on A1	15	8
Portesham Hardy's Monument, 1 mile north off B3157 road, 6 miles north-west of Weymouth	63	11
Reading Forbury Gardens	225	7
Ruislip A40 Oxford road, next to Northolt RAF Station	14	8
Runnymede By the Thames, 2 miles north-west of Staines on A308	224	9
Stoke Row 6 miles north of Reading off B481 road to Nettlebed	24	7
Ulverston Summit of Hoad Hill, near town	48	1
Wick Hill 4 miles east of Chippenham	11	7

Milestones

Location	Page	Map
Cambridge A10, between Cambridge and Royston	16	8
Craven Arms 18 miles south of Shrewsbury at the junction of the A49 and B4368	17	6
East Grinstead A22 to Forest Row	17	9
Esher Just north of the town on A3	17	9
Forest Row A22 to East Grinstead	17	9
Horsebridge 12 miles north of Eastbourne on A22	17	9

Mills

Location	Page	Map
Chesterton Green 6 miles south-east of Leamington Spa off A41	231	6
Great Gransden 6 miles east of St Neots off B1046	230	8
Holbeck The Marshall Mill, 5 miles south-west of Worksop on A60	62	3

Obelisks

Location	Page	Map
Barwick Park 1 mile south of Yeovil, just off A37	11	11
Lindale 2 miles north of Grange-over-Sands	12	1
Plymouth On hill, overlooking Plymouth Sound	105	11
Scarrington 8 miles east of Nottingham off A52	24	5
Wick Hill 4 miles east of Chippenham	10	7

Odd Buildings/Odd Features

Location	Page	Map
Bidston Church Farm, The Wirral, between Birkenhead and Wallasey	51	4
Bishop's Tawton Just south of Barnstaple on A377	22	11
Bradford-on-Avon Tithe barn, in Barton Farm Country Park	36	7
Brewood Speedwell House The main street, 3 miles north of M54, 12 miles east of Telford	234	6
Brixham Olde Coffin House	55	11
Coldstream Marriage House, on bridge	37	2
Eaglesfield Fletcher Christian's Cottage, 4 miles south-west of Cockermouth off A66	238	1
East Bergholt In the churchyard, 6 miles north-east of Colchester off A12	202	10
East Cowes The Shell House, Cambridge Road	57	7 IoW
Fylingthorpe Fyling Hall, 3 miles west of Robin Hood's Bay off A171	239	3
Gayhurst 4 miles north of Milton Keynes on B526	55	7
Grasmere 3 miles north of village on A591	21	1
Greatstone-on-Sea On the sands, 2 miles south-east of New Romney	27	9
Hartsop 7 miles north of Ambleside off A592	236	1
Harvington Hall 10 miles south of Redditch off A435	106	6
Hindlip Hall 3 miles north of Worcester off A449	107	6
Knole Just south of Sevenoaks, off A225	53	9
Londonthorpe 3 miles north of Grantham off B6403	24	5
Markyate Cell 3 miles south-west of Luton off A5	107	8
Masham Nutwith Cote Farm, 10 miles north-west of Ripon off A6108	237	3
Minster Lovell Hall 3 miles west of Witney off B4070	108	7
Much Marcle Hellen's House, 4 miles south-west of Ledbury off A449	97	6
Much Wenlock 7 miles north-west of Bridgnorth on A458	234	6
Newton Linford 4 miles north-west of Leicester off B5327	51	6
Odiham In grounds of parish church, 7 miles east of Basingstoke off A32	207	7
Okeford Fitzpaine Just south of A357, 7 miles north-west of Blandford Forum	23	11
Porthcurno 3 miles south-east of Land's End off B3283	52	11

Public Houses/Inns/Hotels

Pyramids

Signposts/Village Signs/Emblems

Stately Homes

Stones

Sundials

Temples

Tombs/Tombstones/Graves

Towers/Spires

Trees

Villages/Village Crafts

Wells

Windows

Other Oddities (Miscellany)

Acknowledgments

The majority of the illustrations in this book were specially commissioned; others supplied to us, or requiring acknowledgment are listed below.

6 *left* By permission of the British Library. **49** *top* The Zoological Society of London. **79** *top right* Tony Freeman Press Agency. **102** *bottom right* By kind permission of the Marquess of Tavistock and the Trustees of the Bedford Estates. **103** *top and bottom left* By kind permission of the Marquess of Tavistock and the Trustees of the Bedford Estates. **107** *bottom* Still from the film 'The Wicked Lady' by courtesy of The Rank Organisation plc. **108** *top* By kind permission of English Heritage. **125** *bottom left* Dennis Avon. **128** *bottom two* Ralph Holmes and Sons (Fish Merchants) Limited. **189** *bottom* Dennis Avon. **202** *top* Dennis Avon. **205** *bottom three* By the kind permission of the Dean and Chapter, Wells Cathedral. **216** *bottom* Dennis Avon. **227** From the collection of Henry Ford Museum and Greenfield Village.

The maps appearing on pages 242–257 are based upon the Ordnance Survey map with the permission of the Controller of HMSO, Crown copyright reserved.

The publishers wish to express their gratitude to the many individuals and organisations whose specialised knowledge was invaluable in the preparation of this book. Also to Paula Granados for her tireless efforts in the coordination of this publication.

Printed and bound by Jarrold Printing, Norwich